Solid Food for the Mature Believer

by

Kenneth John Marks

2nd Edition
© Copyright 2017, Kenneth John Marks

All Rights Reserved.

No part of this book may be reproduced, stored in a retrieval system, or transmitted by any means, electronic, mechanical, photocopying, recording, or otherwise, without written permission from the author.

ISBN: 978-1-60414-386-7

Scripture quotations are from the ESV® Bible (The Holy Bible, English Standard Version®), copyright © 2001 by Crossway, a publishing ministry of Good News Publishers. Used by permission. All rights reserved.

Table of Contents

DEDICATION v
For the Glory of the One True God vii
INTRODUCTION 1
PART I: In Very Nature God 7
God, Himself 10
The *Divine* Jesus, The Exact Representation Of The Eternal God 16
The Man Entity That Appeared in Heaven and on Earth Before the Incarnation Was the Divine Jesus 22
The Incarnation of YHWH 23
    To the choirmaster: according to Lilies. A Maskil of the Sons of Korah; a love song. 24
The Son of Man Began With the Incarnation 31
The Son, Now the Resurrected Immortal Human Man 33
Jesus (God) the Love Entity 37
The Holy Spirit 41
What Happened at Pentecost 46
A Recap of Part I 54
PART II 56
God's Character 56
    Love 57
    Hatred / Wrath 58
    Mercy 68
    Goodness 70
    Kindness 71
    Grace 74
    God's Sovereign, Righteous Will 77

PART III 80
Living a Life that Pleases God 80
Fear the LORD Your God 83
Walk in His Ways and Obey His Commands 89
Love Him 90
Serve Him With All Your Soul 94
Serve Him With Overwhelming Gratitude (Thanksgiving) 96

Recap of Parts II & III 99

PART IV 101
Some Miscellaneous Topics 101
Tribulation of the World 101
Tribulation of the Saints of God 107
Defilement of the LORD's Table 119
The Unforgiveable Sin 124
Science, Knowledge and Faith 126

PART V 134
My Testimony 134

APPENDIX 1 138
STUDY OF THE HOLY SPIRIT 138
  2. *By allowing us to choose to be filled with Him.* 191
  6. *Gives gifts of supernatural power to perform miraculous works among men.* 195
  3. *By giving God's chosen leaders faithful followers who will do His will.* 200
  4. *By giving us all instruction how to follow the LORD.* 201

APPENDIX 2 203
A FEW OF GOD'S COMMANDS APPLICABLE TO ALL BELIEVERS 203

BIBLIOGRAPHY OF NON-SCRIPTURAL SOURCES 216
INDEX OF SCRIPTURE REFERENCES 219

DEDICATION

Here are a few of God's servants among the dozens and dozens of whom God has used in my life to bring me into the Kingdom, and who have helped me grow in Christ-likeness: Dave and Kay Landers (missionaries through whom Jesus introduced Himself to me in the early 1950s), Salvador Diwa (who brought me to the LORD in 1968), Steven Roy (through whose example God brought me back onto the path of righteousness after I had fallen away) and Mike Pinkerton, whom God used to shepherd me into spiritual maturity.

This list does not include the many godly young men and women through whom God shepherded me during my college days, or the many other godly men and women I have had the very great honor of knowing. He knows who they are. Because of all these godly servants, I kneel every night and give thanks to the God of all love, grace and mercy for them.

For the Glory of the One True God

By the Word of the LORD

I believe that there is one Almighty God. That means that there is one and only one unique transcendent spiritual entity who exists in a timeless present outside of creation as we know and perceive it; who is all knowing, all powerful, and everywhere present; who created the universe and everything else that exists, including all spiritual realms; who defines justice, righteousness, loving kindness, holiness and all the other such things through His own character, being and actions.

Furthermore, I believe that this unique spiritual entity has one mind (one set of thoughts), one consciousness and one will. In short, this entity is one unique person as we understand the word.

Finally, I believe that this Almighty spiritual entity has revealed Himself to us as YHWH (transliteration: Jehovah, pronounced *yah-weh*) as recorded in the Bible, which is my sole authority for spiritual truth, It is YHWH who is incarnate as the unique flesh and blood human being named Jesus Christ, who is alive to this very day, sitting at the right hand of this transcendent spiritual being.

This is God's own truth!

Praise be to this God of Justice,
Righteousness, Love and Mercy
AMEN

INTRODUCTION

The LORD my God, whom I serve with all my heart and soul, has burdened my heart to write this book. I believe its purpose is to stimulate your thinking about the nature and being of our God and the tenets of our faith. There is also a warning in this book to the church in America that the LORD our God is displeased with us, because we have been corrupted by the world.

This is where the modern church is:

> *[11]About this we have much to say, and it is hard to explain, since you have become dull of hearing. [12]For though by this time you ought to be teachers, you need someone to teach you again the basic principles of the oracles of God. You need milk, not solid food, [13]for everyone who lives on milk is unskilled in the word of righteousness, since he is a child. [14]But solid food is for the mature, for those who have their powers of discernment trained by constant practice to distinguish good from evil (Hebrews 5:11–14).*

Therefore, it is imperative that we

> *[1]...leave the elementary doctrine of Christ and go on to maturity, not laying again a foundation of repentance from dead works and of faith toward God, [2]and of instruction about washings, the laying on of hands, the resurrection of the dead, and eternal judgment. [3]And this we will do if God permits (Hebrews 6:1–3).*

The body of Christ in America has succumbed to the illusions of sin and the deceits of the world. One symptom of this is the appalling fact that many of my brothers and sisters cannot distinguish good from evil. Between thirty and forty percent of so-called evangelical

Solid Food for the Mature Believer

Christians voted in the 2008 presidential election for a man who proudly stood for unlimited abortion rights and the wholehearted acceptance of sexual deviancy as a legitimate alternative lifestyle. Another example is the enthusiastic reception of an abomination of a book, *The Shack,* by Paul Young.[1] There are entire congregations that celebrate hatred and vengeance over love and mercy (see the Westboro Baptist Church's website, www.godhatesfags.com), while others burn Bibles that are not of the *correct* translation.[2] We of the body of Christ in the U.S. have indeed fallen on spiritual hard times.[3]

In this book, I will point out some things we have forgotten about how to walk before God, such as how to fear Him properly. Because we have forgotten, or ignored, certain tenets of our faith, the body of Christ in America has become weak and ineffective, an object of ridicule and scorn. Be assured that God will hold the church in America to account for sliding into spiritual and moral corruption, and it will not be pleasant. If you doubt this, read the letter to the Laodicean church in Revelation 3.

I will also attempt to show that the Godhead theology that has gripped the church for the last fifteen hundred years cannot possibly be true, because if it were, none of the distinct persons of the so-called Godhead could be fully God in themselves. Over the past fifteen hundred years it has been taken as truth that if one rejected the Godhead theology, then one must necessarily reject the deity of Christ, e.g. if there is no Godhead, then Christ cannot be God. Refer to my statement of faith under For the Glory of the One True God at the beginning of this book.

---

[1] See *Burning Down the Shack* by James B. De Young, WND Books, New York, NY, 2010 for an issue by issue debunking of Paul Young's atrocious book, which blasphemes God and the gospel with every page
[2] See the *King James Only Controversy* by Dr. James White, Bethany House, New York, NY, 2009.
[3] For more evidence of this, I recommend you read *The Agony of Deceit* by Horton et. al., Moody Press, Chicago, Ill, 1992; and *The Truth War* by John MacArthur, Thomas Nelson, Nashville, TN, 2007. Also google Paul Washer's sermon *Ten Indictments of the Modern Church in America*, dated May 23, 2010.

Solid Food for the Mature Believer starts by discussing the being, nature and character of God. You can't grow in the Spirit unless you are willing to deal with all aspects of God's nature and character, not just the *God is love* mantra the sons of evil use to lull the world (most especially unbelievers) into a sense of false security. Of course, I am not denying that God is love. This book assumes that any mature believer has been thoroughly acquainted with the more pleasant aspects of God's character and nature, that He is full of loving kindness, graciousness, compassion and so forth. What Scripture clearly teaches, however, is that God is much more than love. He is also holy and righteous, a consuming fire, terrifying in aspect, a being to be feared, as we would fear anything dangerous to us. Sadly, we don't understand or take this to heart anymore.

This book is written with the mature believer in mind, one who has read and studied God's word, and who has committed large chunks of it to memory. I quote Scripture extensively to illustrate a point, but there are times when I refer to a passage without quoting it. In this case I would expect a mature believer to look up the passage on his own.

It should therefore come as no surprise that you will need a Bible as you read through this. My intent is to encourage you to pour over the referenced verses. And keep in mind that we who have repented of our sins and accepted the LORD Jesus Christ as our Savior possess the Holy Spirit, given to us to discern truth so that we might be able to *test the spirits to see whether they are from God*...(Excerpt from 1 John 4:1.) Call on the LORD, therefore, to make sure that you are alert to what the testing Spirit in you is telling you.

In this book, with a few exceptions, I refer to and quote from the English Standard Version (ESV).[4] There are times when, for clarity, I

---

[4] Quoted by permission according to https://www.crossway.org/rights-and-permissions/esv/ to wit: *The ESV text may be quoted (in written, visual, or electronic form) up to and inclusive of one thousand (1,000) verses without express written permission of the publisher, providing that the verses quoted do not amount to a complete book of the Bible nor do the verses quoted account for 50 percent or more of the total text of the work in which they are quoted.* In this book about 880 verses *This note is continued on the next page.*

may refer to the NASB or NIV translations. In referencing some verses, I use the designations *a*, *b*, *c*, which mean the first, second, and third clause of the verse.

The ESV does not capitalize the personal pronouns *he* and *him* when they refer to God, whether in the form of YHWH or in the form of His incarnation as Jesus, but in the text of this book I do. I use *italics* to delineate passages quoted from all my sources, including the Bible. I also use italics to indicate a special word or phrase that might otherwise be set apart by quotation marks (""). Here is an example:

> I would also interpret the phrase *streams of living water flowing from him* to mean that this manifestation of the Spirit will cause men to spread the gospel…

Another example:

> He doesn't use the word *distinct* but it goes without saying…

This is to avoid confusion when quotation marks are nested in a passage to indicate that someone (usually Jesus or YHWH) is speaking. There are also times when I use **bold face italics** for emphasis.

In this book I refer to the LORD Jesus rather than to the LORD Jesus as He is referred to in the New Testament. There is no Greek transliteration of YHWH for YHWH that I know of. (I AM would be translated as ἐγώ εἰμί (*egō eimi*) as in John 8:58.) The Greek word translated LORD in the N.T. is κύριος (*kyrios*), which the Greek uses as a name for God Himself (and also θεός pronounced *theos*). Since God **is** YHWH, the terms are interchangeable. For this reason the N.T. writers, when referring to Jesus as LORD, certainly meant to refer to Him as the incarnation of YHWH. According to 1 Corinthians 15:24–

---

are quoted and the number of words quoted amount to about 34% of the text of this book. No complete books of the Bible are quoted. Quotations are copied from the ESV translation as provided in https://www.esv.org/.

28, the LORD (*kyrios*) Jesus as LORD of the Universe will be put in subjection to YHWH (written *theos (God)* in the Greek Text), so the Son of Man is not strictly LORD as a human being. This is neither here nor there, however. The King in any cloak, in this case a cloak of human flesh, is still the King. As far as we are concerned, the incarnation of YHWH, the Son of Man, Jesus Christ, is every bit God (*theos*). Hence the use of LORD as a title for Jesus seems appropriate.

This is the **second edition** of this work. I originally had quoted from the 1984 version of the NIV Bible but find the latest gender neutral edition of the translation troubling, which is why I have substituted the ESV.[5] In addition, have added some material, reorganized Appendix 1 and the section on the Holy Spirit, and added an index of Scripture references, a bibliography and an index of topical references.

For some passages, I have added some clarifying text in the footnotes regarding the Hebrew and Greek words or texts in the source documents for the O.T. and N.T. translations. For this purpose I have used the online *Blue Letter Bible* at https://www. blueletterbible. org/esv/.

The Blue Letter Bible translation of the Old Testament is based on the Masoretic Text, which is the authorized Hebrew and Aramaic text of the *Tanakh*, the Jewish Bible. Whereas Crowssways' ESV's O.T. translation is based on the *Biblia Hebraica Stuttgartensia* (BHS).

In certain passages the BHS varies slightly from the Masoretic Text, as can be seen in differences between the ESV translation and the KJV or NASB translations. For example, in Malachi 2:16a the Masoretic Text reads א שָׁלַח אָמַר יְהוָה אֱלֹהֵי יִשְׂרָאֵלכִּי־שָׂנֵ, or when

---

[5] For an assessment of the 2011 edition, see the following critique, which states: *The Council on Biblical Manhood and Womanhood, one of the leading critics of the TNIV, promised a full review of the updated NIV after it goes to print. In November, when online text of the updated NIV became available, the group released a statement saying it could not recommend the new NIV Bible because of "over 3,600 gender-related problems" that were previously in its critique of the TNIV.* Read more at http://www.christianpost.com/news/new-niv-bible-to-debut-amid-ongoing-concern-49392/#dXGs0VLlmJjpwGpr.99.

translated, *"For I hate divorce," says the* L*ORD, the God of Israel*.... Yet this clause does not appear in the ESV translation of this verse, which reads, *"For the man who does not love his wife but divorces her," says the* L*ORD, the God of Israel*...The reader will see why I have made a point of this as the book progresses.

PART I: In Very Nature God

What follows is a description of the very nature and being of God, e.g. of His person, as He has revealed Himself in the Scriptures.[6] Note that I say person and not persons. In today's church, the most holy of holy doctrines is that God is three distinct persons. This collection of persons is labeled the Godhead.[7]

The term *Godhead,* as I use it in this book, is defined by Dr. James White of Alpha & Omega Ministries as *one being, three persons.*[8] He doesn't use the word *distinct* but it goes without saying if his definition is to have any meaning at all.

Here is the logical conclusion one would reach about the nature of the Godhead as described by Timothy Keller in an otherwise excellent book, *The Reason For God.*[9]

> *The inner-life of the* [Godhead]...*is characterized by mutually self-giving love. When we delight and serve someone else, we enter into a dynamic orbit about him or her...That creates a dance, particularly if there are three persons, each of whom moves around the other two. So it*

---

[6] Who am I to write this, you might ask? I am no one. God reveals Himself to all of us. He is no respecter of persons. One thing I did find as I grew in knowledge of the Scriptures is that what was preached about God our Father and LORD was not what I was reading in His word. This book is the result of what God Himself revealed to me in His word.

[7] According to many writers and theologians, the Godhead theology ranks right up there with the deity and resurrection of Jesus Christ in importance to the Christian faith.

[8] Dr. James White is an awesome Christian man who is the expert's expert on the Bible. Look him up on YouTube. Search keywords *Dr. James White* and *Trinity* to get his lecture on this subject. As I will show, Dr. White is not infallible when it comes to interpreting Scripture.

[9] *The Reason for God* by Timothy Keller, Riverhead Books, NY, NY, 2008, p. 224. The first half of the book refutes arguments nonbelievers use against Christians and is therefore terrific. As to the second half, well, it could be better.

Solid Food for the Mature Believer

> *is, the Bible tells us.*[10] *Each of the divine persons centers upon the others. None demands that the others revolve around him. Each voluntarily circles the other two, pouring love, delight, and adoration into them. Each Person of the* [Godhead] *loves and, adores, defers to, and rejoices in the others.*[11]

To summarize, the so-called triune God consists of three distinct entities, which the Godhead theologians claim are all God in themselves, orbiting each other like planetary bodies, showering love, goodness and light on each other. God is, to put it succinctly, a committee of love.

This description of God cannot be true (and, I believe, is a destructive heresy) if one uses this common sense definition of *a person*:

> a unique living entity with a unique mind as we understand this concept, a unique set of characteristics (in God's case omniscience, omnipotence, etc.), a unique will and character or personality that is matched or owned by no other living entity either in heaven, outside of heaven, or on earth.[12]

The LORD our God is just such a unique living entity.

---

[10] Where does the Bible tell us that the Son entity moves around (orbits) the Father and the Spirit? Or that the Father orbits the Son entity and the Spirit? Or that the Holy Spirit orbits the Father and the Son entity? There is not one shred of Scriptural evidence to back this questionable (maybe absurd is a better word) position.

[11] Sounds like the Godhead is a mutual adoration society, a love committee. I wonder what else these guys do when a judgment has to be rendered. Do they take a vote? I'd like to see any Scriptural evidence that the Father, Jehovah, defers to anyone. Jesus, in His incarnation as the Son of Man, is pretty clear that deferral goes only one way in His relationship with Jehovah God: upward from Him to His Father.

[12] While I define the word *person* for the purposes of this book, I don't intend to define words like *mind, will, personality*, or *character*. I will continue this book using their common meaning.

Because God the Father is beyond our comprehension and literally beyond human language to describe, He has revealed Himself to us through His exact imprint in the Person of Jesus Christ (Hebrews 1:3). The agency of that revelation is the Holy Spirit. Therefore the fact that God exists as Father, Son and Holy Spirit does not mean that He has three distinct minds, wills and characters. If He did, any of these distinct persons would not and could not be fully God in themselves.

Here's why.

What must it mean to say that God is three distinct persons? If the Person of God the Father is distinct from the Persons of God the Spirit and God the Son (neither of these last two titles for Jesus and the Spirit is ever used in Scripture), the Father must have a unique attribute we'll call **F** that distinguishes His Person from the others, though we might not know what **F** is.[13] **F** could be, for example, a single thought or set of thoughts that neither God the Son nor God the Spirit share. Or **F** could be an attribute unique to God the Father, such as omniscience, that neither God the Son nor God the Spirit share. In the same way let **HS** be the distinctive attribute of the Person of God the Holy Spirit. And for God the Son, let the distinctive attribute be **S**. So the Person of God the Father has neither the distinct Holy Spirit attribute, **HS**, nor that of the Son, **S**. Likewise, the Person of God the Son possesses neither the **F** nor **HS** attributes, and the Person of God the Holy Spirit possesses neither the **F** nor **S** attributes.

Since God the Father in the Godhead theology possesses neither the **HS** nor **S** attributes, He in Himself cannot be fully God. The same is true for the God Holy Spirit and God the Son.

Dr. James White unintentionally makes this same point in his book *The Forgotten Trinity*. He writes of Jesus:

> *The third clause of John 1:1 balances out the initial*
> *presentation John is making about the Word. We read,*
> *"...and the Word was God (καὶ θεὸς ἦν ὁ λόγος)." Again,*

---

[13] From the Keller's description of the Godhead, these persons are distinct beings in their own right.

the eternal en (ἦν). John avoids contradiction by telling us that the Word was with God, and the Word was God. If John were making this an equation, like this:

All of the "Word" = All of God

he would be contradicting himself. If the Word is "all" of God, and God is "all" of the Word, and the two terms are interchangeable, then how could the Word be "with" himself? Such would make no sense.[14]

What he is saying is that all of YHWH as He exists as a Transcendent being, of whom Jesus (the Word) is the incarnation (see **The Incarnation of YHWH** on page 23), is not all of God.

This is exactly my point. Thank you Dr. White.

I say again, if the words *person* and *distinct* have any real meaning in the Godhead theology, then this theology must imply that none of the so-called *three persons* are wholly God in themselves. The Godhead theology must therefore be akin to heresy, because it implies that the divine Person of Jesus Christ is not fully God, nor is God the Father, of whom Jesus is sole revelation.

Understanding the personhood of God is absolutely critical to our understanding the Scriptures. Let's start, then, by speaking about God and His transcendent being.

God, Himself

To speak of God's transcendence we must start before the beginning of the timeline of creation. Before the beginning there was God.[15] He has existed from eternity past and will exist into eternity yet

---

[14] From page 52 of *The Forgotten Trinity* by Dr. James White, Bethany House, Minneapolis, MN., 1998.

[15] Genesis 1:1; John 1:1. In the following, I by no means intend to do a complete dissertation on God's nature, being and character. If it were at all possible, which by His very nature it is not, the pages of this book would more than likely fill the *This note is continued on the next page.*

to come (Nehemiah 9:5). Prior to creation (*the beginning*), nothing existed but God. No evil, no devil, no spirits, no angels, no demons, no heaven, no universe, no light and no darkness (as we created beings understand and are able to comprehend these terms). Nothing but God, who is all goodness and light.

Every human being in God's creation has a concept of God, of who and what He is. Even the wicked, who proclaim that there is no God know in their hearts that this is ridiculous. (The Bible calls them fools in Psalm 14:1.) This is because He has revealed Himself to us by making us in His image (Genesis 1:26a); through the complexity of the universe (Psalm 19:1–4);[16] and by setting the concept of eternity—which is the equivalent to the concept of God—in our hearts (Ecclesiastes 3:11b). If He had chosen not to reveal Himself, we could not only not know Him, we could not know of Him or about Him. We could not even conceive of Him, and therefore we could not speak His Name—the LORD—or discuss Him. He is completely beyond our human conception, our ability to understand (Job 36:26; Ecclesiastes 3:11c; Ecclesiastes 8:17b; and Judges 13:18[17]). His thoughts are infinitely higher than our thoughts, His ways are infinitely higher than our ways (paraphrase of Isaiah 55:9).[18] By His very nature, God transcends His creation. He is the **Transcendent Majesty** we know as the I AM, or LORD (Hebrews 1:3 and Hebrews 8:1).[19]

What does *transcend* mean? According to the dictionary, two of its meanings are *Lying beyond the ordinary range of perception,* and *Being above and independent of the material universe. Used of the*

---

universe. John 21:25 gives indication that this is true. I am merely setting a foundation for what must follow.

[16] As for the complexity of the universe and the raging issue of Intelligent Design, see the excellent documentary film released in 2008, *Expelled: No Intelligence Allowed*, 2008 Video Directed by Nathan Frankowski and hosted by Ben Stein.

[17] In Judges 13:18 the ESV has translated the Hebrew word פִּלְאִי *(pil'iy, H6381)* as *wonderful*. It can also be translated as *incomprehensible*.

[18] *As the heavens are higher than the earth* in the referenced passage refers metaphorically to the infinitude of difference between us and God.

[19] I don't know that the writer of Hebrews had the word *transcendent* in his vocabulary, but he certainly understood the concept.

Deity.[20] God exists *outside* the creation and, apart from revealing Himself, is inaccessible to His created beings' understanding or perception in every conceivable way.

He is infinite in extent, meaning that His being knows no physical or spiritual boundaries, nor do His thoughts (1 Kings 8:27; Psalm 119:96).[21] Our finite minds could no more comprehend Him than an amoeba swimming around in a Petri dish could conceive of the vastness of our universe or begin to comprehend it.[22]

Nevertheless, I want to provide an admittedly inadequate picture of the awesome majesty of God's being.

Imagine that you are floating in a hazy, dusty cloud extending as far as you can see, but in which you can make out no solid form: no matter how hard you try, the dust particles are too fine. Now suppose as you drift through the cloud, the individual dust grains begin to grow, and as they become more distinct you can see that each one of them is a sphere with dozens of spokes radiating out in all directions. Imagine that at the end of each spoke is another smaller sphere. It is opaque at first, but as you approach it you can make out something inside it. Getting closer still, you see that in this sphere is a universe full of stars and galaxies. You realize that this could very well be our

---

[20] From *Microsoft Bookshelf*, 1996-1997 edition.

[21] In Psalm 119:96, the ESV translates the Hebrew phrase מְאֹד רְחָב (*m@`od rachab*, H3966, H7342) literally as *exceedingly broad*. A reasonable interpretation of this phrase could be *boundless,* as in the NIV translation. Or, more specifically, *infinite*.

[22] In *Coming of Age in the Milky Way,* Timothy Ferris writes, *And yet the more we know about the universe, the more we come to see how little we know. When the cosmos was thought to be but a tidy garden, with the sky its ceiling and earth its floor and its history coextensive with that of the human family tree, it was still possible to imagine that we might one day comprehend it in both plan and detail. That illusion can no longer be sustained. We might eventually obtain some sort of bedrock understanding of cosmic structure,* **but we will never understand the universe in detail; it is just too big and varied for that.** *If we possessed an atlas of our galaxy that devoted but a single page to each star system in the Milky Way... that atlas would run to more than ten million volumes of ten thousand pages each... and merely to flip through it, at the rate of a page per second, would require over ten thousand years.* From *Coming of Age in the Milky Way* by Timothy Ferris, Anchor Books–Doubleday, NY, NY, 1988, pp. 382–383.

universe. As a chill runs up and down your spine, you find that all the other spheres contain similar universes as vast as our own. You can see that there are billions and billions of dust grains in the cloud, maybe an infinite number, and you know instinctively that each central sphere must support dozens of universes. Now imagine that you are pulling away from the cloud. Suppose you can now see the space in which the cloud rests. You find that it is in another great sphere and that this sphere is resting on the tip of someone's finger.

This is God's finger![23]

The point of this image is not to assert that God might have created billions of universes like our own, although He may very well have. Who can know that? The point is that God's being is immeasurably greater in extent than we can conceive, as is the extent of our own universe, which is infinitesimally small compared to Him.[24]

God's power cannot be measured or even comprehended. Try to imagine power that can bring something as vast and complex as our universe into existence in a split second (aka the Big Bang).

Here are some other aspects of God's being:

God's presence is indescribable. He fills the universe (Jeremiah 23:24).[25] There is nowhere that God is not. He fills every small particle of space. To use a term the mathematicians use when describing a certain class of mathematical fractal objects, God is everywhere self-similar.[26] If I cup my hand, the *amount* of God in terms of character,

---

[23] This sequence of images came to me in a dream. I have assumed it was God Himself speaking to me, so it seemed appropriate to share.

[24] I have read that our universe is between 90 and 156 billion light years in diameter (one light year equals about 5.9 trillion miles; roughly one thousand times the diameter of our solar system). This vast physical system contains over three hundred billion trillion (3×10^{21}) stars–about the same number as all the grains of sand on all the beaches of the earth–in several hundred billion (10^{11}) or maybe even a trillion (10^{12}) galaxies. We can, by definition, have no clue as to what lies *outside* the observable universe.

[25] Ephesians 1:23 and Ephesians 4:10 refer directly to the divine Person of Jesus, who fills the universe.

[26] One such object is the Mandelbrot set.

being and power that occupies the space between my hands is the same as that with which He fills creation.

The LORD is also a consuming fire (Deuteronomy 4:24 and Hebrews 12:29). If He were to remove the protective barrier that allows us to exist in His presence, we would all be destroyed. The universe itself would be consumed, not to mention the earth (Job 9:1–13).[27]

God's understanding and knowledge is beyond measure. He hears every thought and knows the actions of every living thing in the universe, for all time, from eternity past through eternity future. He knows every atom of His creation and understands its past, present, and future energy states. He knows every molecule and the substance containing it. He has even given each of the billions of billions of stars a name (Psalm 147:4). He instantaneously understands all things at once and forever.

God is absolutely sovereign over all creation. He controls and commands all things, both physical and spiritual. All beings (and all other things), whether spiritual or physical—even the devil himself—were created by Him and for Him to serve His righteous purpose. (Proverbs 16:4, Isaiah 45:7, and Psalm 103:19). God is sovereign over evil. He allows evil to exist for His own unfathomable purpose. Were He to decide to end it all, He could do so with but a thought (Job 34:13–15[28]).

God has life in Himself and is the source of all life (John 5:26). We cannot adequately describe what *life* is based on our finite understanding of creation. I challenge any scientist to describe in detail how the DNA molecule can be the source of every aspect of our physical being and yet be nothing but lifeless atoms. In fact, how do lifeless atoms that form lifeless molecules (by which I mean, objects without sentient thought) come together to form animals and men, which do think and understand, as far as God has made them able (Job 39:13–17)? Does anyone understand this? As the cosmologists must

---

[27] This is one example among many. Declarations of God's vast, incomprehensible power in the Bible are quite numerous.
[28] I am extrapolating the content of this passage a little.

admit that they will never understand the universe in its entirety, I would bet that in their heart of hearts, biologists will also admit that they will never completely understand *life*.

God the Father (the LORD or the Transcendent Majesty) is the source of all knowledge and understanding (Proverbs 2:1–8). We cannot describe the mechanism of intelligence that works in our brains or understand how or where it originates. What scientist can tell how a thought is formed in the human brain or where it comes from? Or how the brain works? Or where our identity (our soul) resides?

God is spirit, meaning in His transcendent being, He has no physical qualities as we would understand the word *physical* (John 4:24). We know that God forms the spirit of a man within him (Zechariah 12:1). Yet what is *spirit*? What is its *substance*?

God is eternal, meaning He is *from everlasting to everlasting*, without beginning or end (1 Chronicles 16:36).[29] God has always existed and will always exist. God exists outside the confines of time as we understand the concept.[30]

God has all the qualities of a person, including emotions. He loves, hates, laughs, weeps, reasons, experiences jealousy and wrath.[31] He can be both a tender shepherd (Isaiah 40:11) and, as shown in Ezekiel 9, a merciless executioner (though He is absolutely, perfectly just in His judgment). He can be a tough disciplinarian as well as a doting father (Psalm 38; Proverbs 3:11–12).

God is terrifying (Exodus 20:18; 1 Samuel 11:7; Hebrews 12:21). So terrifying, in fact, that when all the powerful beings of heaven stand

---

[29] This is one of many passages that describe the eternality of the Transcendent Majesty in heaven. Incidentally, all scientists acknowledge *forever* or *eternity* as time going forward from this moment without limit or end. But what about *time* going backward from this moment without limit or end? Who can comprehend it?

[30] In Exodus 3:14, God identifies Himself as I AM without tense or qualification. Repeating this in His visitation on earth, Jesus said to the Pharisees, "... *Truly, truly, I say to you, before Abraham was, I am*" (John 8:58). God lives in an indescribable, incomprehensible eternal present.

[31] The Bible is filled with evidence of these emotions in God. Go to any online or computer-based Bible and do a word search on each one if you doubt it.

before Him, they shudder with awe (Psalm 89:7[32]). How much more should we tremble in His presence? (Jeremiah 5:22; Isaiah 8:13; and Luke 12:4–5). Unfortunately, the modern born-again Christian has forgotten that God is to be feared with a trembling heart. This is why sin and lousy, even heretical, doctrine flourish in the church today.[33]

God's Person and being are expressed in His revealed existence as Father, Son and Holy Spirit. As to *God the Father*, Jesus made clear during His ministry that the Father is the Transcendent Majesty, God, of whom we have been speaking. Jesus—who is, as I will show, God's unique bodily revelation to creation—says, *"You heard me say to you, 'I am going away, and I will come to you.' If you loved me, you would have rejoiced, because I am going to the Father, for the Father is greater than I"* (John 14:28). [34]

It is therefore to the *persons* of the Son and the Holy Spirit that I wish to direct the rest of my discourse.

The *Divine* Jesus, The Exact Representation Of The Eternal God

It has long been known that the LORD Jesus Christ has two coexistent natures, one divine (as spirit, John 4:24) and one human (as a flesh and bone human being in Luke 24:39). The Bible makes it clear

---

[32] Reading between the lines, Jeremiah 2:12; and James 2:19 are but a few more examples.

[33] God tells us in Proverbs 16:6b, *by the fear of the LORD one turns away from evil.* It stands to reason that without such fear, evil can have a field day in our lives. It certainly has in the modern American church.

[34] I believe Jesus is referring to His incarnate self, a human being, not to His existence as Jehovah God. For example, as a human man, Jesus did not know when He was coming again. Jesus in His incarnation as the Son of Man testifies time and again that He, as a human being, does nothing without the Father's approval (John 5:19). Therefore, as a human man Jesus is next to God in power, which makes Jehovah in His Transcendent Majesty greater than His human self. Later, I will show that Jesus, the Son of Man, is in fact the incarnation of God the Father, who has revealed Himself in the O.T. to be YHWH (Jehovah). See **The Incarnation of YHWH** on page 23.

that the divine Jesus, in His incarnation as a flesh and bone human man, is the Son of God.

Scripture also makes it clear that it is through both the divine and human Christ[35] alone that the God of creation is revealed to us. (Matthew 11:27).

In this section I deal with the divine Jesus. In the next, I deal with the Son of Man, the incarnate God, YHWH (John 8:58).

Scripture teaches without equivocation that Jesus, as a spiritual being, is God over all, the Sovereign LORD of the universe. (Romans 9:5 and Jude 1:4). Thus there can be no **other** spiritual being, person, or entity in the universe who reveals God to us. Therefore, as the exact revelation of God, this spiritual being cannot lack anything of God's attributes, character or knowledge.

The following passages talk about both of Jesus' natures:

- Hebrews 1:3: *He is the radiance of God's glory* (as Spirit) *and the exact imprint of His nature* (in Spirit as God has revealed Himself through His word, and as a human being, representing God on earth), *sustaining all things by his powerful word* (as Spirit);[36]
- Colossians 1:15–17: *He is the image of the invisible God, the firstborn of all creation* [as the Son of Man]. *For by him* [as Spirit] *all things were created, in heaven and on earth, visible and invisible, whether thrones or dominions or rulers or authorities—all things were created through*

---

[35] There are two distinct persons here, one completely human and one completely divine, both of them named Jesus. As I understand it, the human person is not a member of the Godhead in the Godhead theology. See a discussion of this at the bottom of page 54.

[36] The *exact imprint of his nature* comes from the Greek text, καὶ χαρακτὴρ αὐτός ὑπόστασις (transliterated as: *kai charaktēr autos hypostasis*: G2532, G5481, G846, G5287), which can be translated as, *and* (kai) *the express image* (charaktēr) *of his* (autos) *person* or *substance* or *being* (hypostasis). I would hazard the opinion that it is just as valid to say the LORD Jesus Christ is the exact revelation of God's being as the exact representation thereof. Notice that ὑπόστασις (hypostasis) is translated as a singular noun, not plural. If God as the deity, divinity or divine nature were three persons, I think it would have been plural.

> *him and for him.* [As Spirit] *He is before all things, and in him all things hold together;*[37]
- As a human being, He is the one in whom *the whole fullness of deity dwells bodily...* (Excerpt from Colossians 2:9);
- As both flesh and bone and spirit, *He was in the form of God* (Excerpt from Philippians 2:6).

What does it mean to be the radiance of God's glory and the exact representation of His being?

Let's take the latter first, which metaphorically describes God's revelation of Himself through the Person of Jesus Christ. Imagine, if you can, an infinite dimensional being folding Himself into a finitely dimensional creation as a representation of this infinite being. By the properties of God's infinitude, not all God's being can be contained in creation (1 Kings 8:27), because creation is finite and God transcends creation in being and nature. So what we see in the LORD Jesus Christ must be a representation of the infinite God in a finite creation.

And as the radiance of God's glory, Jesus in His divine nature proceeds from this infinite dimensional being in some unimaginable way to reveal God's presence to the creation. As the boundaries of a flame and its very existence are revealed by the light it gives off, so does the radiance of God's glory reveal God.[38]

For these two things to be true, the divine Jesus—who, in His incarnation as the Son of Man, is YHWH God incarnate, the eternal entity dwelling in heaven—cannot be distinct from God; His person cannot be distinct from God's Person in any way. This sense of *representation*, of *image*, of *radiance*, and of *bodily form* is the Holy Spirit's finite way of describing what is by nature infinite and

---

[37] This cannot be said of the Son of Man. Scripture makes it clear that Jesus' incarnation began at a point in the timeline of creation, so the Son of Man could not have existed from eternity past.

[38] God's glory is not just a shining light. It is the full measure of the impact or the evidence of all God's work in creation as perceived by creation. The *light* of God's glory reveals God's being, nature and person to creation.

indescribable. I would put it to you that when the Godhead theologians refer to the Son of God coming down from heaven, they must mean (without knowing it, obviously) the eternal, revealed, transcendent God, whom creation cannot otherwise know or experience.[39]

Further, it must have been the Person of Jesus Christ who spoke throughout the Old Testament (O.T.) and says, *"And the Father who sent me has himself borne witness about me.* **His voice you have never heard, his form you have never seen***..."* (excerpt from John 5:37). Yet there are dozens of examples of God appearing to the O.T. saints and speaking to them. For instance, God appeared and spoke to:

- Adam in Genesis 3:8–10;
- Abraham in Genesis 18:1;
- Moses numerous times, even face-to-face as the Spirit testifies in Exodus 33:10–11;
- Jacob in Genesis 32:22–30;
- Joshua in Joshua 5:13–16 ;[40]
- Solomon in 1 Kings 3:5 and 1 Kings 9:2;
- Daniel, starting in Daniel 10:5;[41]

---

[39] Many passages in Scripture describe God or Jesus as coming *down* from heaven. This is a metaphorical allusion to Jesus coming into creation and manifesting Himself among us, whether as an angel (see Isaiah 63:9 as one of many examples) or as a man (see Genesis 18, where the LORD appears to Abraham as a man, among many other examples) or in other perceivable manifestations like a pillar of fire. This is not the same as a bird descending toward us from the sky. There is no unique *down* direction when talking about moving about in creation.

[40] In this appearance Scripture says a *man* appeared to Joshua. We know it was God, first because Joshua falls face down and worships Him, which no angel would allow (see Revelation 22:9); and this man also says to Joshua in Joshua 5:15, *And the commander of the LORD's army said to Joshua, "Take off your sandals, for the place where you are standing is holy."* This is almost word for word what He said to Moses in Exodus 3:5. We also know this is Jesus because the man identifies himself as the commander of the LORD's army, whom we know to be Jesus Christ.

[41] If there are any questions as to the truth of this, compare the appearance of this divine being with Jesus' appearance to John in Revelation 1.

- Ezekiel in Ezekiel 1:26–28, and then in Ezekiel 2:1 through the rest of the chapter.

There are many, many more examples. Is the Spirit contradicting Himself, then, in John 5:37? These passages demonstrate without doubt that God spoke audibly throughout O.T. times and interacted with the people. In the context of this truth, this passage in John must mean that it was God's revelation to creation—Jesus Christ—who spoke and appeared throughout the O.T., not the Transcendent Majesty directly.[42]

Further, Isaiah 44:6 says, *Thus says the LORD, the King of Israel and his Redeemer, the LORD of hosts: "I am the first and I am the last; besides me there is no god."*[43] Jesus says this same thing of Himself in Revelation 1:17, Revelation 2:8 and Revelation 22:13. Since there can only be one First and Last, the Person of Jesus must be speaking to Isaiah. Also, the Apostle John says in John 1:18, *"No one has ever seen God; the only God, who is* [now] *at the Father's side, he has made him known."* These statements cannot be true unless it is God's bodily representation—that is, His revealed self, His divine representation—that speaks throughout the O.T. and who appeared many times to O.T. saints. Another way to think of it is that it is the Transcendent Majesty speaking to us through His revelation of Himself—the divine Person of Jesus Christ.

In short, the Father does everything in His creation through His revealed self, the divine Jesus Christ. Apart from Jesus—the exact representation of God the Father's being and the radiance of His glory—God has no other form or representation to His creation.

Looking down into creation from God's perspective:
- When God speaks audibly, He does so with the LORD Jesus' voice;

---

[42] We could not hear, understand or even conceive of what He was saying if we did not have this self-revealing entity, Jesus Christ, through His Spirit, to reveal Him to us in ways that our finite beings could process.

[43] See also Isaiah 48:12.

- When God looks into creation, He does so with Jesus' eyes;
- When God forms a spirit or a soul or anything else that exists in creation, He does so with Jesus' hands.

Looking up from creation toward heaven:
- We see and comprehend the Transcendent Majesty (the Father) through the Person of the LORD Jesus Christ, and through Him only;
- When we speak to Him our words enter Jesus' mind, which is God's mind;
- All things in creation relate to God through the eternal revealed entity, Jesus Christ.

This comports with Jesus' statement that it is He who reveals to the creation the Person of God, the Transcendent Majesty, or the Father (Matthew 11:27 and Luke 10:22). I say again it is His person and no other. This also is consistent with Jesus' statement that He and the Father are One and that if you've seen Him you have also seen the Father (paraphrase of John 10:30 and John 14:9).

The word *One* means one, as in one being, one entity, one identity, one God (Deuteronomy 6:4).[44,45] I can't for the life of me understand

---

[44] I looked up the Hebrew word אֶחָד (*'echad*, H259) for *one* used by the Holy Spirit here (translated as the number one by the KJV 687 times out of a total of 952 occurrences in the O.T.). It simply means the number one (1). I have heard some say that it can mean things like a unified whole or a unity. This is manifestly false. The hermeneutics of this word would demand that those hearing Moses say this line, and those rabbis who read it for the twelve hundred seventy-three years until the advent of our LORD and Savior would have understood it to mean one God, meaning one God entity, not the unity of three distinct entities. The corresponding exegesis demands that we interpret this the same way, as the number 1.

[45] I had one godly person tell me that he thought of God the Father as a flame and of Jesus as being a spark of that flame (rather than the very radiance and image of the flame as we saw on page 17), which is a natural consequence of this theological error. This misconception of Jesus as some small spark of God goes back to the earliest history of the church.

This note is continued on the next page.

why this is not preached in the modern day. As we have seen previously, the Godhead theology makes no bones about asserting that the divine Jesus (who is God overall) is somehow a distinct entity from the Father (God). This is not just crazy, it is heresy of the highest order, because it has the effect of denying that the Sovereign LORD who bought us is indeed God Himself.[46]

The Man Entity That Appeared in Heaven and on Earth Before the Incarnation Was the Divine Jesus

In this section, I want to explore further how it is that John has said no one has seen God, and yet God appeared to many prior to Pentecost and His incarnation as Jesus Christ.

As demonstrated above, there are many times in Scripture where God is seen in the form of a man, not only when He appears on earth, but also when He appears in heaven. See Ezekiel 1, for example. This revelation of God's being, this *man entity*, has existed from eternity past through eternity future. This man entity is the Person of Jesus, of course.

As mentioned in the previous paragraphs, this man entity is the one comprehensible (*visible* or *physical*) revelation of God to His creation. It's as if when the Transcendent Majesty created all things (through

---

The first church historian, Eusebius of Caesarea (260–339 A.D.), says of Jesus in his *Church History*, "Before all creation and fashioning, visible or invisible, he was the first and only *offspring of* God...the *second cause* of the universe after the Father, the true and only begotten child of God" (Maier, Paul L., *Eusebius–the Church History: A New Translation with Commentary*. Kregal Publications, Grand Rapids, MI, 1999, p. 23).

If these words are taken literally, how can one fail to see Jesus as a distinct entity from God, and a lesser one at that as the mere spark of the flame, a secondary cause of all things—something or someone less than fully God Himself? What this leads to is a gravely erroneous misconception concerning the nature and being of Christ, and I believe a subtle but no less destructive heresy.

[46] 2 Peter 2:1. This is, in Peter's words, a destructive heresy.

Jesus), He wrapped himself in His own creation like One putting on a cloak. It is this *cloak* that we see when God appears throughout Scripture in the form or likeness of a man.

Wherever the Man entity is, that's also where God is in comprehensible form. The Man entity is God and therefore lives in the eternal present of God's existence, even when He walked in human form through the time that defines the creation. The veracity of this is demonstrated when Jesus told the Pharisees that *"... before Abraham was born, I am"* (excerpt from John 8:58). They immediately understood what He was saying. "I am the 'I AM' who spoke to Moses from the burning bush; I am the 'I AM' who revealed God to the world in the Scriptures (meaning the Jewish Bible, or Tanakh). Yes, indeed," Jesus says, "I am that God!" That's why they wanted to stone Him.

That the Person of the LORD Jesus Christ is the revelation to all creation of the Person of God (the Father), the Transcendent Majesty, is not a disputable truth. But I believe the most distinctive way He revealed Himself was through His advent on earth as a human man: the Son of Man.

In the following two sections we look at the human Jesus, as distinguished from the divine Jesus.

The Incarnation of YHWH

What does incarnation mean?

Here's what I hear when the subject is preached. "The Son of God came down from Heaven and…" There is no question in my mind that when that statement is made, the speaker means that the Son of God who came down is somehow a distinct entity from Jehovah God, God the Father.[47] We know that this cannot be true based on the argument concerning the so-called distinctness of the three persons of the Godhead provided on page 9, which shows that the persons in the so-

---

[47] In the Godhead theology Jesus is related to God in some mysterious fashion; *sharing God's essence* (whatever that means) is the way I've heard it put.

called Godhead cannot possibly be distinct from one another if they are fully God; rather, they are indeed one unique *person*, as we understand that term.

Back to my point. Here's what biblical *incarnation* means. The very revealed Person of God the Father, who is Jehovah God, the God of the Old Testament—who appeared and spoke throughout the O.T.—that very person *came down*,[48] metaphorically speaking, from His throne in heaven and assumed the form of a man (John 6:41–42 and Philippians 2:6–8).[49] I say *came down* is a metaphor because when He came to earth as a man, He didn't descend into the earth's atmosphere on angel's wings but was born to a human woman. In that instant, he reached *down* from the vast timelessness of His divine existence, and put His whole character and being into the timeline of creation. The Living God of the O.T. became the Son of Man, a real human being with human flesh (John 1:14 and Luke 24:39). In that instant of time, Jehovah God became *fully man,* as we are wont to say when describing His incarnation.

How do I know that Jesus is the incarnation of YHWH? Because the Scriptures clearly teach this.[50] There are two Psalms that are pertinent here, which are quoted in Hebrews 1:8–12.

First there is this passage from Psalm 45, a song of praise to the LORD:

> **To the choirmaster: according to Lilies. A Maskil of the Sons of Korah; a love song.**
>
> *My heart overflows with a pleasing theme; I address my verses to the king; my tongue is like the pen of a ready*

---

[48] To come *down* as used with respect to Jesus' incarnation is a Biblical metaphor for assuming a lesser quality of existence.

[49] See also 1 Timothy 3:16, which certainly refers to the Living God mentioned in 1 Timothy 3:14–15 that *appeared in a body* here on earth. The term *Living God,* as used to describe God sixteen times in the O.T., can only mean the God who revealed Himself in the Old Testament.

[50] Thanks to Dr. James White of Alpha & Omega Ministries for this teaching. You may view it on YouTube by searching for key words *Dr. James White* and *Jehovah.*

scribe. / ²*You are the most handsome of the sons of men; grace is poured upon your lips; therefore God has blessed you forever.* / ³*Gird your sword on your thigh, O mighty one, in your splendor and majesty!* / ⁴*In your majesty ride out victoriously for the cause of truth and meekness and righteousness; let your right hand teach you awesome deeds!* / ⁵*Your arrows are sharp in the heart of the king's enemies; the peoples fall under you.* / ⁶*Your throne, O God, is forever and ever. The scepter of your kingdom is a scepter of uprightness;* ⁷*you have loved righteousness and hated wickedness. / Therefore God, your God, has anointed you with the oil of gladness beyond your companions* (Psalm 45:1–7).

Then, in Psalm 102 of the O.T., we have this prayer of an afflicted man petitioning the LORD:

A prayer of an afflicted man. When he is faint and pours out his lament before the LORD.

¹*Hear my prayer, O LORD; let my cry come to you!. . .* / ¹²[For] *you, O LORD, are enthroned forever; you are remembered throughout all generations.* / ¹⁸*Let this be recorded for a generation to come, so that a people yet to be created may praise the LORD:* / ¹⁹*that he looked down from his holy height; from heaven the LORD looked at the earth...* / ²⁴*"O my God," I say, "take me not away in the midst of my days— you whose years endure throughout all generations!"* / ²⁵*Of old you laid the foundation of the earth, and the heavens are the work of your hands.* / ²⁶*They will perish, but you will remain; they will all wear out like a garment. You will change them like a robe, and they will pass away,* / ²⁷*but you are the same, and your years have no end* (Psalm 102:1; 12, 18–19, 24–27).

I have quoted these Psalms this way to make sure there is no misunderstanding that each Psalm is about YHWH.

Solid Food for the Mature Believer

Quoting from these Psalms (see bold text), here's what the Spirit tells us of the Son, Jesus, in Hebrews 1:8–12:

⁸*But of the Son he says, "**Your throne, O God, is forever and ever, the scepter of uprightness is the scepter of your kingdom.** / ⁹**You have loved righteousness and hated wickedness; therefore God, your God, has anointed you with the oil of gladness beyond your companions**"* (Hebrews 1:8–9 are from Psalm 45:6–7).

He also says,

¹⁰*And, "**You, LORD, laid the foundation of the earth in the beginning, and the heavens are the work of your hands;** / ¹³**they will perish, but you remain; they will all wear out like a garment,** / ¹²**like a robe you will roll them up, like a garment they will be changed. But you are the same, and your years will have no end**"* (Hebrews 1:10–12 are from Psalm 102:25–27).

The same person is referenced in both passages; Jesus, in His divine nature, is YHWH.[51] In quoting what He'd written before in Psalm 102, the Spirit adds, *O LORD* after *beginning* in the second paragraph. This LORD clearly refers to the LORD, Jehovah, for the

---

[51] The Hebrew word for God used Psalm 45 is אֱלֹהִים (*'elohiym*, H430). When a Hebrew writer wants to identify the LORD as a Sovereign LORD, he will sometimes use אֱלֹהִים יְהוָה ((*'elohiym*)*Yĕhovah* (H3068)), literally *God the LORD*, translated by the ESV as LORD God, as in the book of Genesis. Other times he will use יְהוָה אֲדֹנָי (*'Adonay* (H136) *Yĕhovah* (H3068)), literally meaning *the LORD LORD*, also translated as LORD God, as in, for example, Ezekiel 3:11. The long and short of this is that there is no question when the Hebrew writer refers to God he is referring to the LORD, Jehovah, as the ESV translation attests.

reason just mentioned. Such convention is not followed in the N.T., because the Greeks had no word for YHWH.[52]

Again, how do I know for certain it was the revelation of God the Father, the God of the Old Testament, who came to live in a human body and not the *Son of God* entity that is preached today? Jesus confirms this in John 14:10, where He says, *"Do you not believe that I am in the Father and the Father is in me? The words that I say to you I do not speak on my own authority, but the Father who dwells In me does his works."* Note that Jesus did not say it was the Son of God entity of the so-called Godhead living in Him, which without doubt He would have said if the advocates of the Godhead theology are correct.

Also, when it is preached that Jesus came down off His throne in heaven to come to earth, the distinct impression is given that while Jesus as the Son of Man walked the earth, He left an empty throne in heaven with a sign hanging on it saying, "Out temporarily. Will be back in thirty-three years." Jesus—who is the radiance of God's glory and the exact representation of His being, and who also fills the universe—never stopped being God, who is spirit (John 4:24), while He walked the earth.

When speaking of Jesus' incarnation, Scripture plainly states that the revealed God of the Old Testament, by His Spirit, inseminated a young virgin with a Holy Seed that, when it came to fruition, became a physical man with many of the limitations of naturally born human beings, but without a sin nature. From the very moment of conception, this physical being was inhabited by the Holy Spirit of God and through this, became the physical revelation of God on earth. (Psalm 22:9).[53] All Jesus' power came (and still comes) from God's Holy

---

[52] According to the Godhead theology, the divine Jesus is not God the Father because they are distinct persons. It follows, then, that YHWH, is not God the Father. Well, the Jews of the N.T. believed that YHWH was the Father. See for example Psalm 89:26 and Malachi 2:10. They understood that when Jesus, the Son of Man, spoke of the Father He was referring to YHWH. Wouldn't proper exegesis of these passages in the N.T. demand that we interpret them as referring to God the Father, since that's what the audience understood Jesus to mean?

[53] As we will see later, the Holy Spirit of God is another name for the Person of God interacting with His creation. He is the Spirit *form* of God who lived in Jesus.

Spirit working through Him (Matthew 12:28).[54] None of Jesus' supernatural power came from His physical human body as it existed on earth two thousand years ago, or continues to exist as the transformed immortal human body He inhabits now. Jesus (God) also had to suffer many things as a result of living in a fragile jar of clay (2 Corinthians 4:7). One of them was to learn to deal with His limitations as a man without sinning. For example, when He became hungry in the desert, He had to learn not to give in to what must have been an overwhelming desire to eat but to remain in God's will—that He remain hungry until the proper time.[55]

There is no way we can know the full extent of the human limitations Jesus imposed on Himself while He sojourned with us. What we do know from Scripture is that He got hungry, thirsty and tired. His pre-resurrection human body was mortal, in the sense that it could be killed by the cross.[56] And the human Jesus did not seem to have all the characteristics of omniscience, because He would have known when the Son of Man was coming again, which He Himself said that the Son of Man did not know (Matthew 24:36).[57]

Continuing this line of thought, the Gospel accounts indicate that the Son of Man, while on earth, had other human limitations. For example, in the story of the hemorrhaging woman, when she touches

---

[54] It is clear that Jesus not only drove out demons by the Spirit of God, but did everything else that He did by the Holy Spirit working through Him.

[55] Of Jesus the man learning things, see John 4:1; John 15:15; and Hebrews 5:8. Certainly as the divine being who exists eternally in heaven (apart from His human, immortal body), Jesus never learned anything or had to learn anything because He is omniscient. This idea of *learning* indicates that as a human boy and then a man, He was taught the truths of God just as we are: by reading the word and listening to the Spirit speak. And He never had to become perfect; He was already perfect. Nor was He ever disobedient, but His obedience was perfected, that is brought to its very fullness in Him, as He walked the earth in accordance with God's will.

[56] Jesus as hungry: Matthew 4:2; thirsty: John 4:7 and John 19:28; tired: Matthew 8:24. Of course God (Jesus), the transcendent spiritual being as He exists in heaven (aka YHWH), never goes hungry or thirsts or gets tired or sleeps (see for example Isaiah 40:28c).

[57] The divine Jesus must be omniscient, so this lack of knowledge must exist in the distinct mind of the human Jesus, the Son of Man, as He now exists in heaven.

Him, He turns and asks His disciples, *"Who touched me?"* (excerpt from Luke 8:45). Why did He ask if He knew?[58] This calls into question whether Jesus, the earthly man, had the instantaneous omniscience of God. Again it seems that He did not, at least not in its transcendent fullness.

There were also other limitations He faced. When He went back to Nazareth, Mark states that, *"And he could do no mighty work there..."* because of their lack of faith (excerpt from Mark 6:5).[59] Finally, the writer to the Hebrews said that Jesus *learned obedience through what he suffered* (excerpt from Hebrews 5:8).[60] God (Jesus), the spiritual being, cannot learn anything because He is omniscient.

Look at the world through Jesus the man's eyes. He is human. He gets tired, hungry and all the rest. He feels emotional and physical pain. His human mind has human thoughts running through it.[61] His human body is animated by the natural physical laws that animate all

---

[58] I am fully aware that this could very well have been a rhetorical question. It could be similar to Jesus asking Adam where he was in Genesis 3:9, when He knew perfectly well where he was. But the phrasing of this passage in Luke seems to indicate that the Son of Man did not know who had touched Him.

[59] The Spirit, precisely why their lack of faith inhibited Him, but the Greek words δύναμαι ποιέω οὐ οὐδείς δύναμις (*dynami poieō ou oudeisdynamis*, G1410, 4160, 3756, 1411) translated as *could do no, not one, mighty work* speak for themselves.

[60] I don't believe for one minute this means to imply that Jesus was ever disobedient. We know this because He was without any sin. I believe the Spirit is saying that Jesus' obedience was perfected by the great suffering He endured and persevered through. This is the example we must all follow as children of God.

[61] Jesus says in John 6:38 that He does not do his own will, but the will of Him who sent Him. If, then, the Son of Man has a will apart from God's will, it must exist in His human mind, apart from His eternal Spirit Mind. This may be the point of distinction of person that has been erroneously transferred in the Godhead theology to the Person of the divine Jesus. An alternative theology is that the Son of Man's mind has thoughts running through it that are not the Transcendent Majesty's thoughts, making Him a distinct and fully human person. One clear example of a purely human thought going through the Son of Man's mind is in John 12:27, where He says that His soul is troubled due to his upcoming crucifixion; and again in Mark 14:34 where Jesus says His soul was *overwhelmed with sorrow to the point of death* (KJV). I don't see how the Eternal Majesty, Jehovah God could ever conceivably feel this awful emotion.

human beings. Yet He is also in constant contact with His Father, that is, with transcendent God as He exists eternally in heaven and whose Person inhabits Jesus by means of His Holy Spirit (John 14:10). Therefore it must be that as the human Jesus' earthly senses perceive the world outside His body, He is also getting inspiration from God's Spirit, moment by moment. This is how He taught with such authority without being formally trained. This is how He knew the hearts of men. This is how He performed miracles. By the very nature of the Incarnation itself, Jesus' faith was perfect; His human nature was perfect. But still, by an act of His divine eternal will, He limited Himself as a man, as we have already discussed. It may be that His human physical mind—which had a finite number of neurons that operated via electrical impulses—was not capable of holding all the omniscient knowledge He has as Jehovah God. Nevertheless, the Spirit was speaking to Him without ceasing, informing and empowering Him to complete His ministry.[62]

It also seems obvious to me that when Jesus, the human man, spoke of his Father, He was speaking as any man might speak of his natural father. Jesus did not mean to imply that He, His eternal self in heaven, is somehow distinct from the God entity that fills the heavens and the earth. We know this because, as we have seen, it is the Person of Jesus Himself who fills the heavens and the earth (Ephesians 1:23 and Ephesians 4:10), and there can't be room in creation for two such god-like entities. The intimate relationship that we sense between Jesus as He walked on the earth and His Father in heaven is precisely (taking into account the self-imposed limitations of His physical being) the same expression of any son's relationship with his father. Therefore while Jesus was a man, He was a God entity *and* human Person that was in some sense distinct from the Person of God in heaven, but only by virtue of His finite existence on earth and His humanness.

---

[62] Since we have the same limitations placed on us as created beings, we as believers must strive to emulate Jesus' walk of submission to and dependence upon God, our Father.

The Son of Man Began With the Incarnation

Prior to when the Son of Man was conceived by the Holy Spirit in Mary's womb, He did not exist in the envelope of creation, though YHWH, who inhabited the human vessel known as the Son of Man, has always existed.[63] What He did do by His incarnation was come *down* from the heights of heaven to save us.

After all the speaking He did through the writers of the O.T. revealing Himself to us through them (Hebrews 1:1), He then revealed Himself to us by becoming a physical being—that is, a being made of the earth's dust—to walk in the evil of this reality, to experience it and to save us, when He could otherwise have stayed in the awesome perfection of heaven (Hebrews 1:2).

As the Almighty Spirit and LORD God, Jesus had no beginning and has no end. As the writer of the Hebrews explains when talking about Jesus, the Man Entity now living (as opposed to walking the earth decades before the writing of this letter) in heaven, *He is without father or mother or genealogy, having neither beginning of days nor end of life, but resembling the Son of God he continues a priest forever* (Hebrews 7:3). But as the Son of Man, that is, as the still-living human male progeny of God the Father, the now-eternal Jesus as the Son of Man did have a beginning.[64]

It all started, of course, with His birth to a human woman. For the LORD God says of this event:

> ...*The* LORD *said to me, "You are my Son; today I have begotten you"* (excerpt from Psalm 2:7).

> ...*and the Word became flesh* (John 1:14a).

---

[63] It seems obvious that the human *jar of clay* that God inhabited when He walked the earth, who called Himself the Son of Man, did not exist from eternity past. The Son of Man entered creation at a certain verifiable point in the timeline of creation, and from that point on exists forever. Therefore, when we refer to the eternal Son of Man, we understand that it's not the same quality of eternity as Jesus, the I AM, who existed in heaven from eternity past.

[64] The very term *son* means the male progeny of a human father and mother.

God the Father is saying of His revealed self, I have come into the timeline of creation and become a mortal human male. Of this human being, who was (and still is) Jehovah God in human flesh (Luke 24:39, though now that perishable *flesh* is transformed to the imperishable [1 Corinthians 15:53]), He says, to paraphrase, *You are now my Son, my **human** Son.* His plan was that this Son of Man would exist in a mortal body for a few years, and then rise from the dead and be transformed into a human being with an eternal body.

If Jesus as the Son had existed from eternity past as a human being, that is, as the human male progeny of His Father, there would be no *today* to have become the Son. Also it says of Him that:

> *[18] And he is the head of the body, the church. He is the beginning, the firstborn from the dead, that in everything he might be preeminent. [19] For in him all the fullness of God was pleased to dwell, [20] and through him to reconcile to himself all things, whether on earth or in heaven, making peace by the blood of his cross* (Colossians 1:18–20).

Again there is an idea of a *beginning* of the Son of Man. To emphasize this, Scripture goes on to say of Jesus, *And again, when he brings the firstborn into the world, he says, "Let all God's angels worship him"* (Hebrews 1:6). Clearly this *firstborn* had a beginning by *being brought into the world* and still dwells in the timeline of the creation.[65] And as we shall see, He will continue to dwell as the Son of Man (also seen as the Lamb of God in Revelation 5:6) and as the ruler of creation until the purpose of transcendent God (the Father, of whom He is the incarnation) has been fulfilled (1 Corinthians 15:27–28).

---

[65] To bring a son into the world is a common expression used when a human baby is born. This does not mean that this human baby existed as a human being before he was born. So it is with the Son of Man.

Kenneth John Marks

The Son, Now the Resurrected Immortal Human Man

The LORD Jesus Christ the Son of Man, from whom Paul sends greetings in his letters, *still exists as a human being*, now with a glorified body, living in heaven; an entity distinct from the Spirit YHWH by virtue of his humanity. This human man—indwelt without limit by the Holy Spirit, yet while he was on earth having certain self-imposed limitations—is, apparently, the first human who had a mortal body that was transformed into an eternal human body by resurrection from the dead, as we will all be transformed when Jesus, the Son of Man, comes again (1 Corinthians 15:51–54). This may be what the description *firstborn of all creation* in Colossians 1:15 means.[66] While others were saved before Christ's birth, it must be that they have yet to be clothed with human immortal bodies, though they have some recognizable form. Consider, for example, Moses and Elijah, who are now alive in heaven and who appeared as men alongside the transfigured Jesus.[67]

Who, then, can understand the depths of the mystery that surrounds the exact nature of the eternal Son of Man? It is commonly understood that we will all retain our identities when we get to heaven. We will have minds that are distinct from God's mind and souls that are distinct from God's soul. As the everlasting God, Jesus' soul is not distinguishable from God's soul because there is only one God. But it appears that this human Son entity, in whom the Person of God dwells through the Holy Spirit, may have a mind and a soul distinct from God's mind and soul because of His eternal humanness. Apparently, the risen LORD Jesus Christ, the eternal Son of Man, continues to have

---

[66] He is also called the *first fruits of those have fallen asleep* in Christ in 1 Corinthians 15:20b. I have seen some speculate that as a *firstborn*, the writer is referring to Jesus' being the Heir to His Father's creation, as a firstborn son was heir to his father's wealth in that culture.

[67] For the transfiguration, see Matthew 17:2–3. Clearly Moses and Elijah were saved. For the salvation of O.T.. saints, see discussion of salvation by the Spirit starting on page 45.

certain human attributes, attributes associated with a created mortal being who has been transformed into an eternal being by resurrection from the dead. For example, He can eat (after His resurrection He ate with His disciples), one can touch Him (as Thomas and Mary Magdalene did), and He described Himself as having flesh and bones.[68]

As to the spiritual fruit of Jesus' resurrection, *God exalted him at his right hand as Leader and Savior, to give repentance to Israel and forgiveness of sin* (Acts 5:31).[69] Also, *"[9][Because Jesus obediently died on the cross for the sins of the world] God has highly exalted him and bestowed on him the name that is above every name, [10] so that at the name of Jesus every knee should bow, in heaven and on earth and under the earth, [11] and every tongue confess that Jesus Christ is* LORD, *to the glory of God the Father"* (Philippians 2:9–11).[70] This resurrected Jesus, the Son of Man, has been appointed ruler of everything by God the Father. A living (but transformed) **human man of flesh and bone** is now ruler of all creation! Think about it.

But this exalted place as ruler of everything does not seem to be of eternal duration for the Son of Man. For Scripture suggests that the resurrected Son of Man's relationship to God the Transcendent Majesty is like that of a prime minister to a sovereign king, as, for example, was Joseph's relationship to Pharaoh:

> *[41] And Pharaoh said to Joseph, "See, I have set you over all the land of Egypt."[42] Then Pharaoh took his signet ring from his hand and put it on Joseph's hand,* [thereby exalting him to the highest place in Egypt] *and clothed him in garments of fine linen and put a gold chain about his*

---

[68] As to Jesus eating, see Luke 24:43; as to Thomas touching Him, see John 20:27; as to Jesus having flesh and bones, see Luke 24:39. Nowhere in Scripture is Jehovah God in His transcendent spiritual form described as eating, drinking or being touchable.

[69] In Acts 5:29–30 Peter clearly implies that Jesus was exalted after he was killed on the cross and raised from the dead.

[70] I've added the brackets because Paul also implies that Jesus' exaltation was the reward for his obedience unto death.

neck. [Thereby giving him a name above all other names in Egypt, except of course, Pharaoh himself.] *⁴³And he made him ride in his second chariot* [e.g. second-in-command, sitting at his right hand, so to speak]*, And they called out before him, "Bow the knee!" Thus he set him over all the land of Egypt. ⁴⁴Moreover, Pharaoh said to Joseph, "I am Pharaoh, and without your consent no one shall lift up hand or foot in all the land of Egypt"* (Genesis 41:41–44).

Simply put, Joseph was exalted to Pharaoh's right hand, and he ruled Egypt in Pharaoh's place, though Pharaoh was the final authority.

Compare this to the Son of Man's reign as described in Scripture:

³¹ ...he foresaw and spoke about the resurrection of the Christ, that he was not abandoned to Hades, nor did his flesh see corruption.³² This Jesus God raised up, and of that we all are witnesses.³³ Being therefore exalted at the right hand of God, and having received from the Father the promise of the Holy Spirit, he has poured out this that you yourselves are seeing and hearing.³⁴ For David did not ascend into the heavens, but he himself says, "The LORD *said to my Lord, 'Sit at my right hand,³⁵* **until I make your enemies your footstool**'" (Acts 2:31–35). [71]

And what happens to Jesus' *prime-ministerhood* when all His enemies have been made His footstool? Here's what the Spirit tells us through the Apostle Paul:

²⁰But in fact Christ has been raised from the dead, the firstfruits of those who have fallen asleep. ²¹For as by a man came death, by a man has come also the resurrection

---

[71] Peter quotes Psalm 110:1, which has the capitalization presented here. The difference in the two words LORD and Lord is very significant in this context! This action of exaltation is a onetime event in the timeline of creation and happened to a human man, as the everlasting God, the divine Jesus, by His very nature, has always been exalted over all things.

of the dead. ²²For as in Adam all die, so also in Christ shall all be made alive. ²³But each in his own order: Christ the firstfruits, then at his coming those who belong to Christ. ²⁴Then comes the end, when he delivers the kingdom to God the Father after destroying every rule and every authority and power. ²⁵For he must reign until he has put all his enemies under his feet. ²⁶The last enemy to be destroyed is death. ²⁷For "God has put all things in subjection under his feet." But when it says, "all things are put in subjection," it is plain that he is excepted who put all things in subjection under him. ²⁸When all things are subjected to him, then the Son himself will also be subjected to him who put all things in subjection under him, that God may be all in all (1 Corinthians 15:20–28).

Paul refers to the human Jesus here as the first fruits of those who are to be raised from the dead. Then His reign as prime minister will, according to this passage, cease when the conditions of Psalm 110:1 have been met, namely, that all His enemies are put under His feet. I believe this is why Jesus testified of Himself as the Son of Man, *"You heard me say to you, 'I am going away, and I will come to you.' If you loved me, you would have rejoiced, because I am going to the Father, for the Father is greater than I'"* (John 14:28).

This is another mystery. What will the subordination of the human Jesus to God the Father look like? How will the human Jesus, who has been made subject to God, relate to the transcendent God, YHWH, of whom He will still be the incarnation? Scripture implies that Jesus, the Son of Man, will no longer be considered Ruler of Everything. We will look to God Himself (the revealed God of creation, the Spiritual Jesus Christ) on the Throne of Authority, rather than the eternally human Son of Man.

This passage from Revelation 22 may shed some light on this mystery:

¹Then the angel showed me the river of the water of life, bright as crystal, flowing from the throne of God and of the Lamb² through the middle of the street of the city; also, on either side of the river, the tree of life with its twelve kinds of fruit, yielding its fruit each month. The leaves of the tree were for the healing of the nations.³ No longer will there be anything accursed, but the throne of God and of the Lamb will be in it, and his servants will worship him.⁴ They will see his face, and his name will be on their foreheads.⁵ And night will be no more. They will need no light of lamp or sun, for the LORD *God will be their light, and they will reign forever and ever* (Revelation 22:1–5).

Note that there is only one throne, not two or three thrones: that of God and the Lamb. It says His servants will serve Him, clearly meaning God; it does not say that His servants will serve *them*, meaning both God and the Lamb. It says they will see His face, not *their* faces. So it is impossible to deny that there is just one God entity in this picture, not the two (or three) of the Godhead theology.

The question arises, does the incarnation cease at this point? Does the human Jesus just morph into His spiritual self, like some transfiguration event, after which Jehovah God is always perceived as a man, but no longer as a resurrected human being? Or does Jesus, the Son of Man, become just one of the gang, one of us, who worships at the foot of the throne as we do? What a great mystery this is! We won't know the answer to this mystery until we see it happen.

Jesus (God) the Love Entity

I want to finish this section by talking about another critical theological error made by today's church (and maybe going back hundreds of years). We have forgotten that God is to be feared with a trembling, gut-wrenching fear (Jeremiah 5:21–22), not just regarded with reverent awe as we might look at a mountain or at the Grand Canyon, which is the way the fear of God is preached today.[72]

The modern Christian church has committed the same frightening sin that the Israelites did before their nation was destroyed. Since the Israelites forgot how to fear their God, they did not take His warnings to heart, and neither do we in the church today. This led to Israel's destruction as a nation, and it follows them even today as God continues to carry out against them the curses of Deuteronomy 28. This has also led to all kinds of sin flourishing in the modern American church. It has made the church weak and ineffective as a moral guidepost for this country. If we do not repent, it will lead us to the same Laodicean fate as Israel (Revelation 3:14–22). Doesn't that scare you?

How did we lose the fear of God? As our feel-good, everything-is-okay-as-long-as-no-one-gets-hurt culture developed, we feel increasing discomfort when talking about the consequences of sin and judgment. There is a widespread belief in the church that the *wrathful, vengeful* God of the Old Testament (O.T.), YHWH, is *different* somehow from the God of the New Testament (N.T.), Jesus Christ.[73,74]

To a vast majority of believers, not to mention those who call themselves Christians but aren't, God is love. Period. Many might wave their hands at admonitions of judgment for believers, such as 1

---

[72] For more on how we are to fear God, see the section titled **Fear The LORD Your God** on page 83.

[73] In this book I will refer to the time after Pentecost as belonging to the New Testament (N.T.). The time prior to Pentecost belongs to the Old Testament (O.T.). This is because all Scripture in the N.T. was written after the church age began at Pentecost.

[74] This is what I was taught as a young Christian. Not in so many words, mind you, but in the general tenor of the way the O.T.. and N.T. were preached or spoken of. Having said that, I have seen such distinctions made in so many words in books written by very godly men. It took me years of studying God's word and meditating on it to convince myself that Jehovah and Jesus were the same God. I would bet that this same belief prevailed in the early church and was at the root of the thinking that lead to the Godhead theology, distinguishing the Person of Jesus Christ from that of the Holy Spirit and YHWH.

Corinthians 3:15, but in the church today, Jesus is love, and that's it. The implication is that we can go ahead and sin, and it will be okay.

This is precisely the argument used by active homosexuals who call themselves Christian. They have invented the Law of Love to justify their abominable sexual behavior. They are attacking, sometimes violently, those of us who don't buy their twisted view of Scripture.[75]

If taken to its absurd extreme, this idea means that if God is just love, we don't have to worry about judgment leading to condemnation, because a loving Father would never throw those He loves into hell.[76] In this view of God, He is like a chuckling old grandfather who never punishes sin.[77] How far from the truth this is!

To illustrate how distorted this is, in Luke 19, Jesus tells the parable of the ten minas. He begins by saying,[12] *"A nobleman went into a far country to receive for himself a kingdom and then return..."* (Luke 19:12).

Jesus goes on to say,[14] *"But his citizens hated him and sent a delegation after him, saying, 'We do not want this man to reign over us.'"*[15] He received his kingdom and returned home to reward the servants to whom he had given money to invest while he was gone. (Luke 19:14, and paraphrase of Luke 9:15).

After the king in the parable finishes rewarding the servants to whom he had given the minas, Jesus continues,[27] *"The king then said, 'But as for these enemies of mine, who did not want me to reign over them, **bring them here and slaughter them before me**'"* (Luke 19:27).

This is but the briefest hint of what it will be like in the Judgment for those who reject Jesus as LORD and Savior. And it is certainly

---

[75] See *Can You Be Gay and Christian?* by Michael L. Brown, Front Line Publishing, Lake Mary, Fla., 2014, pp. 6–11.

[76] This is a true statement. God never throws those He loves into hell. See a discussion of God's hatred and wrath in the section **Hatred / Wrath** on page 58.

[77] Think, for a moment, what it would mean if God's defining characteristic were only love. There would be no eternally severe punishment for sin. Jesus would not have had to come to save us. Why should we give our life to Him and suffer as a consequence? (Philippians 1:29). It doesn't take long to see the ridiculous conclusions you must reach if God's only characteristic is love.

Jesus, the Son of Man, who will judge humankind and mete out the terrible punishment that awaits those who rejected Him (Matthew 7:21–23; Matthew 13:47–50; Matthew 22:13; Matthew 24:50–51; John 5:27; and Revelation 20:11–15).

It will also be the Person of Jesus Christ who will lay waste to the earth in the last days (Isaiah 24:1). This is a God who is much more than *love*. He is a God who should indeed be greatly feared. Take heed! Our God is indeed a consuming fire (Deuteronomy 4:24; Hebrews 12:29), and *It is a fearful thing to fall into the hands of the living God* (Hebrews 10:31).

The Holy Spirit[78]

The Holy Spirit is the Person of God interacting with His creation, which is everything that exists *outside of* or *in addition to* His being.[79]

The Holy Spirit dwells within God's being, as any person's spirit dwells within his being. To say that the Holy Spirit is part of God is misleading in that He cannot be separated from God's being. If you were to think of God as an infinitely vast and deep ocean, the Holy Spirit is the water in that ocean. He completely fills God's being.

Therefore, the Person of the Holy Spirit is identical to the Person of the Transcendent Majesty. He carries all God's nature and person with Him when He reveals God to His creation through His actions. Since the Person of Christ (YHWH) is not distinguishable from the Person of God, the Holy Spirit also carries all that there is of the nature and Person of Christ. Here is the proof from Paul himself:

> *[12]Since we have such a hope, we are very bold, [13]not like Moses, who would put a veil over his face so that the Israelites might not gaze at the outcome of what was being brought to an end. [14]But their minds were hardened. For to this day, when they read the old covenant, that same veil remains unlifted, because only through Christ is it taken away. [15]Yes, to this day whenever Moses is read a veil lies over their hearts. [16]But when one turns to the* LORD, *the veil is removed. [17]**Now the Lord is the Spirit**, and where the Spirit of the Lord is, there is freedom. [18]And we all, with unveiled face, beholding the glory of the Lord, are being transformed into the same image from one degree of*

---

[78] In Appendix 1, I have expanded on this idea, and the text here refers to that study of the Spirit's work and actions as testified to by Scripture.

[79] We clearly understand that rocks are not God. Molecules are not God. All the *natural* forces—gravity, electromagnetism, the strong and weak nuclear forces—that keep this universe from flying apart are not God. The creation itself is not God. All these things exist *outside of* or *in addition to* God's being, which is the sense in which I discuss creation here.

*glory to another. For this comes from **the Lord who is the Spirit*** (2 Corinthians 3:12–18).[80]

The Spirit does not exist in addition to God the Father, as the Godhead theology implies. The Spirit is God the Father—the LORD God—and the LORD God is the Spirit, just as the divine Person of Jesus Christ is God, and carries all God's nature and person with Him. And since the Person of Christ is not distinguishable from the Person of God, the Holy Spirit also carries all that there is of the nature and Person of Christ.[81]

The Holy Spirit is referred to in Revelation 1:4; 3:1; 4:5 and 5:6 as the *seven spirits* of God, also translated as the *sevenfold* Spirit of God, because the Holy Spirit operates simultaneously on many different levels in God's creation.

As explained further in Appendix 1, among the many things the Holy Spirit does:

I. Fills creation with the presence of God and sustain creation's existence from nanosecond to nanosecond.[82] Whatever is not God—that does not belong to God's being—is everything that exists as a result of God's creative act, and it continues due to His sustaining power exercised through the Holy Spirit. This includes everything that we might ever be able to comprehend or understand. *For by him all things were created, in heaven and on earth, visible and invisible, whether thrones or dominions or rulers or authorities* (Colossians 1:16a).

---

[80] I have reproduced the entire passage here to leave no doubt to whom Paul is referring when he says that the Lord is the Spirit. Twice. It seems to me that the only possible way to interpret this passage, if the language here is to have any meaning at all, is that the Person of the Holy Spirit is the same as the Person of Person of Jesus Christ, who is the Person of Almighty God revealed to His creation.

[81] See also Romans 8:9 and 1 Peter 1:11, where the Holy Spirit is referred to as the Spirit of Christ (see page 138 in Appendix 1). Romans 8:9 makes it clear that when Paul speaks of the Spirit of God, he is speaking of the Spirit of Christ.

[82] See Hebrews 1:3, where the author combines the work of Christ (the Creator) with the work of the Spirit, who is the sustainer of all things.

II. Breathes life into what would otherwise be lifeless matter. That is, He animates all living things, all plants, animals, microbes, everything in creation outside of God that has life (Job 33:4).[83] Think of Him as the life-giving Spirit, both temporal and eternal.

III. Brings comprehension and understanding to angels, spirits and human beings (Joel 2:28–30; Ephesians 1:17; and 3:4–5). God's Spirit is the source of what we would call intellect or intelligence. He also reveals God's existence to God's children, aka the Spirit of understanding.

IV. Reveals God's truth through His powerful word, and enable sapient beings to believe and comprehend that word by providing eyes that can see and ears that can hear (1 Corinthians 2:14; Deuteronomy 29:4).[84] The Spirit does this through speaking to our souls or giving us visions, and enabling prophetic utterances. He is the revealing, prophetic Spirit.

V. Contends with man[85] and feels grief when we do not obey. He convicts a person of sin, and after completing this process, which could take years, He gives a person the power to accept Christ as his Savior. He then comes in to dwell within him,

---

[83] It is only God who has life in Himself. No single *thing* composed of any matter or created spirit has life apart from the work of God's (Christ's) Spirit.

[84] I use the term *sapient* here to mean a being with intellect, understanding and self-awareness, who can reason complex abstract ideas and use them to gain understanding of his environment, and through this attribute can come to know and love God, if he is willing.

[85] See Genesis 6:3 for *contending*. The ESV for some mysterious reason translates the Hebrew word דִּין (*diyn*, H1777) as *abide in*, when the word is more clearly translated as *strive with* or *contend with*.

bestowing on him eternal life.[86] He can be considered the saving, indwelling and transforming Spirit.[87]

VI. Circumcises (transforms) hearts, shaping God's elect into Christ-likeness, giving them the desire and ability to follow and serve God (Numbers 14:24; Deuteronomy 8:17–18; Zechariah 4:6; Romans 8:2–8; Philippians 2:13 and 4:13).[88] He can also cause non-believers, even wicked men, to carry out His will. He is the Spirit of service through a changed life that results from God's act of salvation.

VII. Enables the believer to know and relate to God personally.[89]

VIII. Bestows talents, skills and abilities as well as spiritual gifts as He sees fit.[90] Provides what we would call miraculous power to any sapient being God chooses as the Spirit of power.[91]

IX. Shapes God's church according to His will (1 Corinthians 3:9–10; 2 Corinthians 5:1; and Ephesians 2:21).

---

[86] This is the *drawing* part of John 6:44. For grieving, see Ephesians 4:30; convicting of sin, John 16:8; indwelling, Acts 2:38 and 2 Corinthians 1:22.

[87] As I will discuss later, the permanent indwelling Spirit of Salvation has been available to man from the time of Adam. It is not true that He first was given as an eternal indwelling deposit at Pentecost.

[88] There are many more. When Scripture says *God works in you,* or its equivalent, it means that He works in you through the Person of the Holy Spirit, which is God's (e.g. Jesus Christ's) very own presence in you. As for making non-believers carrying out His will, see the story of Balaam in Numbers 22.

[89] This falls into the *common knowledge* category. There are probably several dozen verses in the N.T. one could cite that when taken together would prove this, and one could write a thousand pages commenting on all of these. To choose one, I like, *...Christ in you, the hope of glory* from Colossians 1:27. Since the LORD is the Spirit, then Christ dwells in us by His Spirit.

[90] For talents, skills and abilities, see Exodus 31:1–6. For spiritual gifts, see 1 Corinthians 12:1–11.

[91] More specifically, the Son of Man Himself, Jesus Christ, worked by the power of the Spirit. See Matthew 12:28. Also see 1 Samuel 10:6 as an example of God giving the Spirit to Saul, but temporarily. There are dozens of examples in Scripture of the miraculous work done through men by the Spirit of Jesus.

X. Raises the dead whom God has chosen (again the life-giving Spirit, the Spirit of salvation), to all who were, are or will ever be saved in this age (Isaiah 26:19; Acts 2:28–39).[92] Once the saving Spirit is given, He will never be taken away (John 10:28–29; 2 Corinthians 1:22).

In addition to all this, here is an understood truth of Scripture concerning the process of a sinner coming into the Kingdom. In Acts 2, after Peter accuses his people of murdering their messiah and they ask, "What shall we do?" he replies:

> [38]*"Repent and be baptized every one of you in the name of Jesus Christ for the forgiveness of your sins, and you will receive the gift of the Holy Spirit.* [39]*For the promise is for you and for your children and for all who are far off, everyone whom the* LORD *our God calls to himself"* (Acts 2:38–39).

It is clear, then, that when a sinner repents and turns to Christ for salvation, he receives the gift of the Holy Spirit. And we know from other Scripture that this gift is irrevocable (Romans 11:29).[93] And we know that the sinner cannot come to this place without the Spirit working in his life beforehand.

---

[92] These verse references are but a few examples of this truth. In John 6:44 Jesus also says that He, Himself, will raise the dead on that last day, thereby identifying Himself as being one in Spirit and Being with God.

[93] One cannot lose his salvation, because the salvation of any soul is made through God's sovereign choice. None of us did anything to earn that salvation, therefore none of us can do anything to *unearn* our salvation. There is no sin we can commit to cause God to take His Spirit from us, because when He gives His Spirit to us, He knows all the sins we will commit after we get His Spirit. If there was such a sin, He would not have given His Spirit to us in the first place. And Jesus Himself testifies to this truth in John 10:28b. When He says, *"No one will snatch them out of my hand,"* He means the sinner who's saved. To those who think that by doing something awful, they can lose their salvation, consider this: God knew everything you were ever going to do in your life before you received His Spirit, and He gave this gift to you anyway. How then would He change is mind? (See Numbers 23:19.)

I point out these well-known truths here, because there is a common but incorrect belief in religious circles that the Holy Spirit's eternal indwelling presence in human beings, the saving (and transforming) Spirit described by Peter, was not given until Pentecost. This cannot be true, as I will explain next.

What Happened at Pentecost

It is my fervent belief that it was not the eternal indwelling Spirit of salvation that was introduced into the world at Pentecost. The coming of the Spirit in Acts 2 must refer to the work of Comforting Spirit, and the Spirit who gives knowledge and miraculous power. Of course these are all *one* Spirit, manifesting His power in different ways (1 Corinthians 12:9, 13; Ephesians 2:8 and Ephesians 4:4).

I know this assertion may seem outrageous in light of passages like the following:

> [37]*On the last day of the feast, the great day, Jesus stood up and cried out, "If anyone thirsts, let him come to me and drink.* [38] *Whoever believes in me, as the Scripture has said, 'Out of his heart will flow rivers of living water.'"* [39]*Now this he said about the Spirit, whom those who believed in him were to receive, for as yet* **the Spirit had not been given**, *because Jesus was not yet glorified* (John 7:37–39).

This is about as black-and-white a statement as can be. The (supposedly indwelling) Spirit had not been given. Period.

To understand why this passage cannot refer to the permanent indwelling Spirit, we must first recall what our LORD Jesus Christ said concerning the power of the flesh to receive salvation:

> *"No one can come to me, except the Father who sent me, draws him..."* (John 6:44a).

> *⁶³"It is the Spirit who gives life; the flesh is no help at all.*[94] *The words that I have spoken to you are spirit and life.* ⁶⁴*But there are some of you who do not believe." (For Jesus knew from the beginning who those were who did not believe, and who it was who would betray him.)* ⁶⁵*And he said, "This is why I told you that no one can come to me unless it is granted him by the Father"* (John 6:63–65).

Scripture is clear that God draws sinners to Himself only through the work of His Spirit. There can be no other existing entity that draws men to God to enable them to believe in Him. It is also clear that the flesh—man's natural strength and desire—counting for nothing has been true since Adam.

In pre-Pentecostal times, no one could have served God or been saved if the Spirit had not drawn them to Him and then come to dwell in them. The disciples themselves **could not** have been following Jesus had the Spirit not been working in their lives. It is only by God's eternal power and sovereign will that one can approach God, come to follow Him and be saved.[95] If it were true that the Spirit was only given **after** Pentecost, how then did pre-Pentecostal saints—for example, Enoch, Noah, Abraham, Moses, Elijah, and Daniel—come to know and follow God? Jesus' claim about the worth of the flesh shouts at us that they could not have done it through the strength of their own fleshly nature, and they couldn't have decided one day to become worshippers of God. The Holy Spirit **must have been** working in them already.[96]

---

[94] The NIV translates the Greek phrase ὠφελέω οὐδείς *(ōpheleō oudeis)(G5623,G3762) counts for nothing*. The literal translation is *prophets nothing,* which is the KJV translation. I believe the ESV translation given above, which strangely enough seems like a paraphrase to me, is not as strong. In any case, the flesh will never be able to save faith by itself, because it cannot do so according to Romans 8:7. It must come by the Spirit of God working in us, drawing us to God.

[95] John 1:12–13 makes this truth abundantly clear.

[96] All children of God know through personal experience that to be saved, Jesus must work on our hearts before we finally surrender to His call. This is what *drawing* means. This has been true since Adam. It has certainly been true in my life.

That these great saints were granted eternal life is verified by Jesus Himself when He declares that Abraham, Isaac, Jacob and all the Prophets are alive in heaven (Luke 13:28). We also know from Jesus' transfiguration that Moses and Elijah were saved (Luke 9:30). And consider Joseph, Ruth, Boaz, David, Zechariah, Anna, Simeon and other pre-Pentecostal saints mentioned in Scripture. Can there be any doubt that they reside in heaven with Jehovah God? And then there are Jesus' followers who walked with Him. According to Jesus, their names were **written in heaven** before Pentecost (Luke 10:20), which must mean that they were saved.

Therefore, there can be no doubt whatsoever that the saving work of the Holy Spirit occurred prior to Pentecost.[97]

Knowing that once a person is saved he cannot lose his salvation, which would require the Spirit to part from him, it follows that if the Spirit did not come to dwell with the pre-Pentecostal saints forever, God could have somehow taken their salvation away from them. Is it conceivable that Abraham could have lost his salvation? Or Moses? Or David? Or any of the prophets? No indeed!

So to what specific work of the Spirit is the passage referring? As I was pondering this mystery, God spoke to me in words that formed in my mind as clearly as if they had been spoken into my ear. It was the Spirit of the church and also the Spirit of miraculous power that came at Pentecost. (I've seen this spirit described as a *charismatic* spirit.)

I would interpret the phrase *rivers of living water* flowing out of someone's heart (paraphrase of John 7:38b from above quote) to mean that this manifestation of the Spirit will cause men to spread the gospel, encourage and admonish the saints, perform miracles, form churches, and shepherd others into the Kingdom. This is a different manifestation of the Spirit than the Spirit of salvation, just as the manifestation of the Spirit that gives us each a gift from God is different from the Spirit of salvation.

This Spirit of living water flowing out of God's saints is called the Counselor and the Spirit of truth in John 14:17, and a teacher in John

---

[97] It's God's own truth that thousands of people were saved prior to Pentecost. See 1 Kings 19:18.

14:26, John 15:26 and John 16:13.[98] In the context of these verses, this Counselor was sent to help Jesus' disciples understand the truth about Him. The Holy Spirit was also sent to instill in them the testimony about Jesus that they shared with others. Nowhere here does Jesus say that after the Counselor is given, *you will then be saved and live with me forever*. They were already saved.[99] In fact, a careful reading of post-Pentecostal Scripture reveals how the disciples' lives were transformed prior to Pentecost by the power of this indwelling Spirit.[100]

To confirm my reasoning, here is an exegesis of Acts 8:14–17 written by Gordon D. Fee and Douglas Stuart, professors of the N.T. and O.T., respectively. First the passage:

> *[14]Now when the apostles at Jerusalem heard that Samaria had received the word of God, they sent to them Peter and John, [15] who came down and prayed for them that they might receive the **Holy Spirit**, [16]**for he had not yet fallen on any of them, but they had only been baptized in the name of the LORD Jesus**. [17]Then*

---

[98] Note that Jesus says in John 14:17: *"...even the Spirit of truth, whom the world cannot receive, because it neither sees him nor knows him. You know him, for he dwells with you and **will be** in you."* The phrase in the Greek translated *will be in you* is εἰμί ἐν σύ. The Greek word εἰμί (pronounced *eimi*, G1510), is the present tense of the verb *to be*. The ESV notes that some manuscripts have the present tense *is* here for the translation of εἰμί: namely, that the Spirit *is already* dwelling with them. Both the Textus Receptus and the Morphological Greek New Testament use the future tense of word εἰμί, which is ἔσται, or *will be*. I'm not clear on the spiritual difference between dwelling **with** and dwelling **in**, here, made by the Greek word for *will be*. In any case, if they are following God and their names are written in heaven, they must already have the indwelling Spirit.

[99] See 1 John 2:22–23. See also 1 John 4:2–3. Here John makes it abundantly clear that to be able to acknowledge that Jesus is from God, one must have the Spirit of salvation working in him. Also see Luke 10:20, where Jesus Himself says His disciples are saved.

[100] Another example is Abraham. If you study the account of his life, starting at Genesis 12:1, you can see him grow in righteousness and obedience, which must be through the work of the Holy Spirit, as proved by the severe test he passes in Genesis 22:1–14.

> *they laid their hands on them and they received the Holy Spirit* (Acts 8:14–17).

Then the exegesis:

> *About the Samaritan conversions, two things seem to be significant for* [Luke]*:(1) The mission to Samaria, which was the first geographical expansion of the Gospel...* [and] *(2)...it is important for Luke's readers to know that the mission had both divine and apostolic approval, as evidenced by the withholding of the Spirit until the laying on of the apostle's hands...*
>
> *Although we cannot prove this—because the text does not tell us and it lies apart from Luke's concerns—it is likely that what was withheld until the coming of Peter and John was the visible, charismatic **evidence** of the Spirit's presence.* [Emphasis by authors.] *Our reasons for suggesting this are three: (1) All the things said about the Samaritans before the coming of Peter and John are said elsewhere in Acts to describe the genuine Christian experience. Therefore they must have in fact begun the Christian life. (2) Elsewhere in Acts the presence of the Spirit—as here—is **the** crucial element in the Christian life. [Emphasis by authors.] How then could they have begun the Christian life without the crucial element? (3) For Luke in Acts the presence of the Spirit means power (Acts 1:8; 6:8; 10:38), which is usually manifested by some visible evidence.*

They conclude, *Therefore it is probably this powerful, visible manifestation of the Spirit's presence that had not yet occurred in*

Samaria that Luke equates with the "coming" or "receiving" of the Spirit.[101]

Precisely my point. At Pentecost it was not the permanent indwelling Spirit of salvation that was given. It was the Spirit of power and the Spirit of the church. It was an extension of the Covenant of Grace from the Jews as a nation to the whole world through the church. Here is how Paul describes this act of mercy on God's part:

> *[10]...so that through the church the manifold wisdom of God might now be made known to the rulers and authorities in the heavenly places. [11]This was according to the eternal purpose that he has realized in Christ Jesus our LORD, [12]in whom we have boldness and access with confidence through our faith in him. [13]So I ask you not to lose heart over what I am suffering for you, which is your glory* (Ephesians 3:10–13).

Well then, you might ask, what about this passage?

> *[1]...There he found some disciples. [2]And he said to them, "Did you receive the Holy Spirit when you believed?"*
> *And they said, "No, we have not even heard that there is a Holy Spirit."*
> *[3]And he said, "Into what then were you baptized?"*
> *They said, "Into John's baptism."*
> *[4]And Paul said, "John baptized with the baptism of repentance, telling the people to believe in the one who was to come after him, that is, Jesus."*
> *[5]On hearing this, they were baptized in the name of the LORD Jesus. [6]And when Paul had laid his hands on them, the Holy Spirit came on them, and they began speaking in tongues and prophesying. [7]There were about twelve men in all* (Acts 19:1b–7).

---

[101] *How to Read the Bible for All Its Worth* by Gordon D. Fee & Douglas Stuart, Zondervan, Grand Rapids, Michigan, 1981 & 1993, p. 104.

Solid Food for the Mature Believer

Before unpacking this passage, I must digress a moment.

Many times in Scripture, people are quoted as saying something that is untrue or display their ignorance by what they say. For example, in John 7:25–27, Scripture says:

> ^{25}*Some of the people of Jerusalem therefore said, "Is not this the man [Jesus] whom they seek to kill? ^{26}And here he is, speaking openly, and they say nothing to him! Can it be that the authorities really know that this is the Christ? ^{27}But we know where this man comes from, and when the Christ appears, no one will know where he comes from."*

This is not true. The people speaking were ignorant of the prophecy of Micah, which says that the Messiah will come from Bethlehem (Micah 5:2). This very truth was relayed to Herod when he asked the priests and teachers of the law where the Christ would come from (Matthew 2:3–6).

Now back to the passage in Acts 19.

So if these disciples knew nothing of any Holy Spirit, how would they know whether they had received Him or not? The point of Paul's question could have been, "What do you know about how you were saved? Do you understand the gospel message? Do you understand that when you believe in the Name of Jesus, the Holy Spirit comes to dwell in you forever and you are then saved?" These absolute truths of Scripture are not to be denied, and it is clear that these men were ignorant of these truths. Therefore, this passage does not necessarily imply that the indwelling Spirit of salvation was not given until Pentecost.

If one were to take this passage as a literal statement of truth about the timing of when one receives the Holy Spirit, then one would have to believe a) that we only receive the Spirit of salvation once we are baptized (which is demonstrably false as the thief on the cross demonstrates, in addition to the dozens of other verses that also demonstrate this); and b) that one must have hands laid on him to receive the Spirit. Finally, notice that when the Spirit comes upon them they begin speaking in tongues. As pointed out in the exegetical passage above, this was the Spirit of power that came upon them.

Let me apply this to my own experience. Scripture teaches through the words of Peter from Acts 2, quoted on page 45, that when I was saved, the Person of Jesus Christ came to live in me through His Holy Spirit. This happened without anyone laying hands on me, nor did I receive any miraculous powers or speak in tongues. How many of you saints had hands laid on you to receive the Holy Spirit?

Another verse that might call my thesis into question is Psalm 51:11–12:

^{11}Cast me not away from your presence, and take not your Holy Spirit from me. ^{12}Restore to me the joy of your salvation, and uphold me with a willing spirit.

This overwrought verse is typically quoted to justify the claim that the permanent indwelling Spirit of salvation was not given prior to Pentecost. Like this verse, there are many verses that, if read in isolation, seem to contradict what we know to be true.[102]

Since David was saved, he must have been given the deposit that comes with salvation, and he cannot by a wish or any other act lose his salvation.

So what is King David talking about? I believe that he is referring to that aspect of the filling of the Holy Spirit that gives us joy, peace, contentment, as well as the strength and will to serve God and all the rest. That's what the second sentence says in this passage, after all. He wants to be filled with the Spirit at all times. I can see myself pleading with God in these same words because I have sinned against Him, that I not lose the sense of His presence in me and with me and living through me, which He does by the Holy Spirit.

Read also 2 Samuel 23:2–5, where David describes himself as the anointed of God, through whom His Spirit spoke and who made an

---

[102] See, for example, Romans 11:22, which implies that if one does not *continue in [God's] kindness*, he can be *cut off*. One could interpret this *cutting off* to mean that it's possible to lose one's salvation.

everlasting covenant with him, including his salvation (in verse 5). Can anyone doubt that this *everlasting covenant* pertains as much to his salvation as to his kingship over Israel, which is a metaphor used throughout Scripture for the Lordship of Jesus Christ?[103]

The conclusion must then be that the eternal indwelling Spirit of salvation was given prior to Pentecost. And that the post-Pentecostal Spirit was the Spirit of the church age.

A Recap of Part I

I have set out to dispel mistaken notions of the nature of God's being, the Transcendent Majesty, who exists beyond His creation, and is therefore beyond the unaided (or natural) understanding of every sapient being in creation.

This is why He had to reveal Himself to us, and He has done so in the Person of Jesus Christ, whom we can somewhat comprehend because He is this Transcendent Majesty's exact representation. When Scripture uses the prepositions *through* and *in* concerning Christ, it is talking about the everlasting revelation of God's Person through whom the Transcendent Majesty performed all these works. It is this revealed Person of God, the divine Jesus Christ, who spoke to the prophets and manifested Himself to the O.T. saints in a pillar of fire or in the likeness of a man. When he stepped *down* into the reality He created, He became a human male to reveal more of Himself to us.

Scripture is clear that God has revealed to us many of His names: LORD (YHWH); LORD God, the Almighty (or LORD God Almighty); LORD of hosts, etc. Scripture also reveals that God bears this Name: Christ Jesus (which means *the anointed One who saves His people*). That Jesus bears all the names of God, there can be no question, for the Spirit of Christ tells us so in Isaiah 9:6. That the Person of the divine

---

[103] See also Isaiah 55:3, which speaks of an everlasting covenant God will make with all who come to Him for salvation. The Spirit identifies the covenant that God made with David as the same everlasting covenant. It must be the Holy Spirit who enforces this covenant promise in the hearts of the saints, so David must have had the Spirit of Salvation dwelling in him.

Jesus had no beginning and no end is clearly taught by Scripture. (*"Before Abraham was born, I am,"* in John 8:58) But concerning the human Jesus, Scripture speaks about a certain finite point in the timeline of creation called *today* when the Son of Man came into being, the first born and the first fruits of all creation and so forth. And this Son of Man is still a human being, the incarnation of YHWH.

Therefore, if there be a distinction of person between the Son and the Father, it must be between the Person of the Son of Man—the incarnation of the Person of the everlasting Jehovah God—and the Person of YHWH, (aka the divine Jesus) whom the ancient Jews knew to be their Father (1 Chronicles 29:10; Isaiah 64:8; see also Footnote 52 on page 27), and who would have associated with Jesus' Father.

One might ask, why write about this at all? These things that I have written about my LORD and Savior, both as God and as man, are true.

We must be worshippers of God in Spirit and Truth. Failure to do so will hinder our ministries and our walk with the LORD. Also, because the Godhead theology has divided God, as seen by the passage Quoted 7 above, the church has been divided to the point of exploding into thousands of denominations.

If we understand the fullness of the incarnate God's humanity, we will better appreciate the incredible, thoroughly indescribable, sacrifice it was for Him to step down off His throne and join us down here in this filthy world so that He could die for us, though we are born as His enemies (Genesis 8:21; Romans 5:10; and Romans 8:6–7). Isn't that amazing?

PART II
God's Character

This is by no means meant to be an exhaustive study. Rather, I will mention the specific things that the LORD brought to my mind as He prepared me to write this. I believe He wanted me to write these things because we have refused to accept Him in all His majesty and power. We have, instead, created in our minds a god who lives in a tiny box and called Him God. In most churches, for example, if you listen carefully to how God is presented, you will come to believe that God is *not* sovereign over evil. It took me several years of study to get rid of this terrible theological disease. In today's understanding of God, He seems overwhelmed by the evil in the world; He does not have anything to do with the bad things that happen.[104] In today's theology He is presented like a chuckling old grandfather who doesn't mean what He says about the terrible consequences of sin, for believer and unbeliever alike. In this part and in Part III I hope to dispel these errors, which testify that we have truly forgotten how to fear the LORD our God and to worship Him in Spirit *and Truth.*

So then here are a few of the aspects of God's character and being that I will discuss: Love,[105] Hatred/Wrath, Mercy, Goodness, Kindness, Grace, and God's sovereignty.

---

[104] The teaching of Scripture is clear, that God's hand is in all things that transpire in the heavens and on earth. Nothing happens in creation that does not pass through the portal of His will.

[105] In the Hebrew, when the word speaks of God's love, the NASB has translated the nearly untranslatable Hebrew word חֶסֶד (*checed,* H2617) that means, among other things, *kindness, lovingkindness, mercy, goodness,* into *lovingkindness,* whereas the ESV translates it as *steadfast love* (as in Jeremiah 9:24) or *kindness* (as in Genesis 19:19). In the N.T. the word *love,* when speaking of God's love for us, is the Greek word agapē (ἀγάπη, G26), which denotes a benevolent, self-sacrificing type of love, not at all related to eros (ερως) (which does not occur in the Bible) and can signify the erotic, grasping, greedy, self-promoting emotion that substitutes for real love in our defiled and vicious culture.

Love

I believe that the most frequently quoted verse of the Bible, especially from those who have never read it, or those who have read it but don't believe it, is the highlighted part of the following passage:

> *So we have come to know and to believe the love that God has for us.* **God is love**, *and whoever abides in love abides in God, and God abides in him* (1 John 4:16).

I would guess thousands and thousands of books have been written about the love of God, but my favorite testimony of His love is the following verse that, I have read, was found scratched into a prison wall:

> *Could we with ink the ocean fill, and were the skies*
> *parchment made;*
> *Were every stalk on earth a quill and every man a*
> *scribe by trade;*
> *To write the love of God above would drain the ocean*
> *dry;*
> *Nor could the scroll contain the whole, though it stretch*
> *from sky to sky.*[106]

One of the most amazing things about Jesus (YHWH) becoming the Son of Man is that God gave us the ultimate expression of His love by becoming human. He became part of His creation by walking as the Son of Man through the timeline of creation. Given the books and all the rest, I have just one more thing to say about God's love. I would not be writing these lines if He were not Love.

But I do have a warning. People have carried the God-is-Love mantra to such distracting heights that there is a somewhat common notion that even as God's unrepentant enemies are being thrown into

---

[106] The complete story of this verse can be found at http://www.devotions.com/-2003/02/verse-of-favorite-hymn-found-on-wall.html.

hell (by Him), His love somehow follows them there. Brothers and sisters, **there is no love in hell!** God would never throw anyone He loved into hell. Love doesn't work that way. The LORD our God hates those who are in hell and will hate them forever![107]

Hatred / Wrath

Something I must say before I continue. As of the writing of this section, a hateful church in Topeka, Kansas, Westboro Baptist Church, has been in the news. I have visited their website, www.godhatesfags.com, and it is appalling. The words *hate* and *fags* and other vile things are displayed there for all to see, along with God's name. The book you are reading now has nothing whatsoever to do with this abomination of an organization or with its demented pastor, Fred Phelps. Please do not judge the words that follow by Phelps' or Westboro's despicable example. God will make an example of them in His own time. God have mercy on us that such a detestable thing can exist among us and call itself Christian. How I grieve for their eternal souls!

In hearing dozens of preachers preach, I have never heard any one of them attach the word *hatred* to the Name of God. I can understand why in this touchy feely, everything's okay society, but to say that God is just love is not the whole story. God does hate, and it is this emotion that fuels His wrath. Denying this side of God's nature is dangerous. The fires of hell are the eternal expression of God's wrath, which is fueled by His hatred of sin and evil. He also hates people who have purposefully decided to hate Him with all their hearts and souls (see Deuteronomy 7:9–10).[108] He hates those who have lived their

---

[107] Revelation 22:15 testifies to this. He calls those who are in hell *dogs*, the ultimate insult that could be hurled at a person of that era.

[108] We are all born as haters of God, but most of us are unaware of this. These men/women, however, have made a conscious decision to hate God. Dr. Richard Dawkins is a good example of such a person. The referenced Scripture is but one of many examples of this truth. Try also Psalm 11:5.

lives in willful disobedience to Him and want to destroy His church and His children.

When we hear that God might hate something, it is natural to think of God's hatred as being small and ugly like ours. Sinful man hates out of ignorance, bigotry, malice, rage and anger; these emotions are born of unredeemed hearts and spirits as black as pitch and thoroughly corrupt.[109] We hate because hatred is one of the primary motivations of our nature. Our hate is motivated by evil hearts.

The Topeka, Kansas church mentioned above is one unfortunate example of this. Their hatred finds its expression in despicable acts like demonstrating at the graves of our fallen heroes and putting *God hates fags* on its website. Vile hate has also found its expression in hanging black men from trees and in blowing up innocents because they don't worship the same god or gods. It oppresses those who disagree with a person's political, philosophical, scientific or religious point of view. It destroys the reputations of its political enemies through innuendo and outright lies, because they threaten to derail its personal ambitions.[110]

But God does not hate the way we do. His motives are pure and righteous. He hates sin and evil because He is good and just. He hates sin and evil precisely because He is a God of love, and He hates seeing men, whom He came to earth to save, destroying and butchering each other. He looks down on the earth and sees the fruit of sin and evil, every atrocity men can visit on one another, in many cases considering themselves to be doing good! God hates that ugliness with an indescribable passion. And, as I mentioned before, He hates those who, as a pattern of life, with malice aforethought, have chosen to hate Him and who, as a result, make evil choices and contribute to the misery of this world, and He will destroy them (Deuteronomy 32:43b).

---

[109] In the ESV, Jeremiah 17:9a is translated as, *The heart is deceitful above all things, and **desperately sick**,* which lacks a certain punch, don't you think? Try the KJV translation instead, *The heart is deceitful above all things and **desperately wicked**.* To me the latter gives a much better picture of our fallen nature, especially as God sees it.

[110] In short, its name is Leftist Liberalism.

This is not about God hating us run-of-the-mill sinners.[111] Rather, God knows everything there is to know about a person, and He knows whether or not that person will ever bow the knee, confess his sins, and accept the LORD's love and forgiveness, and with that receive His transforming Spirit. He knows whether or not a person will commit terrible acts of destruction out of pure meanness of spirit without the slightest bit of remorse. He knows if a person will ever change, or whether he will always be a vicious murderer in his heart, and He will hate such a person.

There is a caveat. The LORD offers His hand of love to everyone, including such people (Revelation 3:20). While someone may be practicing evil, if he responds to the Spirit calling him to repent and accept the LORD's saving grace, God will turn from this hatred and the repentant sinner will then bask in His love. If, however, the sinner refuses to repent, he has blasphemed the Holy Spirit and there is no hope for him.[112] It's also true that at some point God's offering of love can be withdrawn, and the LORD pushes the unrepentant sinner away from Him and into hell (2 Thessalonians 2:7–12).

Here is one passage that describes how hatred finds expression in God's character:

> *16There are six things that the LORD hates, seven that are an abomination to him: 17haughty eyes, a lying tongue, and hands that shed innocent blood, 18a heart that devises wicked plans, feet that make haste to run to evil, 19a false witness who breathes out lies, and one who sows discord among brothers* (Proverbs 6:16–19).

Note that in this passage the object of His hatred is not just the sin, but also the one who makes it a pattern of life to practice this sin. Here

---

[111] The common saying *God loves the sinner but hates the sin* is true–for most sinners: e.g. those *who cannot tell their right hand from their left.* (Paraphrase of Jonah 4:11) But this is not true for all sinners.

[112] For more on blaspheming the Holy Spirit, see **The Unforgiveable Sin** on page 124.

are more passages that explain God's hatred of sin, evil and those who refuse to repent:

> ⁵*The boastful shall not stand before your eyes; you **hate** all evildoers. ⁶You destroy those who speak lies; the* LORD ***abhors** the bloodthirsty and deceitful man* (Psalm 5:5–6).

> ⁶*Your throne, O God, is forever and ever. The scepter of your kingdom is a scepter of uprightness; ⁷you have loved righteousness and **hated** wickedness. Therefore God, your God, has anointed you with the oil of gladness beyond your companions* (Psalm 45:6–7).

> ²⁰*Is not the day of the* LORD *darkness, and not light, and gloom with no brightness in it?* ²¹*"I hate, I **despise** your feasts, and I take no delight in your solemn assemblies.* ²²*Even though you offer me your burnt offerings and grain offerings, I will not accept them; and the peace offerings of your fattened animals, I will not look upon them"* (Amos 5:20–22).

> *"For I **hate** divorce,"* says the LORD, *the God of Israel, "and him who covers his garment with wrong," says the* LORD *of hosts* (Malachi 2:16 NASB).[113,114]

> *"A woman shall not wear a man's garment, nor shall a man put on a woman's cloak, for whoever does these*

---

[113] I use the NASB here, which is based on the Masoretic Text, because the BHS (the Crossway ESV source document) does not have the *I hate divorce* clause. This is discussed in detail on page 5.

[114] I sure wish the church took this declaration more seriously. If we continue to ignore this and continue to behave like the world by disregarding the sanctity of marriage, we will certainly be judged here on earth, for it is God's promise that He will judge His people (Psalm 50:4; Hebrews 10:30).

*things is an **abomination** to the* LORD *your God"* (Deuteronomy 22:5).

*"You shall not lie with a male as with a woman; it is an **abomination**"* (Leviticus 18:22).[115]

"[15]*A full and fair weight you shall have, a full and fair measure you shall have, that your days may be long in the land that the* LORD *your God is giving you.* [16]*For all who do such things, all who act dishonestly, are an **abomination** to the* LORD *your God"* (Deuteronomy 25:15–16).

[31]*"Do not envy a man of violence and do not choose any of his ways,* [32]*for the devious person is an **abomination** to the* LORD*..."* (Proverbs 3:31–32a).

*The sacrifice of the wicked is an **abomination** to the* LORD*...* (Proverbs 15:8a).

*The thoughts of the wicked are an **abomination** to the* LORD*...* (Proverbs 15:26a).

*He who justifies the wicked and he who condemns the righteous are both alike an **abomination** to the* LORD (Proverbs 17:15).

I mentioned above that God's hand of Love can be withdrawn, and He pushes unrepentant sinners away from the possibility of salvation.

---

[115] Note also that this detestation of homosexuality did not stop with the Cross. Read 1 Corinthians 6:9, which says that homosexual offenders will not enter the Kingdom. Also read Romans 1:26–27. Despite these clear statements of Scripture, how many churches in this country have ordained practicing homosexuals as pastors? How many preach tolerance of sexually deviant behavior? It will be very sad for them on the day of destruction. So very, very sad, indeed!

Here is a passage that shows how the LORD treats those who spit in His face day in and day out by rejecting His gospel:

> ...*the two sons of Eli, Hophni and Phinehas, were priests of the LORD* (1 Samuel 1:3b).
> *[12]Now the sons of Eli were worthless men. They did not know the LORD. [13]The custom of the priests with the people was that when any man offered sacrifice, the priest's servant would come, while the meat was boiling, with a three-pronged fork in his hand, [14]and he would thrust it into the pan or kettle or cauldron or pot. All that the fork brought up the priest would take for himself. This is what they did at Shiloh to all the Israelites who came there. [15]Moreover, before the fat was burned, the priest's servant would come and say to the man who was sacrificing, "Give meat for the priest to roast, for he will not accept boiled meat from you but only raw." [16]And if the man said to him, "Let them burn the fat first, and then take as much as you wish," he would say, "No, you must give it now, and if not, I will take it by force." [17]Thus the sin of the young men was very great in the sight of the LORD, for* [these] *men treated the offering of the LORD with contempt* (1 Samuel 2:12–17).[116]
> *[22]Now Eli was very old, and he kept hearing all that his sons were doing to all Israel, and how they lay with the women who were serving at the entrance to the tent of meeting. [23]And he said to them, "Why do you do such things? For I hear of your evil dealings from all the people. [24]No, my sons; it is no good report that I hear the people of the LORD spreading abroad. [25]If someone sins against a man, God will mediate for him, but if*

---

[116] I have replaced the word *the* in this passage making it [these], because the last sentence in this passage makes it clear that the writer is speaking of Phinehas and Hophni.

> *someone sins against the* L<small>ORD</small>*, who can intercede for him?"* **But they would not listen to the voice of their father, for it was the will of the** L<small>ORD</small> **to put them to death** *(*1 Samuel 2:22–25*)*.

Sermon after sermon, study after study, book after book, we hear only that God loves sinners. And this is true. But Scripture also teaches that there are certain sinners that the L<small>ORD</small> stops loving at some point. Phinehas and Hophni were two of these; I don't see any love for them in this passage. As testified in the Scriptures just presented, The L<small>ORD</small> clearly detested them, so He made it impossible for them to hear their father's rebuke and repent.

This treatment is not only for individuals. The following passage shows how God deals with whole nations that are evil and upon which He has laid His judgment:

> *[18] Joshua made war a long time with all those kings. [19] There was not a city that made peace with the people of Israel except the Hivites, the inhabitants of Gibeon. They took them all in battle.* **[20] For it was the** L<small>ORD</small>**'s doing to harden their hearts that they should come against Israel in battle, in order that they should be devoted to destruction and should receive no mercy but be destroyed**, *just as the* L<small>ORD</small> *commanded Moses* (Joshua 11:18–20).

Just as Phinehas and Hophni had been judged and condemned to death without mercy, so these evil nations, whom the L<small>ORD</small> exterminated through Joshua's armies, had been judged. It is clear that it was the L<small>ORD</small> who caused these people to go to their deaths with no hope of mercy.

The following passage shows that if a nation continues to provoke the L<small>ORD</small>'s anger, He will cease to love that nation. Here is the L<small>ORD</small>'s judgment of the nation of Israel, which had been God's treasured possession:

> *⁵For thus says the* LORD: *"Do not enter the house of mourning, or go to lament or grieve for them, for **I have taken away my peace from this people, my steadfast love and mercy," declares the** LORD. ⁶"Both great and small shall die in this land. They shall not be buried, and no one shall lament for them or cut himself or make himself bald for them. ⁷No one shall break bread for the mourner, to comfort him for the dead, nor shall anyone give him the cup of consolation to drink for his father or his mother"* (Jeremiah 16:5–7).[117]

We know that the story ended badly for Israel:

> *⁸... therefore thus says the* LORD *God: "Behold, I, even I, am against you. And I will execute judgments in your midst in the sight of the nations. ⁹And because of all your abominations I will do with you what I have never yet done, and the like of which I will never do again. ¹⁰Therefore fathers shall eat their sons in your midst, and sons shall eat their fathers. And I will execute judgments on you, and any of you who survive I will scatter to all the winds"* (Ezekiel 5:8–10).

As the city withered under the siege of the Babylonians, the people of Jerusalem did eat their own children to keep from starving (Ezekiel 5:10). This awful thing was from the hand of God. I don't see this as an act of love.

Why, beside the Jew's forsaking God for idols, was the LORD our God against Jerusalem? Here is the LORD speaking to Jeremiah:

---

[117] However, the LORD did not forget the covenant He had made with Abraham and through him with David. In Ezekiel 36:22–23, the LORD makes it clear that He would fulfill the covenant for His Holy Name's sake, not for love of Israel.

> *4 "Because the people have forsaken me and have profaned this place by making offerings in it to other gods whom neither they nor their fathers nor the kings of Judah have known; and because they have filled this place with the blood of innocents, 5and have built the high places of Baal to burn their sons in the fire as burnt offerings to Baal, which I did not command or decree, nor did it come into my mind—6therefore, behold, days are coming, declares the LORD, when this place shall no more be called Topheth, or the Valley of the Son of Hinnom, but the Valley of Slaughter"* (Jeremiah 19:4–6).

This should give the American church and the United States itself pause. We have done everything the LORD judged the Israelis for doing. Founded in the Name of Christ, America has turned away to pagan religions. Our entire culture has surrendered to the idols of money, wealth, fame and fraudulent science—such as evolutionary biology and global warming—to name just a few. America has become a moral cesspool, celebrating grotesque sexual immorality and perverse sexual lifestyles, even to the point of legitimizing homosexual marriage. Likewise, in the name of women's rights, America has murdered upwards of fifty million babies since Roe v. Wade was made the law of the land in 1973.[118] This is the very same thing in God's eyes as if America were casting our children into the burning flames. Yet we continue to shout, "God bless America."[119] Do we really think

---

[118] LifeNews.com puts the estimate at about 58.6 million for 1973 through 2016. Planned Parenthood reports between 1977 and 2014 puts the number at 6.6 million. But they account for around 11% of all abortions performed in the U.S. and these are surgical procedures. PP's numbers do not include chemically induced abortions. See http://www.numberofabortions.com/ for more information on these statistics.

[119] Think about how it must have looked when the people sacrificed their sons and daughters in the fire. In the valley of Ben Hinnom there is a crowd of people surrounding a bonfire, each family with a baby in its arms. As they cast these screaming, helpless infants into the flames, think of the sound of it. In the same way, a fetus screams for help when it is being aborted. Its soul cries out to God for justice. *This note is continued on the next page.*

He will bless us? No, indeed, He will not! Rather, He will destroy this nation if we do not turn from sexual perversion and the horrendous slaughter of innocents.[120]

Finally, this N.T. passage shows how God will lead the world to its final end in the last days:

> *[7]For the mystery of lawlessness is already at work. Only he who now restrains it will do so until he is out of the way. [8]And then the lawless one will be revealed, whom the* LORD *Jesus will kill with the breath of his mouth and bring to nothing by the appearance of his coming. [9]The coming of the lawless one is by the activity of Satan with all power and false signs and wonders, [10]and with all wicked deception for those who are perishing, because they refused to love the truth and so be saved.* **[11]Therefore God sends them a strong delusion, so that they may believe what is false, [12]in order that all may be condemned who did not believe the truth but had pleasure in unrighteousness** (2 Thessalonians 2:7–12).

God will prevent those from repenting who have persisted in their refusal to believe the truth! Since they have never ceased to spit in His face by rejecting the hand of love He extended to them, He will shove them into the eternal fire. This is not an act of love. At this point love has ceased. Hatred of sin and evil and of those who practice these things reigns here, as it did for Phinehas and Hophni. How awful it will be for those who suffer this fate!

O, they will so get that justice when the LORD brings judgment on this nation, which has become despicable in His sight! God bless America, indeed!

[120] I personally believe that God has already become our implacable enemy. But, who knows, if we turn away from our sins as a nation, the LORD might relent and have mercy on America (Jonah 3:9; 2 Chronicles 7:14).

Mercy

I follow this chilling warning with some good news. God has an infinite capacity for mercy, but God limits His mercy for those who are determined to refuse His offer of salvation. And it is God's own truth that showing mercy to sinners is a sovereign choice He makes. Here is the LORD Jesus speaking to Moses:

> *And he said, "I will make all my goodness pass before you and will proclaim before you my name 'The LORD.'* ***And I will be gracious to whom I will be gracious, and will show mercy on whom I will show mercy****"* (Exodus 33:19).

To make sure we do not misunderstand this passage, Paul quotes it in this warning to the Romans:

> *[14]What shall we say then? Is there injustice on God's part? By no means! [15]For he says to Moses, "I will have mercy on whom I have mercy, and I will have compassion on whom I have compassion." [16]So then it depends not on human will or exertion, but on God, who has mercy. [17]For the Scripture says to Pharaoh, "For this very purpose I have raised you up, that I might show my power in you, and that my name might be proclaimed in all the earth." [18]So then he has mercy on whomever he wills, and he hardens whomever he wills* (Romans 9:14–18).

The good news is that God *is willing to make* a sovereign choice to show mercy. He is under no obligation to us to do so. Since God is good and just, the choice He makes of persons to whom He shows mercy will be good and just. To any unbeliever reading this who might wonder whether God would have mercy on him, I shout YES! Just acknowledge your sin to God (confess) and turn from it (repent) toward His saving grace, and commit your life and soul to Jesus Christ. Then believe that God will shower you with goodness and mercy. Accept Him (the LORD Jesus) into your heart, and you will be saved from His horrible wrath.[121]

So what does God's mercy look like? The best example is this: that He, the LORD Jesus Christ—YHWH—came into the world in human flesh for the sake of mankind and died for us all. He did not have to do that. In fact, it's an awesome testament to His mercy that He does not destroy everyone and be done with it all. Justice demands this. But God satisfied justice when He took our sins on His back, carried them away from us and nailed them to the cross.

The second best example is that I have been allowed to write these lines. By an act of God's sovereign will, and because He pursued me without ceasing as a child, and then as a man, I accepted His salvation when I was around eighteen. But then for a variety of reasons I turned from the faith and followed the dark path of sexual promiscuity. I was worthy of death, but the LORD had mercy on me. How grateful I am to Him for the goodness and mercy He has shown me![122]

Here is another example of God's mercy. Nehemiah is praying a prayer of confession and repentance. He says to the LORD:

> [29]*And you warned them in order to turn them back to your law. Yet they acted presumptuously and did not obey your commandments, but sinned against your rules, which if a person does them, he shall live by them, and they turned a stubborn shoulder and stiffened*

---

[121] One may wonder, then, if God makes a sovereign choice to show mercy, how can people be thrown into hell and God still be a just God? I prayed about this for a long time. Then it came to me. I may not get the answer in this life, but I know that on that day, as I stand before God and watch Him throw sinners into hell, I will know in my heart that every one of them deserved this fate. I will know that God's choices were absolutely the right ones. It will be just as if I were witnessing the eternal judgment of Adolf Hitler, Joseph Stalin, Pol Pot, Planned Parenthood, and its enablers like the ACLU. This, of course, includes the unrepentant abortion doctors who have murdered millions of innocent babies. When the books of Judgment are opened, they will be included with all the other gruesome murderers of human history.

[122] See the section called **My Testimony** on page 134.

> *their neck and would not obey. ³⁰Many years you bore with them and warned them by your Spirit through your prophets. Yet they would not give ear. Therefore you gave them into the hand of the peoples of the lands.* ***³¹Nevertheless, in your great mercies you did not make an end of them or forsake them, for you are a gracious and merciful God*** (Nehemiah 9:29–31).

God was patient with Israel for well over eight hundred years, from the time of Moses through the siege of Jerusalem, until He turned away from mercy and His wrath took over, as we have seen above.[123] But even then, after seventy years, God restored the people to the land. Nehemiah is referring to the entire time during which Israel continued to turn their backs on their LORD and God. It's worth noting that Nehemiah is giving thanks in this prayer that he is in Jerusalem getting ready to rebuild the wall, so that the LORD's people might be safe from their enemies.[124]

Goodness

God is good. But *good* doesn't always mean *pleasant*.

Since He has given us an innate understanding of what goodness is, we can understand what this means to a degree. The problem is, in an infantile understanding of God, when we read passages like Romans 8:28, we assume that everything working together for good should be pleasant for us; we assume that the end result of this work will be pleasant. But not every good thing God does to make everything work for good in our lives—and, in some cases, the good place we end up as a result—is pleasant. Some good things He does seem downright horrible to us, but we cannot see reality through God's

---

[123] Moses gave the Law around 1445 B.C. The first captives from Judah were taken to Babylon around 609 B.C., eight hundred thirty-six years later. The Northern Kingdom had long since been destroyed by the Assyrians around 722 B.C.

[124] This prayer was uttered somewhere around 445 B.C., the twentieth year of the Persian king Artaxerxes' reign, one thousand years after the Law was given to Moses.

eyes. If we could, we would see that everything God does *is* good, because He is good.

For example, putting Phinehas and Hophni to death was a good thing because justice was done, and it stopped them from hurting innocent people and bringing dishonor to the Name of God. When the LORD exterminated the evil people of Canaan, it was a good thing, because it was through them that evil was pouring into the world and innocent children were being sacrificed to the flames. He was also putting a stop to their vile sexual practices. When He refrained from totally destroying the Israelites despite their continual disobedience, it was a good thing because it proved that God's covenant with the nation of Israel was irreversible; it also preserved Jesus' line of descent. He also reserved for Himself a remnant that will one day inherit the Kingdom along with the rest of us. When He entered the world encased in human flesh, that was the ultimate good thing, though it was not pleasant for Him, because He did it to reconcile us to Him forever. That is, to reconcile those of us willing to accept His Lordship over our lives.

Kindness

According to the dictionary, *kindness* is the quality of or state of being *kind*.[125] It then defines *kind* as follows:

1. Of a friendly, generous, or warm-hearted nature.
2. Showing sympathy or understanding; charitable: *a kind word*.
3. Humane; considerate: *kind to animals*.
4. Forbearing; tolerant: *Our neighbor was very kind about the window we broke*.
5. Generous; liberal: *kind words of praise*.
6. Agreeable; beneficial: *a dry climate kind to asthmatics*.[126]

---

[125] Microsoft Bookshelf 96–97 edition.
[126] Ibid.

Solid Food for the Mature Believer

From our perspective as believers, God proves this definition because all these things flow out of Him. Everyone who knows the LORD can look at these items and recount to himself how the LORD has exhibited kindness in the context of his life. I will do that here for my life.

1. Re: *Friendly* etc.: God has always wanted to be my friend. One of my earliest memories is of Him introducing Himself to me when I was a little boy of six or seven. He made this possible by moving my non-believing mother to send me to Sunday school at a little one-room Bible church started by Dave and Kay Landers, the two wonderful missionaries mentioned in the dedication to this book. I don't know where their mission field was outside the United States, but for a few years it must have been in my neighborhood. How I thank God for it! It was through their ministry that the LORD revealed Himself to me as Jesus Christ. God has not stopped wanting to be my friend, even when I walked the dark path of sexual promiscuity for many years of my adulthood. God has always been generous to me and approached me with a warm heart.

2. Re: S*ympathy, Understanding, Charitable*: God shows His sympathy to me every day as I struggle with my sin nature. Recently, when I was discouraged by my sin, God came to me and said, "Don't worry, my love. I know that your heart is with me but that your flesh is against me." That was just so very nice (or should I say, kind) of Him![127] God also has been charitable to me as He is to all believers. (And non-believers too, for a time. See Isaiah 26:10.) That's why, when I sin, the LORD does not destroy me, but disciplines

---

[127] This also affirmed for me that the Romans 7 struggle is not about unbelievers, as some think, but about believers. And I am comforted to know that Paul had the same struggles that we all do with our sinful flesh, which is ever battling against the guiding Spirit in us.

me so that I can get back on track. In the case of some believers, God's discipline can lead to death, as it did for Ananias and Sapphira.[128] Since I am aware of this and take God at His word and fear Him, this adds urgency to getting back on the right track if I am straying.

3. Re: *Humane, Considerate*: If God had a pet or was a farmer and raised livestock, or if He rode a horse or donkey, He would be kind to these animals. It says in the Proverbs, *A righteous man cares for the needs of his animal, / but the kindest acts of the wicked are cruel* (Proverbs 12:10). I think God hates with particular intensity those who mistreat animals. If you say you love and know the LORD, you will be kind to animals.[129] How much kinder, then, will the LORD be to humans who seek Him?

God has been more than considerate of me. He has always been gentle with me. This is because He always tells us to relate gently to one another, and He always leads by example. Gentleness is key to how Christians should relate to one another, especially when one is in need of correction because he has fallen off the path of righteousness. Being gentle is the hallmark of showing consideration for others.

4. Re: *Forbearance and Tolerance*: I believe that God will overlook the occasional minor transgression if we go to Him and confess our sin right away.[130] I think of

---

[128] See Acts 5:1–11. This passage illustrates that if we insist on living in disobedience, God will take us home, where we have the 1 Corinthians 3:12–15 experience waiting for us.

[129] This is not meant to give PETA and other loony, vicious extremist groups biblical cover for their worship of animals and the terrorist acts they commit in the name of this idol. They are delusional at best, but most are little more than common vicious thugs. They will have a rude awakening when the unrepentant among them step through death's door into eternity to see a wrathful God waiting for them.

[130] 1 John 1:9 says He has forgiven us. But the Glory of the LORD demands that there be consequences to all sin (see for example Numbers 14:20–23). I'm saying here that God may forbear to rain them down on us who are saved.

forbearance as being identical to patience. God has been infinitely patient with me in my Christian walk, as He demonstrated during the twenty-five years I walked the dark path. God not only did not destroy me (because He had other plans for me, plans for good and not for harm as in Jeremiah 29:11), but He protected me from getting any STDs during this time. That's not to say that I don't suffer the consequences of my bad choices; God has not allowed me to marry or to have children because of the path I chose.

5. Re: *Generous and Liberal*: God has lavished His love on me (Ephesians 1:7–8; 1 John 3:1). I know this for the reasons stated above, and for how He has shepherded me through my entire life, even when I was walking the dark path.[131]

6. Re: *Agreeable and Beneficial*: It goes without saying that knowing God has been beneficial for me. He has continued to bless me with abundant blessings, the greatest of these being that I know that He loves me and is concerned about my welfare.

Grace

Grace is unmerited favor. When God saves us, He does it because He is good and loves us, not because we deserve it or because we have earned it through *good works*. When He blesses us, He does it because He is good and loves us, not because we deserve to be blessed. What every human deserves, rather, is to be destroyed. But God, being good,

---

[131] This does not mean that God is a political liberal. As it is practiced today, political liberalism is the pure expression of the laws of Satan, among which are: murder, ethical corruption, greed, viciousness, pride, self-righteousness, intolerance for any dissent from their liberal views, hypocrisy, sexual deviancy and a deep contempt for the truth and for those who do not profess their kind of liberalism. To prove my point, the head of the Department of Homeland Security, Janet Napolitano, issued a report declaring that anyone who disagrees with the despicable liberal point of view is at best a rightwing extremist and at worst a terrorist. This from someone who refuses to call the Muslim murderers of children terrorists!

will not do that until humanity has slapped His gracious hand away one time too many, and the LORD Jesus' love for the world is replaced with hatred, as expressed by His wrath.

I would bet the vast majority of Christians alive today believe that grace began with the resurrection of our LORD and Savior, that it is a purely a post-Pentecostal phenomenon. This is not true. Grace started when Eve and then Adam sinned against the LORD, and they were not destroyed. God showed incredible grace to Noah (and to mankind) by saving him (and mankind through him) from destruction of the flood. He showed tremendous grace to Abraham when He became his friend, as He did to Moses and all pre-Pentecostal saints. It was an act of astounding grace to choose Isaac's descendants to be His treasured possessions, to give them the law and the prophets, and through them, to give us God's word and ultimately our incarnate LORD, Jesus Christ. In addition, thousands of saints who lived prior to Pentecost were saved (given eternal life) by the work of God's Holy Spirit in their lives. Here are some O.T. passages where the word *favor* (meaning grace)[132] is used explicitly:

> *[8]Hear, my son, your father's instruction, and forsake not your mother's teaching, [9]for they are a graceful garland for your head and pendants for your neck* (Proverbs 1:8–9).[133]

> *[34]Toward the scorners* [the LORD] *is scornful, but to the humble he gives favor. [35]The wise will inherit honor, but fools get disgrace* (Proverbs 3:34–35).

> *If favor is shown to the wicked, he does not learn righteousness; in the land of uprightness he deals*

---

[132] In the following verses the Hebrew word חֵן (*khān*, H2603) is translated as *favor* by the ESV. As I read its definition in the *Blue Letter Bible* it can also mean *grace*.

[133] I don't believe the words *garland of grace* here are used in the colloquial way, meaning to make one's appearance more beautiful.

> *corruptly and does not see the majesty of the* LORD (Isaiah 26:10).[134]

> *"And I [the* LORD] *will pour out on the house of David and the inhabitants of Jerusalem a spirit of grace and pleas for mercy, so that, when they look on me, on him whom they have pierced, they shall mourn for him, as one mourns for an only child, and weep bitterly over him, as one weeps over a firstborn"* (Zechariah 12:10).[135]

This section on grace would be incomplete if it did not include this most famous statement about grace, which is found in the post-Pentecostal Scriptures:

> ¹*And you were dead in the trespasses and sins* ²*in which you once walked, following the course of this world, following the prince of the power of the air, the spirit that is now at work in the sons of disobedience—* ³*among whom we all once lived in the passions of our flesh, carrying out the desires of the body and the mind, and were by nature children of wrath, like the rest of mankind.* ⁴*But God, being rich in mercy, because of the great love with which he loved us,* ⁵*even when we were dead in our trespasses, made us alive together with Christ—**by grace you have been saved**—* ⁶*and raised us up with him and seated us with him in the heavenly places in Christ Jesus,* ⁷*so that in the coming ages he might show the immeasurable riches of his grace in kindness toward us in Christ Jesus.* ⁸***For by grace you***

---

[134] In the Masoretic Text, the word *though* begins the verse, changing the emphasis to the second phrase: *he does not learn...*

[135] Notice how the LORD refers to the one they have pierced as both *me,* meaning Himself, and *Him,* meaning the Son of Man. Thus does the Almighty Spirit, Jehovah God, identify Himself with the human man.

have been saved through faith*. And this is not your own doing; it is the gift of God, ⁹not a result of works, so that no one may boast* (Ephesians 2:1–9).

All these acts of God were acts of goodness, mercy and grace. God made a sovereign choice to set His love on the world and to die for it, to give every person a way to escape from the consequence of his sins. The LORD made a sovereign choice to set His loving kindness on each of you who have received salvation from His outstretched hand of love. Too bad the world has turned its back on that wonderful act of kindness. The entire earth, and its unbelieving inhabitants, will be destroyed as a result (Isaiah 24:1–3).

God's Sovereign, Righteous Will

That God is sovereign is an aspect of His divine nature rather than His character, but God is also righteous. When He exercises His sovereign will, He always does so in righteousness, sometimes motivated by love, goodness and mercy; at other times, by justifiable hatred, leading to wrath and deserved vengeance. He is always just. This seems a good place to speak of God's sovereignty, because Scripture teaches that nothing happens in all creation that does not pass through the portal of the LORD's sovereign will. ²⁹*"Are not two sparrows sold for a penny? And not one of them will fall to the ground apart from your Father. ³⁰But even the hairs of your head are all numbered"* (Matthew 10:29–30).

Therefore, as a sovereign, God bears the ultimate responsibility for everything that happens, whether He initiates it or allows someone else, such as Satan, to initiate it. As our Sovereign LORD and revelation of the Transcendent Majesty, Jesus Christ makes certain choices. As we have seen, He chooses on whom to have compassion and mercy, and who to deny these blessings. As Paul says, it does not depend on man's desire, but on God's sovereign will.

Solid Food for the Mature Believer

God also created all things that exist, including Satan, and, through him, the darkness in which evil dwells. Here are two passages that say this unmistakably:

> ^{5}"*I am the* LORD, *and there is no other, besides me there is no God; I equip you, though you do not know me,* ^{6}*that people may know, from the rising of the sun and from the west, that there is none besides me; I am the* LORD, *and there is no other.* ^{7}*I form light and create darkness, I make well-being and create calamity, I am the* LORD *who does all these things*" (Isaiah 45:5–7).

And again:

> ^{15}[The LORD Jesus Christ] *is the image of the invisible God, the firstborn of all creation.* ^{16}*For by him all things were created, in heaven and on earth, visible and invisible, whether thrones or dominions or rulers or authorities—all things were created through him and for him.* ^{17}*And he is before all things, and in him all things hold together* (Colossians 1:15–17).[136]

Before God's creative act, there was nothing that existed other than His being. No evil beings, no good beings, no angels, no hell, no heaven, no universe, no light or darkness (as we created beings understand these last two terms). God made all these for His own pleasure and righteous purposes. Here is what the LORD says:

> "*I the* LORD *speak the truth; I declare what is right*" (Isaiah 45:19c).
> "*...I am God, and there is none like me,* ^{10}*declaring the end from the beginning and from ancient times things*

---

[136] All powers and rulers include the rulers of darkness, including Satan himself.

> *not yet done, saying, 'My counsel shall stand, and I will accomplish all my purpose'...* "[137] (Isaiah 46:9c–10).

When He created Lucifer and lavished wisdom and beauty on him (Ezekiel 28:12-13), He knew that Lucifer would rebel, and that through his rebellion evil would enter creation. When He created man, He knew that Adam would fall into sin. When He gave His covenant Law to the Hebrews, He knew that they would forsake Him and that He would destroy their nation.[138]

God created the dark kingdoms and allows them to exist for His own righteous purposes. For example, the devil, or Satan, obeys God when He tells him to do something or not to do something, as we see in Job, chapter 1. We also see that the demons are subject to His will as Jesus casts them into the abyss. In the last days, it will be an act of God's righteous, sovereign will to destroy all evil and unrepentant sinners, even all creation itself, and then remake it anew (2 Peter 3:12).

---

[137] The Hebrew word חֵפֶץ (*chaphets*, H2654) translated as *purpose* by the ESV can also mean pleasure. For example the NIV translation of v. 10 reads, *"I make known the end from the beginning, from ancient times, what is still to come. I say, 'My purpose will stand, and I will do all that I please.'"*

[138] See, for example, Deuteronomy 31:20 and the warning preceding it in Deuteronomy 28:63. This last verse is horrifying. It clearly says that it will please God to ruin and destroy Israel if they fall away from worshipping Him. While God takes no pleasure in the death of the wicked (Ezekiel 33:11), He does take pleasure in exercising justice and righteousness (Jeremiah 9:23–24). Justice and righteousness trump mercy. Therefore if the body of Christ in America continues to displease Him as a church, it will please Him to take our lampstand away, or, as He often says in Scripture, to break off the unfruitful branches and throw them into the flames (John 15:6).

PART III

Living a Life that Pleases God

What every saint should desire with all his heart and soul is to receive the following praise from the LORD when he stands before Him in the Judgment, *"Well done, good and faithful servant!"* (Matthew 25:23). But living a life that pleases God is not about *blindly* following a set of rules, hoping that will please Him. We know the fate of the counterfeit Christians who try to find justification in good works. See, for example, Matthew 7:21–23.[139] So, how do we attain this highly coveted praise from the very LORD of all things?

Pleasing God starts with where your heart is (Job 11:13–20). As the LORD said of David, here is a man after my own heart (1 Samuel 13:14). With this in mind, here is a simple passage that says it all:

> *12"And now, Israel, what does the LORD your God require of you, but to fear the LORD your God, to walk in all his ways, to love him, to serve the LORD your God with all your heart and with all your soul, 13and to keep the commandments and statutes of the LORD, which I am commanding you today for your good?"* (Deuteronomy 10:12–13).[140]

Here are five commands that come from this passage:

    A. Fear God;
    B. Walk in His ways;

---

[139] Note that in this passage, those whining to God about what great works they have done do not mention His grace or mercy, thinking that their works should qualify them for entrance into the Kingdom.

[140] Doing all the things on this list will not get you into heaven. We do not get to heaven by obeying rules, no matter how lofty they are. Doing things on this list, through the work of the Spirit in your life, will please God and get you that *good and faithful servant* welcome.

C. Love Him;
D. Serve Him with all your heart and all your soul;
E. Obey His commandments.

The reason God has given us these instructions is so that we can do these things for our own good, which will manifest itself in this life and in the next (Matthew 19:29). But this verse also implies that if we do not obey these commands, we will come to harm. How true this passage in Deuteronomy is! As true now as then.[141]

"But," many in the modern church will say, "this verse is all about commands and decrees, and everyone knows that we (post-Pentecostal Christians) are not under law but under grace." True enough. But what they don't understand is that it has always been true that humanity lived by grace, prior to as well as after Pentecost. For all human history, if one wanted to live a life pleasing to God, one had to live a life of faith, which is a gift of God that comes through His grace, motivated by His goodness and mercy. Without faith, it is impossible to please God (Hebrews 11:6). This principle is eternal. Therefore pleasing God is never about finding justification leading to salvation through following a set of rules. That's what tripped up the Israelites. As Paul says:

> [30] *What shall we say, then? That Gentiles who did not pursue righteousness have attained it, that is, a righteousness that is by faith;* [31] *but that Israel who pursued a law that would lead to righteousness did not succeed in reaching that law.* [32] *Why?* ***Because they did not pursue it by faith, but as if it were based on works.*** *They have stumbled over the stumbling stone,* [33] *as it is written, "Behold, I am laying in Zion a stone of*

---

[141] Because the church in the America has forgotten how to obey these commands, as a body we also stand in danger of God's righteous anger being poured out on us. See **Tribulation of the Saints of God** on page 107.

Solid Food for the Mature Believer

> *stumbling, and a rock of offense; and whoever believes in him will not be put to shame"* (Romans 9:30–33).[142]

Therefore there can be no justification before God by trying to live by a set of rules or by counting on our works of righteousness.[143] Our only justification comes through the cleansing work of the blood of Christ.[144]

I do not mean to imply that Christians should not do works of righteousness. We are called to live a righteous life, one worthy of our calling as children of God (Colossians 1:10). These works must proceed not out of a desire to justify ourselves before God, but out of our faith, which gives us a desire to please God. It is this heart that pleases the LORD (Ephesians 2:10 and 4:1; and James 2:14–17). And we are without question called to be obedient to God's will, not as embodied in the O.T. covenant Law that God made with Israel,[145] but as embodied by the foundation of all the Law and the Prophets, love the LORD your God with all your heart and all your soul, and love your neighbor as yourself (Matthew 22:37–39, excerpts). Jesus said, "If you love me, you will keep my commandments" (John 14:15, 21).[146]

I have not counted the number of commands in the N.T., but I would bet there are well over a hundred. They are all related to the truths expressed in Deuteronomy 10:12. What many in the modern church have forgotten (or choose willfully to ignore) is that for the

---

[142] Paul quotes Isaiah 8:14 and Isaiah 28:16.

[143] Isaiah 64:6a, *We have all become like one who is unclean, and all our righteous deeds are like a polluted garment.*

[144] I would bet that when the Apostle Paul stands in the judgment and Jesus asks him to give an account of his life, even though his works were monumental, he will not boast. Rather he will say, "All I have to justify me is your blood O LORD, shed on the cross for my sins," because this is true of him and all of us who are saved.

[145] The O.T. Covenant Law was intended to set Israel apart as a nation; to make them a light to the gentiles; to show how wise they were; and to glorify God. (Deuteronomy 4:6). The Covenant Law was never intended as a path to the righteousness that God accepts (Romans 3:20; Romans 4:13, Romans 5:20). Rather, righteousness has always come through living one's life by faith. (Habakkuk 2:4).

[146] This entire passage is about this truth; I've quoted the first sentence.

believer the consequences of disobedience are not pleasant in this life (Acts 5:1–10; 1 Corinthians 11:30), and one can suffer loss in the next (1 Corinthians 3:14–15).

It is in this light of revelation that we should view Deuteronomy 10:12. There are five simple commands. But they are fraught with danger for us if we do not understand how to obey them or how necessary obeying them is.

The Spirit had a reason for ordering these commands as He did. So let's find out why the first command is to:

Fear the LORD Your God

The Scriptures tell us that *the fear of the LORD is the **beginning** of wisdom* (Psalm 111:10a).[147] If fearing the Living God is the beginning of wisdom, there is a very strong implication that if we don't know how to fear Him, we cannot attain any wisdom at all that will be useful in serving Him. This makes it all the more unfortunate that modern theologians explain the word *fear* away, saying all it means is to hold God in high esteem, to regard Him with awe. Esteem and awe are not the fear of God, though they are certainly two of its many results.

Let's reason together on this.

What does it mean to fear something? Fear, according to the dictionary, is an emotional state of apprehension and anxiety caused by the presence or imminence of danger.[148]

---

[147] See also, Job 28:28; Psalm 34:11–16; Proverbs 9:10; Proverbs 15:33; and Isaiah 33:6.

[148] The entire definition reads:

> *1. a. A feeling of agitation and anxiety caused by the presence or imminence of danger. b. A state or condition marked by this feeling: living in fear. 2. A feeling of disquiet or apprehension: a fear of looking foolish. 3. Extreme reverence or awe, as toward a supreme power. 4. A reason for dread or apprehension: Being alone is my greatest fear (Microsoft Bookshelf, op. cit.).*

Note that in item 3, the dictionary has defined *fear* in the sense that the modern day church preaches it. This item demonstrates that fear as it is preached in the modern church is not the same as definitions 1 or 2, when it should be. If the fear of God *This note is continued on the next page.*

Solid Food for the Mature Believer

Consider your common day experience. Go to the top of a skyscraper and look over the edge, and you realize the danger that falling poses. Build a large fire and think about jumping into it. You know what it's like to get burned, and you don't go through with it. Think about a tidal wave a thousand feet high bearing down on you as you stand and watch helplessly. Or think of being trapped at the base of a volcano as it erupts, and a several thousand-degree ball of plasma rolls down toward you.[149]

In the last two cases, there would be nothing we could do except run and hope to escape, which is not likely, though it's easy to imagine the terror we would feel. In the first two cases, fear is a warning device that prevents us from doing something that will cause us harm. In the last two, it just tells us that we're very probably going to die. Both of these types of fear are an appropriate way to regard the power, majesty and wrath of God.

In the Bible godly fear is presented as a **healthy behavior-changing emotion** that the LORD our God gave us to protect ourselves from experiencing His righteous and terrifying judgment. As Moses told the trembling Israelites who thought they would die in the presence of God, *"Do not fear* [you are not going to die today]*, for*

---

were appropriately understood in modern church teaching, there would be no need for definition 3; it would go without saying.

[149] After Mt. St. Helens erupted in May 1980, I read stories in the press about an incident involving a cloud of very hot plasma ejected by the eruption. Apparently a person who was trying to photograph the eruption *up close and personal* was vaporized by a five thousand degree ball of gas issued from the volcano. As the stories went, all that was left of him and his car was an iron hulk, and the metal legs and feet of a camera tripod standing on the roof of the car. If this was true, we can see that this person obviously did not respect the power of the volcano, despite repeated warnings from the governor of Washington to stay away, and he paid for it with his life.

In this same way, when the LORD comes to destroy the earth, all those headed for hell will then know what the fear of the LORD is. When the infinitely hot plasma of God's wrath comes upon them, they will watch helplessly as they and the entire earth are consumed. Then they will fear! But then it will be too late for them.

84

God has come to test you, that the fear of him may be before you, that you may not sin"[150] (Exodus 20:20).

In this society, we have been trained to think that being in the presence of God is *not* the same thing as being in the presence of imminent danger. How foolish! God's presence—by His very nature and being, by His incomprehensible power—is the very essence of imminent danger. That's why He has been called a consuming fire (Deuteronomy 4:24; Hebrews 12:29). This is what our God meant when He said to Jeremiah, *[20]"Declare this in the house of Jacob; proclaim it in Judah: [21]Hear this, O foolish and senseless people, who have eyes, but see not, who have ears, but hear not. [22]Do you not fear me?" declares the* LORD. *"Do you not tremble before me?"* (Jeremiah 5:20–22a).[151] The correct way to fear God, which we have forgotten in this modern age, much to our hurt and potentially to our destruction as well, is to tremble in His presence.[152]

If the body of Christ in America today were more spiritual—that is, more willing to accept the guiding of God's Spirit—we would understand how to fear the LORD as He intended. Here is the chief reason we should fear God: The consequences of sin are terrible, even for a believer, though a child of God cannot lose his salvation. God demonstrated this fiery aspect of His being to Aaron's sons Nadab and Abihu in Leviticus 10:1–2, when they offered unauthorized fire before Him, and fire came out from Him and consumed them. They took the LORD too lightly and paid for it. In today's church, we assume that God would never do to us what He did to Adab and Abihu. Well, then,

---

[150]For us who are saved, there is a difference between fearing God and being afraid of God. I feared my Dad, for example, but I was not afraid of him; my fear of him did not keep me from running into his loving arms. On the other hand there is no difference if you are living a disobedient lifestyle. He will not let it go unpunished. Then be very afraid!

[151]Because they did not fear God, they did not take seriously His warnings through all the prophets to stop sinning. What resulted was the awful destruction of Jerusalem and its people, described graphically by Jeremiah and Ezekiel, especially in Ezekiel 9.

[152] See also Exodus 15:14; 1 Chronicles 16:30; Psalm 96:9; Psalm 114:7; and Isaiah 66:5. It also means to be terrified of His wrath and anger as in Job 23:15.

how about Ananias and Sapphira in Acts 5? They were taken the very moment they sinned. And what was the result? *Great fear seized the whole church and all who heard about these events* (Acts 5:11). This fear was clearly more than the *extreme reverence* or *awe* that is preached today. It is just as true that the mere presence of God is terrifying; when the majesty of God is manifest to people in the Scriptures, they fall flat on their faces, unable to breathe or move.[153]

Many in the body of Christ in America (an overwhelming number) walk in a way that shows they believe that the fear of God is only an O.T. concept. As God was imprinting the meaning of the fear of the LORD on my heart, I asked one of the godliest men I knew about what the N.T. Scriptures said about the fear of God. He said he didn't think they mentioned it that much. So I did a word search and found at least twenty-two passages in which the concept of fearing God appears. Here's one of the most dramatic examples, where Jesus is speaking to His disciples:

> *"And do not fear those who kill the body but cannot kill the soul. Rather fear him who can destroy both soul and body in hell"*(Matthew 10:28).
> *"Yes, I tell you, fear him!"* (Luke 12:5b).[154]

As to not fearing one who can kill the body only, I can't imagine anyone who, if faced with an imminent death at the hands of one of the human monsters of that horrific religion Islam—or through any vicious beast, like a roaring tiger in the wild—wouldn't be petrified. It's in this context that Jesus uses the word *fear*, saying that we are to fear God more than any earthly danger because of His vast, incomprehensible power, and because the consequences of repeatedly refusing to obey Him are just too terrible to contemplate—much, much

---

[153] See, for example, Daniel 10:7–10. See also Revelation 1:17.
[154] I have appended these passages because this last clause is not recorded in Matthew 10:28, though Jesus issues the same warning in Luke 12:4-5.

worse than anything on this earth.[155] The entirety of creation is in imminent danger, so to speak, from God's wrath.[156] The reason we haven't experienced its awful consequences (as a people, though Israel did as a nation) is His great love, mercy and patience. We should fear Him because God will hold everyone to account, both in this life and in the next, and it will not be pleasant for those whom Jesus finds wanting.[157]

This is what the Israelites forgot. This is what led to their horrifying destruction. Fear of an angry God is what led Ezra to tear his clothes and sit alone in a room *appalled* when he learned that the Israelites had married *foreign* women. As Ezra the scribe and teacher of the Law says:

> *³As soon as I heard this, I tore my garment and my cloak and pulled hair from my head and beard and sat appalled. ⁴Then all who trembled at the words of the God of Israel, because of the faithlessness of the returned exiles, gathered around me while I sat appalled until the evening sacrifice* (Ezra 9:3–4).[158]

Some wash their minds of any idea of fearing God with the notion that we have a loving Father who has saved us. Of course it is true that

---

[155] I am not talking about the day-to-day slipups we all face. Even Paul seemed to experience bouts of disobedience. See Romans 7. What I am talking about here is where the pattern of one's life is shaped by a disobedient spirit; that is, one who constantly, willfully, and knowingly blasphemes God by disobeying Him, living in sin, and the like.

[156] Again, refer to Isaiah 24:1–3.

[157] Hebrews 4:13 is just one of many passages that declare this truth.

[158] This was the passage that led me to start asking myself (and God through prayer) what it meant to fear God. I noticed that no one in today's church ever tore their clothes when sin was found among us. And I noticed that there was plenty of sin in the church (rampant divorce, for example). It was then that I realized that we had lost all sense of the destructive power of God, a power that He will not hesitate to use if it is the righteous and just thing to do. I believe that the modern church in America is headed for a firsthand experience of God's scourging discipline in the not too distant future if we do not repent.

Solid Food for the Mature Believer

God is loving. When I mentioned the notion of trembling before God to one of my most godly friends, he seemed to think that our loving relationship with our Father in heaven should preclude that, but that's not true. I had a wonderful dad who was kind and good to me. I was well loved by him. I never thought to doubt his love for me. He never abused me or harmed me in any way, but still I feared him. I feared the consequences of disobedience, even though we had a loving relationship.

Nevertheless, here's a chilling warning from the Apostle Paul that seems to be glossed over when I hear Romans preached:

> *[19]Then you will say, "Branches were broken off so that I might be grafted in." [20]That is true. They were broken off because of their unbelief, but you stand fast through faith. So do not become proud, but fear. [21]For if God did not spare the natural branches, neither will he spare you. [22]Note then the kindness and the severity of God: severity toward those who have fallen, but God's kindness to you, provided you continue in his kindness. Otherwise you too will be cut off* (Romans 11:19–22).[159]

The admonition to *be afraid* seems pretty black and white to me. I will leave it you to do a word study on the fear of God. In almost every case, it is mentioned as a behavior-changing emotion that is meant to keep His holy ones obedient.

So what are we to do? We have to convince ourselves that when Scripture says that the fear of God is the beginning of wisdom, we understand that this fear will cause us to tremble in His presence. If we are living according to His word, we carry this *fear* in reserve, but we are not afraid of Him. See, for example, how David runs into the arms of the LORD in 2 Samuel 24:14, right into His very exacting discipline! Therefore, we do not walk around with hunched shoulders waiting for

---

[159] Also, see Jesus' admonition to the Laodicean church in Revelation 3:14–19.

the lightning of God's anger to strike us at any moment. Rather, we need to find a balance between fearing God, and loving Him and feeling safe in Him. In this *feel-good* society, it's not easy to accept that we must fear God. But fear Him we must, or we can wander off the path and not grow spiritually, and then suffer the consequences. Because the modern American church has forgotten the fear of the LORD, it has become corrupt, bordering on detestable in the LORD's eyes.[160] It may be destroyed as a result.[161]

Walk in His Ways and Obey His Commands

What are God's ways? There are hundreds of verses in the Bible that tell us. One of my favorites is Micah 6:8, *He has told you, O man, what is good; and what does the LORD require of you but to do justice, and to love kindness, and to walk humbly with your God?* Another passage comes from Colossians 3:12–16:

> *[12]Put on then, as God's chosen ones, holy and beloved, compassionate hearts, kindness, humility, meekness, and patience, [13]bearing with one another and, if one has a complaint against another, forgiving each other; as the LORD has forgiven you, so you also must forgive. [14]And above all these put on love, which binds everything together in perfect harmony. [15]And let the*

---

[160] When I reread this, I couldn't believe I'd written it. The church, bordering on detestable? I was ready to strike the sentence when God made it clear to me that He's talking not just about the body of Christ in America, though this community has indeed been corrupted by the world, but about all so-called churches which pretend to represent Him, but which commit the most ghastly sins, such as denying the truth of God's word or ordaining sexually active homosexuals as pastors, bishops, priests, etc. This is especially true when the leaders of one these apostate organizations look the other way when they become aware of the abuse of children in the care of corrupt pastors or priests.

[161] See the letter to the Laodicean Church in Revelation 3:14–22. Godly individuals who have not forgotten the fear of the LORD will be spared, however. See Isaiah 3:10–11, which occurs in the context of a major tribulation coming from the LORD into the earth.

Solid Food for the Mature Believer

> *peace of Christ rule in your hearts, to which indeed you were called in one body. And be thankful.* ¹⁶*Let the word of Christ dwell in you richly, teaching and admonishing one another in all wisdom, singing psalms and hymns and spiritual songs, with thankfulness in your hearts to God.*

Anyone who knows the LORD our God will know by the urging of the Spirit what His ways are. The Spirit of Truth, our Counselor, will show us.

Walking in God's ways is not easy, as obeying His commands is not easy. Nothing in the Bible suggests that walking in God's ways is easy. See, for example, Romans 7, which convinces us that it is the hardest possible thing we can do. In fact, it is impossible for us to do with our own strength. Praise God that He has given us His Spirit who can give us the will, ability and power to win our struggle with sin and then to obey His commands (Romans 7:24–25a, Romans 8:1–11 and Philippians 2:13). We have but to surrender to Him, which, by the way, is not easy either, as anyone who knows the LORD has discovered.

To emphasize that the idea of obeying God's commands did not go out of style when the N.T. books were written, Appendix 2 consists of a table of a few of the commands that come out of the N.T. (with a few out of the O.T. as well). Appendix 2 is by no means exhaustive. I did not make Appendix 2 exhaustive due to space limitations, and it is not intended to be a substitute for getting into God's word, studying it and storing it up in your heart. What I do hope, however, is that the sheer volume of this list gives you pause and makes you think how serious God is when He commands us to *walk in His ways*.

Love Him

Loving God doesn't necessarily have anything to do with experiencing the warm fuzzy feelings we associate with the genital-driven love our vile and defiled culture worships. While it's not impossible (and is, in fact, appropriate) for us to have soul-warming feelings about the One who died for us, our love of Him is not accurately measured by our feelings at any given moment.

When we stand before our LORD in the Judgment, He will measure the love with which we loved Him by how well we lived according to the following words, *²³Jesus answered him, "If anyone loves me, he will keep my word, and my Father will love him, and we will come to him and make our home with him. ²⁴Whoever does not love me does not keep my words. And the word that you hear is not mine but the Father's who sent me"* (John 14:23–24).[162]

He gives a new dimension to the obedience He expects by saying, *²⁶"If anyone comes to me and does not hate his own father and mother and wife and children and brothers and sisters, yes, and even his own life, he cannot be my disciple. ²⁷Whoever does not bear his own cross and come after me cannot be my disciple"* (Luke 14:26–27). I can't imagine that Jesus expects us to actually hate our families. What He must be saying is that nothing in this life should come between us and serving Him. And this can only happen if we love Him more than our very own lives. Here's how Paul put Jesus' command into practice:

> *⁷But whatever gain I had, I counted as loss for the sake of Christ. ⁸Indeed, I count everything as loss because of the surpassing worth of knowing Christ Jesus my LORD. For his sake I have suffered the loss of all things and count them as rubbish, in order that I may gain Christ ⁹and be found in him, not having a righteousness of my own that comes from the law, but that which comes through faith in Christ, the righteousness from God that depends on faith—¹⁰that I may know him and the power*

---

[162] Who is **we** in *we will come to him*? This might seem to contradict my one God person theology. One will undoubtedly say that Jesus must be referring to the Son of God entity referred to as part of the Godhead. I don't think so. As I have mentioned before, I believe there is a distinction of person between Jesus the Son of Man, and Jesus (Jehovah) the revealed God of creation. See example regarding His coming again given on page 28. This can only be true if the Person of the Son of Man, a human man, is distinct from the Person of Jehovah.

> *of his resurrection, and may share his sufferings, becoming like him in his death, [11]that by any means possible I may attain the resurrection from the dead* (Philippians 3:7–11).

It's just that simple (but not easy!). We measure our love of God by how well we submit to His authority, surrender our lives and our will to Him and obey His commandments. If we love Him, we will not love what He hates or hate what He loves. Those who say they love Him and support such vile cultural horrors as abortion and homosexual rights are fooling themselves. The love of God is not in them, nor, in all likelihood, is His saving Spirit.

Another measure of our love for Him will be how we love our brothers and sisters in Christ. John said,

> *[20]If anyone says, "I love God," and hates his brother, he is a liar; for he who does not love his brother whom he has seen cannot love God whom he has not seen. [21]And this commandment we have from him: whoever loves God must also love his brother* (1 John 4:20–21).

And from the LORD Jesus:

> *[34]"A new commandment I give to you, that you love one another: just as I have loved you, you also are to love one another. [35]By this all people will know that you are my disciples, if you have love for one another"* (John 13:34–35).

If you love God you will feel the urge to praise Him and to mean such praise with all your heart and soul:

> *[1]I will give thanks to the LORD with my whole heart; I will recount all of your wonderful deeds. [2]I will be glad and exult in you; I will sing praise to your name, O Most High* (Psalm 9:1–2).

Note in the following passage that loving God makes us able to rejoice in Him no matter what: *Rejoice in the* LORD *always; again I will say, Rejoice*[!] (Philippians 4:4).[163]

To love God is to delight in Him, His ways and His word: *Delight yourself in the* LORD, *and he will give you the desires of your heart* (Psalm 37:4).

And again:

> *¹Blessed is the man who walks not in the counsel of the wicked, nor stands in the way of sinners, nor sits in the seat of scoffers; / ²but his delight is in the law of the* LORD, *and on his law he meditates day and night* (Psalm 1:1–2).

Yet again:

> *⁴⁶I will also speak of your testimonies before kings and shall not be put to shame, ⁴⁷for I find my delight in your commandments, which I love. / ⁴⁸I will lift up my hands toward your commandments, which I love, and I will meditate on your statutes* (Psalm 119:46–48).

Finally, to love the LORD our God is to put our trust in Him:

> *And those who know your name put their trust in you, for you, O* LORD, *have not forsaken those who seek you* (Psalm 9:10).[164]

---

[163] It is God's own truth that if He gives us a command, He will also give us the strength and will to carry it out (Philippians 2:13). See also Psalm 96:1–2 and following, which implies that we are to sing to the LORD at all times and in all circumstances!

[164] It is inconceivable that one could really know God and not love Him. To know God one must know His word, His precepts, His character. The more we know about Him the more we will love Him (and fear Him too!). This is what the Spirit means when He says *those who know your name* in the quoted passage. If you would know God's Name as the Bible uses this phrase, then you must know Him personally.

Solid Food for the Mature Believer

And again:

> [8] *But I am like a green olive tree in the house of God. I trust in the steadfast love of God forever and ever.* / [9] *I will thank you forever, because you have done it. I will wait for your name, for it is good, in the presence of the godly* (Psalm 52:8–9).

Note also how trust and praise are linked in the last two passages.

In ourselves we cannot love God. *If we love Him, it is because He first loved us and gave up Himself to die for us* (paraphrase of 1 John 4:10). Nor does our love for Him come from our own fleshly strength. It is impossible for us to love Him without Him giving us His Spirit to dwell in us. Therefore once we have that Spirit, the measure of our love for Him will come from our willingness to be in communion with Him in prayer, and in reading and meditating on His word, and learning to obey Him. It is through these spiritual disciplines that we increase our love for and knowledge of God.

Serve Him With All Your Soul

God created us to serve Him. Serving Him must be the most important desire of our hearts. The true servant of God serves Him not because he hopes to get a blessing (although serving God does bring great blessing), but because it his duty (from Luke 17:7–10, quoted on the next page). He also serves God because he realizes that it is a great privilege to be called to serve the living God, who created all things. The LORD Jesus does not need us to serve Him. He has millions upon millions of angels, supernatural beings of immense power, to serve Him, but because He has set His heart on loving us, He has called us, unworthy as we are, to serve Him.

I think Paul best expresses the appropriate servant's attitude when he says in Romans 1:9: [It is] *God, whom I serve with my whole heart in preaching the gospel of his Son...*(NIV)[165] And the following passage shows what a great servant can be called to sacrifice to serve Him:

> *⁹For I think that God has exhibited us apostles as last of all, like men sentenced to death, because we have become a spectacle to the world, to angels, and to men. ¹⁰We are fools for Christ's sake, but you are wise in Christ. We are weak, but you are strong. You are held in honor, but we in disrepute. ¹¹To the present hour we hunger and thirst, we are poorly dressed and buffeted and homeless, ¹²and we labor, working with our own hands. When reviled, we bless; when persecuted, we endure; ¹³ when slandered, we entreat. We have become, and are still, like the scum of the world, the refuse of all things* (1 Corinthians 4:9–13).

Paul went through terrible hardship to serve the LORD his God. We should be willing to do the same. This absolute self-sacrificing commitment (as in *present*[ing our] *bodies as a living sacrifice* (Romans 12:1b)) is what the LORD requires and, as our Creator, is worthy of and has a right to demand of us.

And we must also do it with the proper attitude. Jesus summarizes the attitude of dutiful servant in this sobering passage in Luke:

> *⁷"Will any one of you who has a servant plowing or keeping sheep say to him when he has come in from the field, 'Come at once and recline at table'? ⁸Will he not rather say to him, 'Prepare supper for me, and dress properly, and serve me while I eat and drink, and afterward you will eat and drink'? ⁹Does he thank the*

---

[165] Here is the ESV version of Romans 1:9: *For God is my witness, whom I serve with my spirit in the gospel of his Son, that without ceasing I mention you.* I like the NIV's translation of this, because *my whole heart* rather than *my spirit* is really what I think Paul meant.

> servant because he did what was commanded? *¹⁰So you also, when you have done all that you were commanded, say, 'We are unworthy servants; we have only done what was our duty'"* (Luke 17:7–10).

One of the life-changing realizations for me when I read this passage. I had always thought I was doing God a favor by serving Him. Nothing could be farther from the truth. God is doing *me* and all of us a favor by allowing us to serve *Him*. And if we are faithful we will get that praise from Him that we all yearn for: *Well done, good and faithful servant* (Matthew 25:21a).

Serve Him With Overwhelming Gratitude (Thanksgiving)

What Deuteronomy 10:12–13 (as quoted on page 80) does not explicitly say, but what is prevalent throughout Scripture, is this admonition:

> *Let the word of Christ dwell in you richly, teaching and admonishing one another in all wisdom, singing psalms and hymns and spiritual songs, with **thankfulness in your hearts to God*** (Colossians 3:16).[166]

That Jesus Himself gave thanks to God is recorded in all the Gospels. Paul either gives thanks to God or commands that we give thanks to Him about nineteen times in his letters. The four Living Creatures are seen giving thanks to God in Revelation 4:9. In Revelation 7:11–12 all the angels in heaven, the elders on their thrones, and the four Living Creatures are seen falling on their faces in gratitude to God. In the O.T., the act of giving thanks to God is seen in over forty verses.

But why?

---

[166] See also Leviticus 7:13, 15; Ezra 3:11; Nehemiah 11:17; Nehemiah 12:8, 24, 27, and 46; Psalm 69:30; Psalm 95:2; Psalm 100:4, and on and on.

To those of you who know the LORD and who serve Him with all your heart and soul, this is the stupidest question in the universe. You would reply, "How can we not?" But I'm going to provide some answers anyway:

- He has given us life and made us in His image (Genesis 1:26–27).
- He has given us minds to understand and emotions with which to feel (Exodus 31:3; Proverbs 2:6; Job 32:8).
- He has chosen to reveal Himself to us (Numbers 12:6; Matthew 11:27).
- He has loved us despite the fact that we broke His heart in the garden and that by our sin we break His heart every day (Psalm 78:40 and Ezekiel 6:9, just two of dozens of other examples).[167]
- He wants to have a personal relationship with us. Imagine, the King of creation wants us to know Him as He knows us! (Job 29:4; Jeremiah 9:23–24).
- He, therefore, proactively pursues us so that we might come to know Him and dwell with Him (Psalm 23:6).[168]
- He has saved us from our sins, even when we were His enemies and at the greatest cost imaginable, so that we might come into His presence at the end of days (Romans 5:6–10).
- He provides good things for us (Psalm 65:4; Psalm 103:5; Romans 8:28 and dozens of other examples).

---

[167] The ESV translation of Ezekiel 6:9b God says, ...*how I* [God] *have been* **broken** *over their whoring heart*. But the NASB translation reads: ...*how I have been* **hurt** *by their adulterous hearts*. The NASB translation seems much more personal to me; much easier to relate to. Much more powerful.

[168] The Hebrew word in this famous verse, רָדַף (radaph, H7291)—translated as *follow* by both the NAS and ESV (but not in the NLT)—has the sense of a hunter pursuing his prey, or of someone diligently searching for a treasured article. The NLT does use the word *pursue*.

- He showers us with grace and love and forgiveness day in, day out (2 Corinthians 9:8, 14; Ephesians 1:1–7; 1 Timothy 1:14 and many others).
- He wants the very best for us (John 10:10).
- He disciplines us when we stray from the path of righteousness (Proverbs 3:11–12; Hebrews 12:5–11).
- He has given us eternal life (1 John 5:11).
- He will live with us and we with Him forever in a state of bliss unimaginable in this world (Revelation 22:3–5).

To sum this up, the ways God has been good to each of us, and therefore deserves our gratitude, are beyond our ability to count or declare in their fullness (Psalm 40:5).[169]

The next question is, when do we give thanks? Just when we feel like it? When things are going well? When all our needs are met? When we're healthy?

Of course not!

The Spirit answers this question in no uncertain terms through Paul when He says, *[16]Rejoice always, [17]pray without ceasing, [18]give thanks in all circumstances; for this is the will of God in Christ Jesus for you* (1 Thessalonians 5:16–18).

The rubber of our faith hits the hard, rocky pavement of reality when we find ourselves in dire straits. If we can with a clear mind and a devoted heart render heartfelt gratitude to God during hard times, then we love Him in Spirit and Truth, and our faith is proved to be built on solid ground. If, however, we only give thanks when things are going our way, we are like little children, weak in a faith that is built on shifting sands, and we are like *a wave of the sea that is driven and tossed by the wind* (James 1:6b).

One might ask, How can I find it in myself to give thanks during hard times? Well, you can't, *in yourself,* but you can pray for strength to get through the trial and not displease God by having an ungrateful

---

[169] See also Psalm 103, which was clearly written by a heart filled to overflowing with gratitude.

spirit. And, of course, God will grant you the strength you need. One thing I take comfort in during hard times is that even when things are going very wrong, nothing has happened to me that God hasn't either allowed or brought on me Himself.[170] Since God works everything together for good in my life, I know that this particular trial comes from God's loving hand. James makes no bones about it when he says, *²Count it all joy, my brothers, when you meet trials of various kinds, ³for you know that the testing of your faith produces steadfastness. ⁴And let steadfastness have its full effect, that you may be perfect and complete, lacking in nothing. ⁵If any of you lacks wisdom, let him ask God, who gives generously to all without reproach, and it will be given him* (James 1:2–5).

Therefore, give thanks to God, always. Let the last words out of your mouth before you drop off to sleep at night, and the first thing when you awake in the morning, be, "Thank you, LORD."

Recap of Parts II & III

I hope the reader of these pages will take away a much more sober view of who God is and what He does. I hope you will come away with a better appreciation for your LORD's majesty and power. Everyone who professes to know God must realize that though God is love, He is much, much more. In emphasizing the love aspect of God's character and ignoring all the others, we are guilty of misleading generations of people who think they're saved when they are not.[171] And what incentive is there to get saved if God is just love? Surely if God is just love, there's nothing to worry about as far as sin goes; a loving God would never throw anyone into hell. Understand that God hates sin and evil, and it is this emotion that fuels His wrath. Recall that it is a terrible thing to fall into the hands of the Living God. I hope

---

[170] See the section on God's sovereignty beginning on page 77.

[171] This *God is [only] love* theology has manifested in the modern church in such a way that many pastors no longer preach confession and repentance of sin. Therefore, when people ask Jesus into their hearts without acknowledging and repenting of their sin, they have not really acknowledged Him as LORD (Romans 10:9) and are never really saved.

everyone who reads these pages will take this warning to heart. I also hope that the body of Christ in America, and throughout the world, will learn to tremble in the LORD's presence.

PART IV

Some Miscellaneous Topics

I have added this part because there are some things that God has taught me that I feel are worth sharing with you. Again, I am not the sole repository of Truth. I am no one. All of you who know the LORD Jesus Christ have His testing Spirit in you. On your own, by study, prayer and meditation, you can decide if the following discussion is of any value to you in your Christian walk. I hope the following discussion will stimulate your thinking about such things as the Tribulation; the sin of taking grape juice instead of fermented wine at the LORD's table; what the unforgivable sin is; and so forth. I hope you find these few remaining pages interesting.

Tribulation of the World

There has been endless debate about what will happen to the church during the last days, the Great Tribulation (only once referred to by this title in Revelation 7:14). These are the days that we should:

> [18] *"Pray that it may not happen in winter.* [19] *For in those days there will be such tribulation as has not been from the beginning of the creation that God created until now, and never will be.* [20] *And if the LORD had not cut short the days, no human being would be saved. But for the sake of the elect, whom he chose, he shortened the days"* (Jesus speaking in Mark 13:18–20).

This passage tells us without question there will be believers who must go through the Great Tribulation. The Spirit enforces this inescapable conclusion as He speaks to John through one of the twenty-four elders in the following passage from the Revelation:

> ^{13}Then one of the elders addressed me, saying, "Who are these, clothed in white robes, and from where have they come?" ^{14}I said to him, "Sir, you know." And he said to me, "These are the ones coming out of the great tribulation. They have washed their robes and made them white in the blood of the Lamb.
>> ^{15}"Therefore they are before the throne of God, and serve him day and night in his temple; and he who sits on the throne will shelter them with his presence.
>> ^{16}They shall hunger no more, neither thirst anymore; the sun shall not strike them, nor any scorching heat.
>> ^{17}For the Lamb in the midst of the throne will be their shepherd, and he will guide them to springs of living water,
>
> and God will wipe away every tear from their eyes" (Revelation 7:13–17).

It is a well-known scriptural truth that everyone who is saved is part of the body of Christ, e.g. the church. It is clear, then, at least part of the body of Christ will have to endure this terrible time. The question remains whether the whole body of Christ will experience it. There are some who believe, despite this clear teaching, that Jesus will come prior to the Tribulation, at which time the not-yet-completed church (the body of believers that exists at that time) will be *raptured*, taken up to meet Him in the clouds.[172] (O, how I wish that were true!) As I was listening to a famous (and very godly) TV preacher preach the Pre-Trib point of view one Sunday morning, the LORD spoke to me and said, "Nope. Post Trib." The LORD my God told me that the entire body of Christ on the earth during those days will go through this awful time. The LORD then gave me the scriptural passages to prove it.

---

[172] What sense does it make to take part of the church, which is the body of believers, out of the world when it is not yet complete?

Here is what Scripture teaches about the timing of the church's departure to be with Christ:

1. The people the elder referred to in this passage are identified in Revelation 7:9 as:

   ...a great multitude that no one could number, from every nation, from all tribes and peoples and languages, standing before the throne and before the Lamb, clothed in white robes, with palm branches in their hands.

   Sounds like the whole body of Christ, doesn't it?

2. As the Apostle Paul writes:

   *^{13}But we do not want you to be uninformed, brothers, about those who are asleep, that you may not grieve as others do who have no hope. ^{14}For since we believe that Jesus died and rose again, even so, **through Jesus, God will bring with him those who have fallen asleep**. ^{15}For this we declare to you by a word from the L*ORD*, that we who are alive, who are left until the coming of the L*ORD*, **will [certainly] not precede those who have fallen asleep**. ^{16}For the L*ORD* himself will descend from heaven with a cry of command, with the voice of an archangel, and with the sound of the trumpet of God. And **the dead in Christ will rise first**. ^{17}**Then we who are alive, who are left,** will be caught up together with them in the clouds to meet the L*ORD* in the air, and so we will always be with the L*ORD** (1 Thessalonians 4:13–17).[173]

---

[173] I inserted the word *certainly* in brackets in verse 15, because the Greek words translated *not* by the ESV are οὐ μή (*ou mē, G3756, G3361)*, which can mean, *never*, *This note is continued on the next page.*

In the penultimate sentence of this passage, Paul describes the so-called rapture of the church. But one thing must *certainly* happen before the church is taken out of this world. The dead in Christ must rise first. The question is, when does this happen with respect to the events described by Christ in Mark 13 quoted above?

3. The Bible only talks about two resurrections of the dead, the first being that of those who sleep in Christ. Afterward those destined for eternal condemnation (those who refused God's salvation) will rise. Paul's writings tell us unequivocally that the first of these resurrections must happen *before the rapture*. So, does Scripture tell us without equivocation when this will be? Yes! The first resurrection of the dead is recorded in Revelation 20, after all the events of the Tribulation have taken place, and just before the thousand year reign of Christ.[174] Here is the passage:

> *⁴... Also I saw the souls of those who had been beheaded for the testimony of Jesus and for the word of God, and those who had not worshiped the beast or its image and had not received its mark on their foreheads or their hands. They came to life and reigned with Christ for a thousand years. ⁵The rest of the dead did not come to life until the thousand years were ended.* **This is the first resurrection.** *⁶Blessed and holy is the one who shares in the first resurrection! Over such the*

---

or *no more at all*. The single word *not* is not a fair representation of the emphasis that Paul puts on the certainty of the dead in Christ rising before we who are still alive will be gathered up with Christ in the air. To this end the NIV translation of this verse also inserts *certainly*.

[174] I'm making the relatively obvious assumption that the sequence of events matches the sequence of their mention in these verses.

second death has no power, but they will be priests of God and of Christ, and they will reign with him for a thousand years (Revelation 20:4b–6).

This passage tells us that the first resurrection is that of all who have been saved, "Those who had been beheaded because of their testimony for Jesus and because of the word of God."[175] God revealed to me that this word *beheaded* is the equivalent of Paul saying in Romans 6 that we have all died with Christ:

*¹What shall we say then? Are we to continue in sin that grace may abound? ²By no means! How can we **who died to sin** still live in it? ³Do you not know that **all of us who have been baptized into Christ Jesus were baptized into his death?** ⁴We were buried therefore with him by baptism into death, in order that, just as Christ was raised from the dead by the glory of the Father, we too might walk in newness of life. ⁵**For if we have been united with him in a death like his, we shall certainly be united with him in a resurrection like his**. ⁶We know that our old self was crucified with him in order that the body of sin might be brought to nothing, so that we would no longer be enslaved to sin. ⁷For one who*

---

[175] *Those who have been beheaded* is a figure of speech, not to be taken literally. God uses many obscure descriptions in Scripture to prevent the purely intellectual mind from grasping the truth of Scripture. I think of them as traps, or pits that an unbeliever (or arrogant believer) will fall into as he reads the word and tries, in his prideful heart, to understand it on his own without God's help. God has purposefully made the wisdom of the prideful and unrepentant as foolishness before Him. (See Matthew 13:13–14, in which Jesus quotes Isaiah 6:9–10.) Only by the revelation of the Spirit can one understand these codes and obscure passages. I had read this passage many times before and thought that it referred only to a certain class of Christians, those who had been martyred by decapitation. Of course that doesn't make sense when you consider the import of the verse. But God had to open my eyes to see what the passage really says and, now so very clearly to me, means.

> *has died has been set free from sin. ⁸**Now if we have died with Christ, we believe that we will also live with him.** ⁹We know that Christ, being raised from the dead, will never die again; death no longer has dominion over him. ¹⁰For the death he died he died to sin, once for all, but the life he lives he lives to God* (Romans 6:1–10).

It goes without saying that one who has been beheaded will die; that is, his body will die. But it goes deeper than just experiencing this *death* to sin. It means that we have a new mind, no longer conformed to the ways of this world but transformed by a constant renewal (Romans 12:2). We have, in a sense, been given a new head, from which the glory of Christ will shine.

So to believe that the church will be *raptured* before the Great Tribulation is to ignore the description of the saints in Revelation 7, and to believe that somehow the events leading to the first resurrection in Revelation 20 have occurred before the events recorded in chapters 4 through 19, in which the Tribulation occurs. This is too hard to believe for me, personally, but I don't have to reason it out this way, for God has told me what will happen and I believe Him.[176]

---

[176] The LORD spoke to me at a time when I had made it a steadfast purpose in life to avoid controversial issues such as the timing of the rapture, believing that engaging in such controversies leads to evil. See, for example, 1 Timothy 1:3–4 and 1 Timothy 6:4. But at the time I heard this pastor speak, by the grace of God, I had been studying the book of Revelation for some time. When He spoke to me, I also, by His Spirit, was reading 1 Thessalonians 4. This is when I recalled, by His Spirit, this opaque (and therefore extremely interesting) passage in Revelation 20. It was these two passages of Scripture that the Spirit weaved together in my mind to prove what God had said to me. That I was not looking for such knowledge at the time, but, rather, had steadfastly avoided looking into it on my own, tells me that God had another plan for me. Writing these lines is a partial fulfillment of that plan.

Tribulation of the Saints of God

But let's assume *arguendo*, as the lawyers say, that the church will not go through *the* Great Tribulation. It is sad but true that Scripture makes it abundantly clear that the saints of God (and therefore the church) will go through *a* terrible tribulation nonetheless. We get this prediction from Daniel, from Paul and also from John's Revelation. I will quote these passages extensively so that there can be no mistaking their context.

The first passages are from Daniel 7, after the prophet has seen the frightening vision of the four beasts coming out of the sea. In this vision, very much like John's in Revelation, Daniel finds himself standing before the Throne of God where Jesus (YHWH)—the eternal God of heaven, the image and perfect representation of God—enters and sits (Daniel 7:9).[177] There are other celestial beings standing in the throne room, one of whom Daniel asks to explain his vision of the four beasts.

> [16]"*I approached one of those who stood there and asked him the truth concerning all this. So he told me and made known to me the interpretation of the things.* [17]'*These four great beasts are four kings who shall arise out of the earth.* [18]*But the saints of the Most High shall receive the kingdom and possess the kingdom forever, forever and ever.*' [19]***Then I desired to know the truth about the fourth beast, which was different from all the rest, exceedingly terrifying, with its teeth of iron and claws of bronze, and which devoured and broke in pieces and stamped what was left with its feet,*** [20]***and about the ten horns that were on its head, and the other horn that came up and before which three of them fell, the horn that had eyes and a mouth that spoke***

---

[177] That the Ancient of Days is Jesus is verified by the vision He presents to Daniel, which corresponds to Jesus' appearance to Ezekiel in Ezekiel 1 and to John in Revelation 1.

great things, and that seemed greater than its companions. ²¹**As I looked, this horn made war with the saints and prevailed over them**, ²²until the Ancient of Days came, and judgment was given for the saints of the Most High, and the time came when the saints possessed the kingdom" (Daniel 7:16b–22).

This passage suggests that as the fourth beast is defeating the saints, he is also crushing and devouring them.

The next passage goes on to explain this vision further:

²³"Thus he said: 'As for the fourth beast, there shall be a fourth kingdom on earth, which shall be different from all the kingdoms, and it shall devour the whole earth, and trample it down, and break it to pieces. ²⁴As for the ten horns, out of this kingdom ten kings shall arise, and another shall arise after them; he shall be different from the former ones, and shall put down three kings. ²⁵He shall speak words against the Most High, **and shall wear out the saints of the Most High**, and shall think to change the times and the law; and **they [the saints of God] shall be given into his hand for a time, times, and half a time.**[178] ²⁶But the court shall sit in judgment, and his dominion shall be taken away, to be consumed and destroyed to the end. ²⁷And the kingdom and the dominion and the greatness of the kingdoms under the whole heaven shall be given to the people of the saints of the Most High; their kingdom

---

[178] This is also the time frame associated with the Great Tribulation. Quite a coincidence if this war on the saints is not taking place during that time. Also note that the phrase *shall wear out the saints* is translated in the NIV as *shall oppress the saints*.

shall be an everlasting kingdom, and all dominions shall serve and obey them'" (Daniel 7:23–27).[179]

How did this king get his power? And does Scripture give him another name? In Daniel 8, the prophet describes a vision of a ram and goat making war on each other. The goat overpowers the ram and then this happens:

*[8]Then the goat became exceedingly great, but when he was strong, the great horn was broken, and instead of it there came up four conspicuous horns toward the four winds of heaven. [9]Out of one of them came a little horn, which grew exceedingly great toward the south, toward the east, and toward the glorious land. [10]It grew great, even to the host of heaven. And some of the host and some of the stars it threw down to the ground and trampled on them. [11]It became great, even as great as the Prince of the host. And the regular burnt offering was taken away from him, and the place of his sanctuary was overthrown. [12]**And a host** [**of the saints**] **will be given over to it together with the regular burnt offering because of transgression**, and it will throw truth to the ground, and it will act and prosper* (Daniel 8:8–12).

This passage mentions a time of lawless rebellion, which we are seeing today. Especially inside the church, God have mercy on us, a silent rebellion is occurring, as the influence of Satan, resulting in such heresies flourishing as the hyper-grace movement, has become more marked around the world. Then there's divorce, abortion, sexual immorality and other corruptions from the world, and various

---

[179] The *times, time and half a time*, is thought to measure seven years, which many biblical scholars equate to the term of the Tribulation on earth. The Spirit does not leave us despairing. After the saints have gone through this time they will be vindicated and given justice by the LORD our God.

corruptions of church doctrine.[180] Later in the passage the angel Gabriel tells Daniel that the four horns of the goat are four kingdoms. It is clear in this passage (which is speaking of the last days and, therefore, of the Great Tribulation) that the kingdoms mentioned—Media, Persia and Greece—are not only the historic kingdoms of that day, but are also kingdoms that will exist during the Great Tribulation.[181] Then the angel continues:

> [22]*As for the horn that was broken, in place of which four others arose, four kingdoms shall arise from his nation, but not with his power.* [23]*And at the latter end of their kingdom, when the transgressors have reached their limit, a king of bold face, one who understands riddles, shall arise.* [24]***His power shall be great—but not by his own power;*** *and he shall cause fearful destruction and shall succeed in what he does,* ***and destroy mighty men and the people who are the saints***. [25]*By his cunning he shall make deceit prosper under his hand, and in his own mind he shall become great. Without warning he shall destroy many. And he shall even rise up against the Prince of princes, and he shall be broken—but by no human hand* (Daniel 8:22–25).

Who has given this fierce *stern-faced* king power to destroy the mighty men and the holy people (another word for *saints*)? Only God

---

[180] One of the most serious such corruptions is the so-called Gay Christian movement, where a thing created out of thin air called the Law of Love completely perverts the gospel message. It asserts that since God is love, active homosexuals will be accepted into the Kingdom of God. I wish they'd take seriously 1 Corinthians 6:9–11, not to mention Leviticus 18:22 and 20:13.

[181] Media and Persia may represent Iraq and Iran, but they surely represent all the evil that is flowing out of all the Islamic countries, who are controlled by Allah, a demon god that sits at Satan's table. They represent all eastern or Islamic thought that has as its only goal the destruction of the west, which had its beginnings in Greek and Roman culture and thought, but was largely influenced by Christian doctrine during the first millennium A.D.

alone can have given him this power. Scripture teaches clearly that no ruler rises apart from the permissive will and Power of God, not even Satan himself (Proverbs 8:15–16).

Daniel 10 and 11 tell of a great war between the king of the North and the king of the South (the goat and the ram, apparently), wherein the king of the North will prevail.[182] After this, Jesus says:

> *²⁹"At the time appointed he shall return and come into the south, but it shall not be this time as it was before. ³⁰For ships of Kittim shall come against him, and he shall be afraid and withdraw, and shall turn back and be enraged and take action against the holy covenant. He shall turn back and pay attention to those who forsake the holy covenant. ³¹Forces from him shall appear and profane the temple and fortress, and shall take away the regular burnt offering.* [See the passage from Daniel 8:8–12 quoted above.] *And they shall set up the abomination that makes desolate. ³²He shall seduce with flattery those who violate the covenant, but the people who know their God shall stand firm and take action. ³³And the wise among the people shall make many understand,* **though for some days they shall stumble by sword and flame, by captivity and plunder.** *³⁴When they stumble, they shall receive a little help. And many shall join themselves to them with flattery, ³⁵and some of the wise shall stumble, so that they may be refined, purified, and made white, until the time of the end, for it still awaits the appointed time.*
>
> *³⁶"And the king shall do as he wills. He shall exalt himself and magnify himself above every god, and shall speak astonishing things against the God of gods. He shall prosper till the indignation is accomplished; for what is decreed shall be done. ³⁷He shall pay no*

---

[182] As mentioned previously, the person speaking to Daniel here is Jesus Himself. His description in Daniel 10:5–6 matches His description in Revelation 1.

> *attention to the gods of his fathers, or to the one beloved by women. He shall not pay attention to any other god, for he shall magnify himself above all. [38]He shall honor the god of fortresses instead of these. A god whom his fathers did not know he shall honor with gold and silver, with precious stones and costly gifts. [39]He shall deal with the strongest fortresses with the help of a foreign god. Those who acknowledge him he shall load with honor. He shall make them rulers over many and shall divide the land for a price"* (Daniel 11:29–39).

Daniel 12 then tells us precisely when this will happen:

> [1]***"At that time shall arise Michael, the great prince who has charge of your people. And there shall be a time of trouble, such as never has been since there was a nation till that time.*** *But at that time your people shall be delivered, everyone whose name shall be found written in the book.* [2]*And many of those who sleep in the dust of the earth shall awake, some to everlasting life, and some to shame and everlasting contempt.* [3]*And those who are wise shall shine like the brightness of the sky above; and those who turn many to righteousness, like the stars forever and ever"* (Daniel 12:1–3).

That is, this will all happen as part of the Great Tribulation. (Sorry if you were hoping for a more specific answer.)

We see the two resurrections happening here, that of the righteous and that of the wicked. This prophecy does not distinguish between these in time, I would guess on purpose; God was playing His cards close to His vest it seems. But we know from Revelation 20:4–5 that the first resurrection will be that of the righteous (or wise). Then the second resurrection of those who will go into hell will happen after the thousand-year reign of Christ is ended. Scripture is not clear as to how long after the thousand years this second event will occur.

The story is not yet over. There are two more passages of Scripture that shed light on this awful time for the church. The first I will quote is from Paul in 2 Thessalonians 2:

> *¹Now concerning the coming of our LORD Jesus Christ and our being gathered together to him, we ask you, brothers, ²not to be quickly shaken in mind or alarmed, either by a spirit or a spoken word, or a letter seeming to be from us, to the effect that the day of the LORD has come. ³Let no one deceive you in any way.* **For that day will not come, unless the rebellion comes first, and the man of lawlessness is revealed, the son of destruction,** *⁴who opposes and exalts himself against every so-called god or object of worship, so that he takes his seat in the temple of God, proclaiming himself to be God* (2 Thessalonians 2:1–4).

This is the same rebellion mentioned in Daniel. This tracks closely with the passage from Daniel about the nature of the stern-faced king. *"And the king shall do as he wills. He shall exalt himself and magnify himself above every god, and shall speak astonishing things against the God of gods"* (The LORD speaking in Daniel 11:36a). It is not too large a leap of logic to assert that this stern-faced king is the man of lawlessness of whom Paul speaks.

But there's more:

> *⁵Do you not remember that when I was still with you I told you these things? ⁶And you know what is restraining him now so that he may be revealed in his time. ⁷For the mystery of lawlessness is already at work. Only he who now restrains it will do so until he is out of the way. ⁸And then the lawless one will be revealed, whom the LORD Jesus will kill with the breath*

> *of his mouth [e.g. the Holy Spirit]*[183] *and bring to nothing by the appearance of his coming. ⁹The coming of the lawless one is by the activity of Satan with all power and false signs and wonders, ¹⁰and with all wicked deception for those who are perishing, because they refused to love the truth and so be saved.* **¹¹Therefore God sends them a strong delusion, so that they may believe what is false,** *¹²***in order that all may be condemned who did not believe the truth but had pleasure in unrighteousness*** (2 Thessalonians 2:5–12).[184]

The man of lawlessness must be let loose by the power of God. He will work according to the power of Satan. This is described in the following passage from Revelation 13:

> *¹And I saw a beast rising out of the sea, with ten horns and seven heads, with ten diadems on its horns and blasphemous names on its heads. ²And the beast that I saw was like a leopard; its feet were like a bear's, and its mouth was like a lion's mouth. And to it the dragon gave his power and his throne and great authority. ³One of its heads seemed to have a mortal wound, but its mortal wound was healed, and the whole earth marveled as they followed the beast. ⁴And they worshiped the dragon, for he had given his authority to the beast, and they worshiped the beast, saying, "Who is like the beast, and who can fight against it?" ⁵And the beast was given a mouth uttering haughty and*

---

[183] See, for example, John 20:22 where the breath of Jesus clearly represents the Holy Spirit. The word for Spirit used here is the Greek word for breath, πνεῦμα (*pneuma*). In the O.T.. the word for Spirit is the Hebrew word for breath רוּחַ (ruwach).

[184] I've highlighted the passage that says how God will send a powerful delusion to insure that those who have refused to believe the truth will continue to believe the lie, so that their souls will be destroyed in the judgment.

> *blasphemous words, and it was allowed to exercise authority for forty-two months. ⁶It opened its mouth to utter blasphemies against God, blaspheming his name and his dwelling, that is, those who dwell in heaven. ⁷Also it was allowed to make war on the saints and to conquer them. And authority was given it over every tribe and people and language and nation, ⁸and all who dwell on earth will worship it, everyone whose name has not been written before the foundation of the world in the book of life of the Lamb who was slain.*
>
> > ⁹*If anyone has an ear, let him hear:*
> > ¹⁰*If anyone is to be taken captive, to captivity he goes;*
> > > *if anyone is to be slain with the sword, with the sword must he be slain.*
>
> *Here is a call for the endurance and faith of the saints* (Revelation 13:1–10).

Note that it is God who has given the beast the power to make war on the saints to conquer them. Verse 9, stating, *If anyone has an ear...* is speaking of the saints. Many will be martyred during this time. Also, this beast must be the fourth beast Daniel saw in Daniel 7, the one who crushes and devours the whole earth according to Daniel 7:23–25.

Finally, see the description of the man of lawlessness in Revelation 13, where John goes on to say:

> ¹¹*Then I saw another beast rising out of the earth. It had two horns like a lamb and it spoke like a dragon.* ¹²*It exercises all the authority of the first beast in its presence, and makes the earth and its inhabitants worship the first beast, whose mortal wound was healed.* ¹³**It performs great signs, even making fire come down from heaven to earth in front of people,** ¹⁴*and by the signs that it is allowed to work in the*

> *presence of the beast it deceives those who dwell on earth, telling them to make an image for the beast that was wounded by the sword and yet lived.* **¹⁵And it was allowed [by God] to give breath to the image of the beast, so that the image of the beast might even speak and might cause those who would not worship the image of the beast to be slain.** *¹⁶Also it causes all, both small and great, both rich and poor, both free and slave, to be marked on the right hand or the forehead, ¹⁷so that no one can buy or sell unless he has the mark, that is, the name of the beast or the number of its name* (Revelation 13:11–17).

I believe this is the man of lawlessness about whom Paul speaks, who does the work of Satan by following the first beast, who is Satan's agent (Revelation 13:4). It follows that since he speaks like a dragon, he is also the dragon's agent who serves the first beast, and in serving him makes war on the saints. The first beast is clearly a spiritual being through whom Satan controls the man of lawlessness. The man of lawlessness appears not to be a spiritual being, since men interact directly with him, as they do the stern-faced king in Daniel 8.[185]

So we have seen that whether or not the church is taken up to be with Christ (raptured) prior to the Great Tribulation, there will be a time of great suffering for the saints. This suffering will be wrought by the hands of Satan (to the extent permitted by the LORD our God) working through the beast with steel jaws and bronze claws who, in turn, will work through a human man, the man of lawlessness. All these entities have been given power by God to work this work.

As I read Daniel and the Revelation together, these pieces all fell into place, and I have attempted to describe them here. One night, when I realized what the Spirit was telling me, I was horrified. I got on my knees and asked, "Why, LORD, would you give power to Satan and

---

[185] Here is what the LORD has taught me. Daniel 7–8 and 10–12 are visions of the same sequence of events, told from different points of view by the Holy Spirit. These prophecies are repeated by Paul and also in the Holy Spirit's revelation to John.

his agents to make war on the saints, to oppress them and murder them?" **Maybe** the following passages, one from Deuteronomy and another from Hosea, are the answer:

> [58] *"If you are not careful to do all the words of this law that are written in this book, that you may fear this glorious and awesome name, the* LORD *your God,* [59]*then the* LORD *will bring on you and your offspring extraordinary afflictions, afflictions severe and lasting, and sicknesses grievous and lasting.* [60]*And he will bring upon you again all the diseases of Egypt, of which you were afraid, and they shall cling to you.* [61]*Every sickness also and every affliction that is not recorded in the book of this law, the* LORD *will bring upon you, until you are destroyed.* [62]*Whereas you were as numerous as the stars of heaven, you shall be left few in number, because you did not obey the voice of the* LORD *your God.* [63]***And as the* LORD *took delight in doing you good and multiplying you, so the* LORD *will take delight in bringing ruin upon you and destroying you. And you shall be plucked off the land that you are entering to take possession of it*** (Deuteronomy 28:58–63).

And again from Hosea:

> [1]*Hear the word of the* LORD, *O children of Israel, for the* LORD *has a controversy with the inhabitants of the land. There is no faithfulness or steadfast love, and no knowledge of God in the land;* [2]*there is swearing, lying, murder, stealing, and committing adultery; they break all bounds, and bloodshed follows bloodshed.* [3]*Therefore the land mourns, and all who dwell in it languish, and also the beasts of the field and the birds of the heavens, and even the fish of the sea are taken away.* [4]*Yet let no one contend, and let none accuse, for*

> *with you is my contention, O priest.* ⁵*You shall stumble by day; the prophet also shall stumble with you by night; and I will destroy your mother.* ⁶***My people are destroyed for lack of knowledge…***" (Hosea 4:1–6a).

Reading what happened to the Jews in the light of these Scripture passages some eight hundred years after the words were preached to them (in the case of Deuteronomy), I realized that God brought calamity on His people in the O.T. when they had become corrupt. Look at the church in the United States today, riddled with divorce, ugly conflicts that lead to church splits, fornication, destructive false doctrine, downright disobedience and even abortion! We have trashed the Name of God and ruined our testimony. What moral authority do we have to lecture the world around us about the sanctity of marriage when the divorce rate is as high in the church as it is in the world? What moral authority do we have to speak against the horrendous slaughter of innocent children, when millions of so-called evangelical Christians voted for a man who supported unlimited abortion and homosexual rights?[186]

As to the tribulation of the church, Scripture makes clear that not everyone who dies during this time will be corrupt, just as every Jew who died during the siege of Jerusalem was not corrupt. We know from Ezekiel 9 that there were many godly men and women in Jerusalem during those last horrible days. We also know from the Revelation that there will be many saints slain because they refused to worship the beast or his image. Nevertheless, the church is in for a terrible time. This is clear from God's word.

---

[186] In the November 4, 2008 election, the candidate who supported abortion on demand and homosexual rights probably won the election because of the votes of the evangelical community. This marks, I believe, the beginning of the end of America as a superpower, maybe even as a national entity altogether. Be that as it may, the church in America will have a lot to answer for.

Defilement of the LORD's Table

When the modern church decided to offer unfermented wine (grape juice) when celebrating the LORD's Supper, it committed a terrible sin. Here's a story from the O.T. that explains why God will judge this as an awful sin of disobedience.

Recall that when Saul was the king of Israel, the LORD told him to wipe out the entire nation of Amelech. Here's what the LORD said through the prophet Samuel:

> *[1] And Samuel said to Saul, "The LORD sent me to anoint you king over his people Israel; now therefore listen to the words of the LORD. [2] Thus says the LORD of hosts, 'I have noted what Amalek did to Israel in opposing them on the way when they came up out of Egypt. [3] Now go and strike Amalek and devote to destruction all that they have. Do not spare them, but kill both man and woman, child and infant, ox and sheep, camel and donkey'"* (1 Samuel 15:1–3).

So Saul went out, destroyed all their cities, all the men, women and children—well, except for Agag their king—and the livestock—well, except for the best of the cattle and sheep. But, hey, Saul did intend to devote them to the LORD, after all. This is how the LORD responded to Saul's *good intentions*:

> *[10] The word of the LORD came to Samuel: [11] "I regret that I have made Saul king, for he has turned back from following me and has not performed my commandments." And Samuel was angry, and he cried to the LORD all night. [12] And Samuel rose early to meet Saul in the morning. And it was told Samuel, "Saul came to Carmel, and behold, he set up a monument for himself and turned and passed on and went down to Gilgal"* (1 Samuel 15:10–12).

So Samuel got up the next morning and went out to find Saul, to give him the LORD's message. Here is what ensued:

> ^{15}Saul said, "They have brought them from the Amalekites, for the people spared the best of the sheep and of the oxen to sacrifice to the LORD your God, and the rest we have devoted to destruction." ^{16}Then Samuel said to Saul, "Stop! I will tell you what the LORD said to me this night." And he said to him, "Speak." ^{17}And Samuel said, "Though you are little in your own eyes, are you not the head of the tribes of Israel? The LORD anointed you king over Israel. ^{18}And the LORD sent you on a mission and said, 'Go, devote to destruction the sinners, the Amalekites, and fight against them until they are consumed.' ^{19}**Why then did you not obey the voice of the LORD? Why did you pounce on the spoil and do what was evil in the sight of the LORD?**" ^{20}And Saul said to Samuel, "I have obeyed the voice of the LORD. I have gone on the mission on which the LORD sent me. I have brought Agag the king of Amalek, and I have devoted the Amalekites to destruction. ^{21}But the people took of the spoil, sheep and oxen, the best of the things devoted to destruction, to sacrifice to the LORD your God in Gilgal." ^{22}And Samuel said, "Has the LORD as great delight in burnt offerings and sacrifices, as in obeying the voice of the LORD? Behold, to obey is better than sacrifice, and to listen than the fat of rams. ^{23}For rebellion is as the sin of divination, and presumption is as iniquity and idolatry. Because you have rejected the word of the LORD, he has also rejected you from being king" (1 Samuel 15:15–23).

After this, Samuel himself took a sword and cut Agag into pieces so that the LORD's wrath would not break out against Israel.

On that Day, will we have the same whiny excuse as Saul? "We did obey the LORD. Our 'wine' was just not fermented, that's all. What's the harm in that?"

Before I describe what's wrong with that, a little history is in order.

How did it come about that the church decided to disobey the word of the LORD with respect to taking wine at His table? It turns out that the inventor of grape juice, Thomas B. Welch, who lived from 1825 to 1903,[187] joined the *Wesleyan Methodist Connexion* religious movement in 1843, which preached against making, buying or drinking any alcoholic beverage (which is absolutely not supported by Scripture). During the LORD's Supper, they used what they called *unfermented wine*, grape juice, though it had not been discovered how to preserve it so as to keep it from fermenting. Mr. Welch experimented with various ways to achieve this and discovered that it could be done through a pasteurization process. Though his religious affiliation may have spurred him in this quest, he seemed to have had an eye to selling his product, which he did to other churches in the late-nineteenth century. His motives, whether they were pure or not, are immaterial. One can always give *good* reasons for disobeying God, just as Saul did.

People who suffer from alcoholism or its effects on people they've known, such as parents or spouses, have good reason to refrain from drinking any alcoholic beverage themselves. And that's okay with God, as long as they are very careful to keep their vow of abstinence.[188] And it is certainly the duty of all saints to preach, teach and admonish against getting drunk on or becoming dependent on any alcoholic beverage (Ephesians 5:18).[189] But it is not up to any saint to decide for anyone else whether or not he will drink wine or other fermented drink, much less the church as a whole. This is especially true when God has commanded that we drink wine at the communion table. This command was obeyed by the church through the eighteen hundred years leading up to the formation of the Methodist church,

---

[187] See http://fundyreformed.wordpress.com/2006/08/03/welchs-grape-juice-worldly-wisdom-and-wine/. See also *Wikipedia Encyclopedia* regarding Thomas Bramwell Welch for additional information.

[188] A good example of keeping such a vow is that of the Rechabites found in Jeremiah 35.

[189] And not only on fermented drink but on any other drug.

with its doctrine of false righteousness found in forbidding fermented drink at Christ's table. Note how Paul would have reacted to this false righteousness:

> ¹*Now the Spirit expressly says that **in later times** some will depart from the faith by devoting themselves to deceitful spirits and teachings of demons,* ²*through the insincerity of liars whose consciences are seared,* ³***who forbid marriage and require abstinence from foods** that God created to be received with thanksgiving by those who believe and know the truth.* ⁴*For everything created by God is good,* ***and nothing is to be rejected if it is received with thanksgiving***, ⁵*for it is made holy by the word of God and prayer* (1 Timothy 4:1–5).[190]

As I mentioned before, we are in those *later times*. God has made it very clear to me that this was a terrific mistake. If Paul's statement to Timothy above is not enough, recognize that God has never declared any alcoholic beverage unclean in itself, except when one vows to abstain for some reason.[191] Yet by trading wine for grape juice the church has declared wine unclean. The mature believer will recall that in Acts, when Peter was shown the vision of unclean animals and refused God's order to kill and eat, God said, *"What God has made clean, do not call common"* (Acts 11:9).[192]

There is just too much Scripture to quote wherein God affirms that the drinking of wine and fermented drinks is not only okay, but desirable on certain occasions. See, for example, Numbers 28 where God specifies that a ***fermented*** drink is to be offered as a drink

---

[190] It is absolutely clear that the modern church's doctrine with respect to fermented drink has not been informed by this passage. Clearly, a large segment of the modern church has largely rejected the truth of this passage.

[191] As in the vow of the Nazirite described in Numbers 6.

[192] Acts 11:4–10 gives the whole vision.

offering (Numbers 28:7).[193] My favorite quote from the O.T. is this, however, where God is speaking of the tithes to be brought by those who live too far away from the temple to bring them to Jerusalem:

> *[24] And if the way is too long for you, so that you are not able to carry the tithe, when the L*ORD *your God blesses you, because the place is too far from you, which the L*ORD *your God chooses, to set his name there, [25] then you shall turn it into money and bind up the money in your hand and go to the place that the L*ORD *your God chooses [26] and spend the money for whatever you desire—oxen or sheep or wine or* **strong drink**, *whatever your appetite craves. And you shall eat there before the L*ORD *your God and rejoice, you and your household* (Deuteronomy 14:24–26).

God is saying, in essence, when you bring your tithe have a party, drink a little and enjoy yourselves.[194]

Just so you don't think this just an O.T. issue, recall that Jesus not only drank wine Himself, He made wine at the wedding in Cana. It wasn't just any wine, mind you. It was good wine.[195] Apparently Jesus drank enough fermented drink during His stay that some of the Jewish leadership accused Him of being a drunkard (Matthew 11:19 and Luke 7:34).

So, you might ask, where's the sin in choosing to drink grape juice? It's harmless, after all; no one ever got intoxicated on grape juice. Well, if one has declared wine unclean for himself, then, according to Scripture, for that person, grape juice and even the skins

---

[193] The NIV uses the words *fermented drink* whereas the ESV uses the words *strong drink*.

[194] See also Psalm 104:15, which states that God has made wine (and I would guess other alcoholic beverages as seen from the passage just quoted) specifically for man's enjoyment.

[195] See John 2, specifically see John 2:10. The passage also implies that the guests were already intoxicated when Jesus made this wine for them.

and seeds of the grapes are also unclean (Numbers 6:1–4). Anything made from grapes is unclean. So we've doubled up on our sin. We have substituted our righteousness for God's, and we've also been drinking an unclean beverage anyway. You can't have it both ways. If wine is unclean, then so is anything made from the fruit of the vine.

Recall what happened to the Corinthian church for defiling the LORD's table (1 Corinthians 11:27–30). It was weak, some were afflicted with illness and others died. I would put it to you that the church in this country shows the same symptoms. It is weak spiritually, and it is dying. It has certainly died as a meaningful representative of God's wishes as to how America should be governed, as it no longer has any influence in how moral or political decisions are made. So to the church in the United States, repent, I say, or we will continue to suffer God's judgment.

The Unforgiveable Sin

Jesus says, *[31]"Therefore I tell you, every sin and blasphemy will be forgiven people, but the blasphemy against the Spirit will not be forgiven. [32]And whoever speaks a word against the Son of Man will be forgiven, but whoever speaks against the Holy Spirit will not be forgiven, either in this age or in the age to come"* (Matthew 12:31–32).

So what does it mean to commit the unforgiveable sin?

Many preachers believe that this sin was only committed by the Pharisees one time and cannot be committed by anyone after. It's incredible that a person can be a Christian for many decades, even a teacher of the word, and not know that this is false; that they do not know what this sin is, and that it can indeed be committed today, and is committed by all those who are destined for hell.

To understand what it means to blaspheme the Spirit, one must understand what the word *blaspheme* means in the scriptural context. Fortunately, the Bible tells us in the following passage from Numbers 15:

> *"But the person who does anything with a high hand, whether he is native or a sojourner, reviles [blasphemes] the LORD, and that person shall be cut off from among his people"* (Numbers 15:30). [196]

To blaspheme is to sin defiantly, to willfully and continually ignore God's commands as a pattern of life. Therefore one who blasphemes the Holy Spirit for the purposes of Jesus' condemnation is either 1) willfully, over many years, defying His call to the repentance that leads to salvation; 2) claiming over and over again, without chance of repentance, that God in the Person of the Holy Spirit is a liar by stating that the Bible, which was written by Him, is not the true and inerrant word of God; or 3) he is, without any thought of repentance, associating the Spirit's work with the devil, as the Pharisees did.

The only way we can come to the repentance and surrender that leads to salvation is to yield to the urgings of the Spirit. These urgings can go on for years. If, however, they do not yield, there is no other way for one to be saved. Once one irrevocably refuses to believe the truth about God's salvation, one has committed an unpardonable sin: One has rejected the only forgiveness there can possibly be, which is the truth concerning repentance and surrender to Christ's Spirit. Indeed, refusal to accept God's salvation is a sin, and it cannot be forgiven because one has refused the very forgiveness that would have saved him!

---

[196] The word *reviles* in this passage in the Masoretic Text is the Hebrew word גָּדַף (*gadaph*, H1442), which means to revile or reproach men and blaspheme God.

Science, Knowledge and Faith [197]

Being a scientist who searches for knowledge about how creation works, and being a man of godly faith who has a true personal relationship with the LORD—that is, being a person who lives by faith in the saving power and word of Jesus Christ—are not mutually exclusive. In fact, if the church had better understood God over the centuries, more members of the body would have been at the forefront of many great scientific discoveries.[198] God is more than eager to show His children how His creation works. But many, if not most, in the Body of Christ here in America seem to disdain such scientific exploration, because we fear that something might be discovered that will challenge the truth of God's word. Here is a trustworthy principle: insofar as God's word *intends* to tell us how creation works or was assembled, if what science says contradicts God's word, then His word must prevail. Nevertheless, realize that the Bible's purpose is not to instruct us in the details of how creation works (for example: how to calculate how old the universe is); its purpose is, among many other things, rather, to give credit to God for creating all of reality. Having said that, we will see soon that the Bible can be and has been used by evil men through the centuries to deny reality and to lead people into terrible error. These evil men who claimed to speak for God destroyed anyone who disagreed with their doctrine because such people were branded heretics. They were shown no mercy.

---

[197] It has always galled me that the church throughout its history has stood in the way of scientific advancement. This opposition is not always bad, as in the case of opposing the use of human embryos for scientific research. But I think one of the reasons we are not more successful in stopping this type of horrible research is that our history is marred by our seemingly general opposition to the advancement of human secular knowledge in general and science in particular. I believe this tendency dishonors God and that He is not pleased with us in this respect, so I've added this section.

[198] Many of the great scientists of the fifteenth, sixteenth and seventeenth centuries were devoted men of God. One such was Sir Isaac Newton, one of the greatest minds ever put on the earth. He believed in and knew God. Oh, and he rejected the Godhead theology.

As our culture and the church have evolved, what seems to be an irreparable separation between science and religion has formed. As the centuries have progressed, scientists in general have turned away from God, even the idea of a god. I know there are scientists in the world today who love the LORD, but I would bet they are a very small minority of the intellectual and scientific community. This could be why we only hear of the ones who hate what they call *organized religion* and the idea of a Supreme Being. While such people have fabulous God-given intellects, they are no more than fools in God's eyes. The necessary result of their foolishness is in this passage of Scripture:

> *The fool says in his heart, "There is no God." They are corrupt, they do abominable deeds, there is none who does good* (Psalm 14:1).

Thus, in God's eyes, these fools are necessarily men and women of low moral character.[199]

Part of the reason they reject religion is their overweening pride. In a purely worldly sense they have every reason to be proud. They are much smarter than most of us, and many have notable worldly accomplishments to brag about. They are scientists because they have a great hunger to know things and to push the envelope of human knowledge. They are mostly to be commended for this. But in their soul-damning pride, they believe that the human intellect is the measure of all things.[200]

---

[199] We can see that as those who hate God and His word gain more and more power, the world becomes an increasingly awful place. In America today, the moral climate of this society is filthy, corrupt, and full of liars and deceivers who only want to gain control over other people's lives. Abortion rights come directly from this affliction, as does the demonstrably false theory of evolutionary biology.

[200] This is a paraphrase of a statement by the Pre-Socratic philosopher, Protagoras, who lived between 490 and 420 B.C. He is quoted by Plato as saying, *Man is the measure of all things: of things which are, that they are, and of things which are not, that they are not.* The statement is generally paraphrased as: *Man is the measure of all things.* However, Protagoras' statement lacks a specific context which might *This note is continued on the next page.*

There is also another very understandable reason why they hate religion. In the past centuries there have been abundant examples of *organized religion* oppressing the people and keeping them ignorant. Scientists have seen through the centuries, as we in the body of Christ have, that many religious men and women have always been, and are still, satisfied to dwell in ignorance of the world around them. It's no wonder that many intellectuals hate religion! Scientists want to know things, and, as they see it, all religion wants to do is pander to an ignorant person's tendency to superstition.

During the Middle Ages and well into the Renaissance, the Catholic church held as inviolable doctrine that the earth was the center of the universe. (This is the *geocentric theory* of the universe.) They ruthlessly oppressed anyone who dared disagree with this doctrine. And, evil upon evil(!), they used the Holy Scriptures to justify their false doctrines, imprison people or execute them in the most horrible ways for challenging what became demonstrably false doctrine.[201]

The belief in the geocentric theory of the universe was common to many ancient cultures. It was taught by such eminent ancient Greek scholars as Aristotle and Ptolemy.[202] And during the early days of the church, this idea became cast-in-stone church doctrine. What is amazing about this is that these early church theologians used the Bible to convince themselves that this theory was true.[203] In fact, there is at least one member of the Catholic Church today who still argues for the geocentric theory. To see this, incredible as it may seem, go to

---

illumine what he meant by it. Nevertheless, I do not believe I am overstating a point when I say that many modern scientists seem to think that the oft-quoted paraphrase be literally true.

[201] The geocentric theory was disproved without question in the seventeenth century.
[202] This was not the only view of the universe taught in ancient Greece. The Pythagoreans taught the heliocentric theory, as early as the fifth century B.C.
[203] One such passage of Scripture is Joshua 10:12–13, where the LORD commands the sun to stand still for one day. It was argued by Martin Luther and others that if the sun stood still, this must be God's confirmation of the geocentric theory. For more on this see *Martin Luther, Geocentrism, and the Bible vs. Science* at http://www.blogos.org/scienceandtechnology/martin-luther-geocentricism.php.

the website www.scripturecatholic.com/geocentrism.html. This website consists of pages and pages of quotes from the Bible, as well as Papal edicts and other theological declarations that state that *the Bible says* the earth is the center of the universe. Since, in their view, the Bible says so, and since the Bible is the inerrant word of God (which is true), then objective reality cannot disprove this. The person who set up this website states that the heliocentric theory has never been conclusively proven. Can you imagine?

So the geocentric theory became the holiest of holies for the church (kind of like the Godhead theology is today). It held that esteemed position for many hundreds of years, but in the seventeenth century came Galileo Galelei, who asserted that the earth orbits the sun (the *heliocentric theory*), which he proved conclusively by his observations of the sun and planets.[204] He was persecuted by the church for his so-called heretical assertions and threatened with the Roman Inquisition. According to Wikipedia, *Galileo was eventually forced to recant his heliocentrism and spent the last years of his life under house arrest on orders of the Roman Inquisition.*[205]

This kind of denial is very disturbing on many levels, of course, but two come immediately to mind. First, it blasphemes the word of God, which is intended to lead us to truth, not to falsehood. Second, it provides evidence of the type of small-minded, self-centered—and evil—*religious* minds that scientists have had to battle for centuries, evil men and women who will deny the plain-as-the-nose-on-your-face truth to satisfy their twisted faith. They even think they are glorifying God by doing this! To tell the truth, if this kind of wacky doctrine,

---

[204] Johannes Kepler, who was a contemporary of Galileo, also discovered the physical laws of planetary motion, providing mathematical proof of Galileo's assertions.

[205] The modern church has its own version of a demonstrably false doctrine like the geocentric theory. Many hold to the ridiculous idea that the universe is only 6,000 years old when observation has proven beyond question that it is billions of years old. And, of course, just like the priests and theologians of the Middle Ages, they claim that the Bible supports their theories. How stupid we must seem to those who are watching us from outside the Kingdom! How so very awful for our testimony and for God's Name!

reasoning and teaching were preached openly today, I could see myself hating *religious* people and *organized religion* too. When these evil men and women stand before God in the Judgment they will not like how God judges them (see Matthew 7:21–23).

Having said this, there are times when opposition to certain scientific methods is justified, such as objecting to cloning human life, or the demonstrably false and destructive theory of evolutionary biology, or using human embryos for scientific research. Scientists who ignore God-given moral boundaries in their attempt to understand the universe will have much to answer for before the Creator. It is right for God's people to oppose them when they violate the moral laws of God in pursuit of knowledge, but thousands of priests and monks, and a whole line church leaders who hated knowledge and truth will also have much to answer for, more than the unbeliever, because they had the word of God to teach them and should have known better.

Religion, in this case a professed belief in a supernatural, all-powerful, all-knowing God, has no monopoly on denying reality. Modern science has at least one version of its own religion where the scientists' god is their own intellect. This and their intense hatred of God leads them to the Theory of Evolution, which denies the plain-as-the-nose-on-your-face truth that creation and the development of life on earth did not happen by accident.[206] When you boil it all down, evolutionary biology, which is demonstrably false, states that life on earth happened by accident, evolving at random in the primordial oceans, which were filled with various hydrocarbon compounds that were the precursors of life. According to this ridiculous theory, these compounds combined randomly over a billion years or so to form RNA and DNA molecules, which then became part of living single-celled organisms. If a person who knows anything about randomness

---

[206] Yes, scientists do have great faith, faith in their intellects and scientific tools. See, for example, Leonard Susskind, *The Black Hole War: My Battle With Stephen Hawking to Make The World Safe For Quantum Mechanics*, Little Brown Company, NY, NY, 2008. He uses the word *faith* many times in this book to describe his belief that science can indeed come to the right answers regarding the nature of the universe.

and statistics thinks objectively just about forming a single DNA molecule by accident—not even considering how complicated one living cell is—he would quickly come to the conclusion that this theory simply cannot be true.

The typical DNA molecule has about two hundred twenty million base pairs of nucleotides called pyrimidines and purines, each consisting of between ten and fifteen atoms; they are linked together in so that these molecules can function as the templates for making proteins. For the DNA molecule to function properly, these two hundred twenty million base pairs have to be linked exactly in the right way.[207]

To illustrate the sheer impossibility of this occurring randomly, get a computer and have it try to write the phrase *the theory of evolution* by randomly putting together, in just the right order, the twenty-six letters of the alphabet and a space character. It would take over twelve billion times the age of the universe (estimated to be around fifteen billion years) if the computer did a billion picks per second.[208] Therefore it is patently absurd to believe that it is possible to randomly assemble even one DNA molecule, a life-code with two hundred twenty million *letters*. In fact, it's beyond absurd. It provides evidence of a quasi-psychotic break with reality. The Theory of Evolution is so

---

[207] This reasoning is based on the Theory of Irreducible Complexity, first advocated by biochemist Michael Behe in 1996. The theory says that for a single system composed of several well-matched interacting parts that contribute to the basic function, removing any one of these parts would cause the system to effectively cease functioning (*Molecular Machines: Experimental Support for the Design Inference* by Michael Behe [1997] at http://www.arn.org/docs/behe/mb_mm92496.htm).http://www.apologetics.org/MolecularMachines/tabid/99/Default.aspx

[208] The number of operations required would be 23^{27}= 5.84 * 10^{36}. Divide this by the number of seconds in a year times 10^9 picks per second. The result is 1.85 * 10^{20} years, which is about 12.4 billion times the age of the universe (1.5 x 10^{10} years). If a computer did one trillion picks per second, then the time would be shortened to 12.4 million times the age of the universe. Of course, in the primordial seas, atoms and molecules wouldn't be combining willy-nilly in one spot one billion times per second.

sacred to the scientists who believe it they have their own inquisitors who do everything they can to destroy the reputations and careers of those who disagree with them, in the spirit of the grand inquisitors of the church many centuries ago.[209]

The reason this absurd theory has stood the test of time is its intended effect of willfully denying that it was the Judeo-Christian God who created all life, including the DNA molecule, and who also gives life to every living thing in the universe. How do I know this? Here is a well-known statement concerning evolution that appeared in a *Scientific American* article by Dr. George Wald, professor emeritus of Biology at Harvard University and Nobel Prize winner:

> *The reasonable view* [concerning the origins of life; *reasonable* only to the psychotic deniers of reality] *was to believe in spontaneous generation; the only alternative, to believe in a single, primary act of supernatural creation.* **There is no third position**. *For this reason many scientists a century ago chose to regard the belief in spontaneous generation as a "philosophical necessity." It is a symptom of the philosophical poverty of our time that this necessity is no longer appreciated. Most modern biologists, having reviewed with satisfaction the downfall of the spontaneous generation hypothesis,* **yet unwilling to accept the alternative belief in special creation,** *are left with nothing.* ***One has only to contemplate the magnitude of this task to concede that the spontaneous generation of a***

---

[209] To get a wonderful perspective on how silly this theory is and how viciously its adherents defend it, see the documentary film *Expelled, No Intelligence Allowed*, directed by Nathan Frankowski, written by Kevin Miller and Ben Stein, released in April, 2008. See the web address: www.imdb.com/title/tt10916 17/ for more information on this excellent documentary. The theory of evolution is essentially a religion, among the worst of all religions because there is absolutely no verifiable evidence to support its hypotheses.

living organism is impossible. *Yet here we are. As a result, I believe, of spontaneous generation.*[210]

The above quotation seems quite clear. Scientists know that spontaneous generation, another name for evolutionary biology, is impossible, yet Dr. Wald says that it would be inherently unreasonable to accept the idea of a creative God. Hence the *philosophical necessity* of believing in the impossible. So they are left with nothing. The rest of the article goes on to rationalize why they might cling to this *reasonable view* despite everything that tells them it is impossible. The willful self-deception evidenced in this article is mind-boggling. And it is this Creator God, in whom Dr. Wald and others refuse to believe, who will hold all these evil men accountable for their actions.

---

[210] "The origin of life," by Dr. George Wald, *Scientific American*, August 1954 p.46, quoted on this web site: http://bevets.com/equotesw.htm.

PART V

My Testimony

I, myself, am no one. I am the least of the least of God's people. But the LORD my God has charged me to write this book, so I have. Notwithstanding this, you ought to know who's speaking so that you may better judge what you've read and test it with the Spirit God gave you. (That is, if you have put your faith in His Son, Jesus Christ.)[211] By His grace and mercy, I have put my faith in Him and do have His Spirit living in me. This is how it came to be.

In April 1948, I was born to wonderful, devoted, loving, but unbelieving parents in San Francisco, California. We moved to the East Bay when I was about three. When I was about seven or eight, God, through His Spirit, moved my mom to send me to Sunday school at a little one-room Bible church near our home. It was run by a missionary couple, Dave and Kay Landers, who were on furlough. It was at this little church that Jesus introduced Himself to me. A year or so later, Dave and Kay were sent back to the mission field, but before they left, they gave me a Bible with their inscription as a parting gift. I still have it. I remember them standing in our living room, brightly lit by the sunshine streaming in, handing the Bible to Mom but smiling down at me. From that day on I read that Bible.

God never let go of me. He pursued a relationship with me. Though I did not go to church until I was eighteen or nineteen years old, I still became His. There is no other way to explain why I read my Bible or stayed in touch with Him in an environment where there was no church family or spiritual teaching and preaching to encourage me. The LORD Jesus arranged for several godly Christian men to be my roommates at college. He also arranged for a godly man to work with

---

[211] Here is a grave warning: Do not fool yourself. If you have not repented of your sins and accepted Jesus as the only way to salvation, you do not know God and you do not have His Spirit living in you.

me in the summers during my college years. It was this great man, Salvador Diwa, who led me to accept Jesus as my LORD and Savior.

This was in 1967. It was also the year that Mom passed away. A year later I fell away from God by giving in to the temptation to have sexual intercourse. For the twenty-five years during which I was sexually promiscuous, I did not read the Bible regularly. I don't think I opened it more than two or three times during that period. But God was faithful. He brought me back onto the path of faith in 1992. Since then I have devoted myself, heart, mind and soul, to seeking Him and His truth.

It is instructive to know how my return to the path of righteousness happened. I was driving to an early morning tennis match, and I happened to be surfing the channels of my car radio. I *just happened* to land on a religious station (the type that I never listened to) and the speaker was quoting from Ezekiel 36:

> *^{24}"I will take you from the nations and gather you from all the countries and bring you into your own land. ^{25}I will sprinkle clean water on you, and you shall be clean from all your uncleannesses, and from all your idols I will cleanse you. ^{26}And I will give you a new heart, and a new spirit I will put within you. And I will remove the heart of stone from your flesh and give you a heart of flesh. ^{27}And I will put my Spirit within you, and cause you to walk in my statutes and be careful to obey my rules. ^{28}You shall dwell in the land that I gave to your fathers, and you shall be my people, and I will be your God. ^{29}And I will deliver you from all your uncleannesses"* (Ezekiel 36:24–29a).

For some time prior to this, I had been feeling the urging of God's Spirit to return to the path of faith. It *just happened* that I worked in an office building in downtown Portland that *just happened* to be across the street from the church I attended as of the writing of this book. I worked in that office for several years, staring at that church but never yielding to God's urging to go over and give it a shot. But that morning, when I heard these promises that God gave me through the prophet Ezekiel, I knew He was bringing me back. Soon after, I gave in to God's pursuit of me, and I was brought back into the *land* from the place into which I had been *scattered*. These verses from Ezekiel have been life verses for me since that day.

I have sought God's truth with all my heart and soul, but needless to say, I am far from perfect. I have not yet attained the degree of perfection that Jesus commanded us in His Sermon on the Mount, *"You therefore must be perfect, as your heavenly Father is perfect"* (Matthew 5:48). I, like all believers, struggle with sin and disobedience. However, this struggle tells me that Jesus is working on me, as He is working in everyone who knows Him and loves Him. I do take some small comfort that Paul, the greatest Christian who ever lived in my view, also struggled with sin and disobedience, as recorded in Romans 7. We can all take comfort that Paul strove and struggled to attain perfection in his life as well. As he wrote in his letter to the Philippians:

> [8] *Indeed, I count everything as loss because of the surpassing worth of knowing Christ Jesus my LORD. For his sake I have suffered the loss of all things and count them as rubbish, in order that I may gain Christ* [9] *and be found in him, not having a righteousness of my own that comes from the law, but that which comes through faith in Christ, the righteousness from God that depends on faith—*[10]*that I may know him and the power of his resurrection, and may share his sufferings, becoming like him in his death,* [11]*that by any means possible I may attain the resurrection from the dead.* [12]*Not that I have already obtained this or am already perfect, but I press on to make it my own, because Christ Jesus has made me his own.* [13]*Brothers, I do not consider that I have made it my own. But one thing I do: forgetting what lies behind and straining forward to what lies ahead,* [14]*I press on toward the goal for the prize of the upward call of God in Christ Jesus* (Philippians 3:8 –14).

Though I am several orders of magnitude less a servant than this great servant of God, I strive to take hold of Christ and the life change He has promised. It is in this vein that I offer this book to all of you who want to know Christ more, the God I know and love with all my heart. It is my fervent hope that He will find this endeavor acceptable.

Now go with God. Examine yourself carefully, and by the power of His Spirit working in you, repent of any sins He reveals to you. Rest in God's incredible love, be always filled with the Spirit, and let His glorious peace rest in your hearts.

AMEN

APPENDIX 1
STUDY OF THE HOLY SPIRIT[212]

Note: The Greek word used throughout the N.T. for *spirit* or *Spirit* is πνεῦμα (pneuma, G4151), which means *breath*, or *current of air*. Similarly, the Hebrew word רוּחַ (ruwach, H4707), which also means *breath* or *wind*, is translated as *spirit* or *Spirit*. When the following Scriptures refer to God's breath, they are always referring to His Holy Spirit.

What follows is an expansion of the section on the Holy Spirit starting on page 41. This is by no means an exhaustive study of the person and being of the Holy Spirit. One could write a million books on the Spirit of God and not cover every aspect of His work in creation. Rather, I hope this will stimulate a reader's thinking as he contemplates the Person and Being of Almighty God.

The Person of the Holy Spirit is identical to the Person of the LORD, but it's critical to understand that the Holy Spirit belongs to the Person of Jesus Christ. My authority for stating this is the Apostle Peter:

> *[10]Concerning this salvation, the prophets who prophesied about the grace that was to be yours searched and inquired carefully,*

---

[212] As each topic is addressed in this study I have included Scripture texts to illustrate the point. Following the passage, I may make a comment on what I learned from it. As with the main body of this book, in some passages, I add emphasis by using bold font. In some cases I will indicating the point of the following text that I want to highlight. There are many times when I let the Scriptures speak for themselves. As with all Scripture, very few passages have only one point or purpose. I am not attempting in this brief study to exhaust all the possible implications of each passage. I am merely trying to illustrate the truth or truths concerning the Person and purpose of the Holy Spirit, as God has made Him known to me.

*¹¹inquiring what person or time **the Spirit of Christ** in them was indicating when he predicted the sufferings of Christ and the subsequent glories. ¹²It was revealed to them that they were serving not themselves but you, in the things that have now been announced to you through those who preached the good news to you by the Holy Spirit sent from heaven, things into which angels long to look* (1 Peter 1:10–12).[213]

Peter is clearly referring to the O.T. prophets. He points out that the Holy Spirit mentioned in the O.T. is the Spirit of Christ, and the Spirit of Christ must have spoken to the prophets with the voice of Christ (e.g. YHWH, see John 5:37).[214] Peter goes on to identify that Spirit as the same Spirit who empowered the preaching of the gospel in the church age. How can one, reading this passage, think that there is any distinction between the Person of Christ and the Person of the Holy Spirit? They speak with only one voice. It is the voice of the revealed God of creation, the Sovereign LORD—YHWH, who is incarnate as Jesus Christ. See, for example, Revelation 2:7, 11, 17 and 29, and Revelation 3:6, 13 and 22, where the LORD Jesus Christ identifies Himself as speaking with the voice of the Spirit of God.

Here is a more detailed account of some of the things the Sevenfold Spirit does, as referred to on page 42 and following.

What the Holy Spirit Does (in part):

I   Fills creation with the presence of God and sustain creation's existence from nanosecond to nanosecond.

---

[213] The Apostle Paul also refers to the Spirit of Christ in Romans 8:9.

[214] How is the voice of YHWH different than the voice of the Father that Jesus mentions in this verse and others? Who can know for certain? The mystery that is God is great. My guess is that the Father is the totality of God in His transcendent fullness, which we cannot comprehend. If He were to speak to us directly rather than through His revealed self, we would not be able to comprehend Him. In fact, the Jews at Mt. Sinai thought they might die if the Father spoke directly to them. So YHWH is this incomprehensible God revealed to us. The voice of YHWH is the Transcendent Majesty's voice spoken through the LORD Jesus.

As to filling creation with His presence, see for example Jeremiah 23:23–24:

> *²³"Am I a God at hand, declares the* L<small>ORD</small>*, and not a God far away? ²⁴Can a man hide himself in secret places so that I cannot see him?" declares the* L<small>ORD</small>*. "Do I not fill heaven and earth?" declares the* L<small>ORD</small>*.*

This is one of many passages that talk about how God is so much greater than His creation that it cannot contain Him. (For others see 1 Kings 8:27, 2 Chronicles 2:6, and 2 Chronicles 6:18.)

We know also from passages such as Psalm 139:7–10 that the L<small>ORD</small> is everywhere in His creation.[215]

As for the moment-to-moment sustenance of Creation by God, the writer of Hebrews puts if very succinctly:

> [The Son]*is the radiance of the glory of God and the exact imprint of his nature, and he upholds the universe by the word of his power* (Hebrews 1:3).

How does the Word come forth? It comes via breath and that breath is the Spirit of God.[216] If God spoke creation into existence, He must also sustain that existence from moment to moment. Since there is only one agent through whom He interacts with creation, the Holy Spirit, it must be His Spirit who is the breath that carries the divine Jesus' Word out in power to affect this.

---

[215] These verses say that there is nowhere that He is not. Same difference.
[216] As explained earlier, the words *radiance* and *exact representation* show that the divine Jesus Christ is the revelation of Jehovah God to His creation.

Here is another passage confirming that God sustains living beings from moment to moment. In it Paul is speaking to a crowd in Athens:

> ^{24} *"The God who made the world and everything in it, being* LORD *of heaven and earth, does not live in temples made by man,* ^{25}*nor is he served by human hands, as though he needed anything,* **since he himself gives to all mankind life and breath and everything.** ^{26}*And he made from one man every nation of mankind to live on all the face of the earth, having determined allotted periods and the boundaries of their dwelling place,* ^{27}*that they should seek God, in the hope that they might feel their way toward him and find him. Yet he is actually not far from each one of us,* ^{28}*for 'In him we live and move and have our being'*^{217}*; as even some of your own poets have said, 'For we are indeed his offspring'"* (Acts 17:24-28).

II Breathes life into what would otherwise be lifeless matter. That is, He animates all living things.[218]

For example:

    A. Job 12:10: *"In [God's] hand is the life of every living thing and the breath of all mankind."*

---

[217] Paul is paraphrasing Job 12:10.

[218] In the following passages quoted from Job, who is speaking to his friends, the Hebrew words for breath are *nasham,* which can be translated as a puff, i.e. wind, angry or vital breath, divine inspiration, intellect, or (concretely) an animal; and *ruwach* (always used for the word *Spirit*), which can be translated as wind; by resemblance breath, i.e. a sensible (or even violent) exhalation; figuratively, life, anger, insubstantiality; by extension, a region of the sky; by resemblance spirit, but only of a rational being (including its expression and functions). The word *nasham* is used in the above passages, but I don't think it can be denied that this *breath* is the same breath that otherwise would be described as the Holy Spirit. I base this conclusion on the fact that in the New Testament, the Greek word for breath, *pneumea,* is always used to describe the Holy Spirit, or any spirit.

B. Job 4:9: *"By the breath of God they perish, and by the blast of his anger they are consumed."*

C. Job 33:4: *"The Spirit of God has made me, and the breath of the Almighty gives me life."*

D. Job 34:14–15: *¹⁴"If he should set his heart to it and gather to himself his spirit and his breath, ¹⁵all flesh would perish together, and man would return to dust."*²¹⁹

Comment:

It seems clear from the last two passages that it is the Spirit of God who gives human beings life. This goes to the understanding that the Spirit of God is often referred to as the breath of God. When God breathed life into Job, that breath was the life-giving power of the Holy Spirit. (That is to say natural human life, not eternal life.) But He certainly resided in Job as a Savior as well.²²⁰

E. Psalm 104:29–30: *²⁹When you hide your face, they are dismayed; when you take away their breath, they die and return to their dust. / ³⁰When you send forth your*

---

[219] There are two words used here that can be translated Spirit or breath. As mentioned previously, there's רִיחַ (*ruwach*, H7306); and the second is נְשָׁמָה (nĕshamah H5395), which the ESV translates as breath, but it can also be translated as *spirit*. Regarding the word translated as *spirit,* since this verse is clearly referring to God, I can't for the life of me understand why it is not capitalized. What other Spirit does God have except the Holy Spirit? If this is an artifact of the Godhead theology, it means that the God entity referred to here is not the Holy Spirit entity of the Godhead. This suggests that there must be at least two God-like entities in heaven which is certainly the highest form of heresy. One God means one God entity, not two or three.

[220] That Job was saved is absolutely beyond dispute. See Job 19:25–27, where Job testifies that He will see God after his body has been destroyed by death. Therefore he simply had to have the permanent indwelling Spirit of God.

Spirit, they are created, and you renew the face of the ground.[221]

III Brings comprehension and understanding to angels, spirits and human beings (Joel 2:28–30; Ephesians 1:17; and 3:4–5). God's Spirit is the source of what we would call intellect or intelligence. He also reveals God's existence to God's children.

For example, Job 32:8 says that, *"But it is the spirit in man, the breath of the Almighty, that makes him understand."*

1. He also helps us test the spirits to see if they are from God.

John 4:1–3: *¹Beloved, do not believe every spirit, but test the spirits to see whether they are from God, for many false prophets have gone out into the world. ²By this you know the Spirit of God: every spirit that confesses that Jesus Christ has come in the flesh is from God, ³and every spirit that does not confess Jesus is not from God. This is the spirit of the antichrist, which you heard was coming and now is in the world already.*

IV Reveals God's truth through His powerful word, and enables sapient beings to believe and comprehend it by providing eyes that can see and ears that can hear (1 Corinthians 2:14; Deuteronomy 29:4). The Spirit can cause this through visions, dreams, and enabling prophetic utterances.

1. He searches out the deep aspects of God, makes them known to us and enables us to recognize them as being from God.

For example:

---

[221] Here the passage, the word *they* refers to the non-human living inhabitants of the earth.

1 Corinthians 2:6–15: *⁶Yet among the mature we do impart wisdom, although it is not a wisdom of this age or of the rulers of this age, who are doomed to pass away. ⁷But we impart a secret and hidden wisdom of God, which God decreed before the ages for our glory. ⁸None of the rulers of this age understood this, for if they had, they would not have crucified the* L{\sc ord} *of glory. ⁹But, as it is written,* **"What no eye has seen, nor ear heard, nor the heart of man imagined, what God has prepared for those who love him"**— *¹⁰these things God has revealed to us through the Spirit. For the Spirit searches everything, even the depths of God. ¹¹For who knows a person's thoughts except the spirit of that person, which is in him? So also no one comprehends the thoughts of God except the Spirit of God. ¹²Now we have received not the spirit of the world, but the Spirit who is from God, that we might understand the things freely given us by God. ¹³And we impart this in words not taught by human wisdom but taught by the Spirit, interpreting spiritual truths to those who are spiritual. ¹⁴The natural person does not accept the things of the Spirit of God, for they are folly to him, and he is not able to understand them because they are spiritually discerned. ¹⁵The spiritual person judges all things, but is himself to be judged by no one.*

2. **It is because the Spirit of God is working in us that we know the Bible is true.**

While archeology, textual comparisons and other things can be used as external worldly evidence the Bible is true, it is only by the Spirit testifying with our spirit that we know this for a fact. In fact, it is impossible to believe Scripture is true without the conviction the Holy Spirit gives us.

   A. See, for example, Romans 8:16.

   B. See also 1 John 4:13.

   C. See also 1 John 5:6.

3. ***And He reveals God's truth through His servants, enabling prophetic utterances.***

   A. Matthew 22:43–44: *[43][The LORD] said to them, "How is it then that David, **in the Spirit**, calls him LORD [or LORD], saying, [44]'The LORD said to my LORD, Sit at my right hand, until I put your enemies under your feet'?"*[222]

   B. 2 Timothy 3:16–17: *[16]All Scripture is **breathed out** by God and profitable for teaching, for reproof, for correction, and for training in righteousness, [17]that the man of God may be competent, equipped for every good work.*

   C. 1 Timothy 4:1–3: *[1]Now **the Spirit expressly says** that in later times some will depart from the faith by devoting themselves to deceitful spirits and teachings of demons, [2]through the insincerity of liars whose consciences are seared, [3]who forbid marriage and require abstinence from foods that God created to be received with thanksgiving by those who believe and know the truth.*

   Comment:

   Sadly, brothers and sisters, we are in those days. There are many *Christian* churches that forbid the consumption of alcohol, which is clearly not scriptural, as pointed out in the main body of this book. As the otherwise believing man substitutes his own ideas of righteousness for God's, he grows further away from God and becomes increasingly unable to withstand the dark forces of evil arrayed against him.

---

[222] Jesus is quoting Ps 110:1, where this verse in Hebrew reads: יְהֹוָה (Yĕhovah, H3608, The LORD) נְאֻם (nĕ'um, H5002, says) אֲדֹנָי ('Adonay, H136, to my Lord)… Therefore I have capitalized the different words for *Lord* as shown.

I would argue this is why we don't see any (or very few) real demonstrations of God's miraculous power in America. I have heard it said by some Christians that the reason God does not perform any miracles in this country is because our church is too *advanced*. They cite the lack of miracles as proof of this questionable doctrine. This is a circular argument if I've ever heard one. I believe God would perform miracles here, such as healing the sick as described in James 5:14–15, if we were stronger believers. It is God's own truth that a lack of miracles is a sign of our weak faith, not of any unwillingness on God's part to demonstrate His incomprehensibly vast power to us. See, for example, Mark 6:4–6.

D. In Genesis 41, it is recorded how the Spirit enabled Joseph to interpret Pharaoh's dreams and give him advice concerning the coming famine. Here is the conclusion Pharaoh reached:

> *^{37}This proposal pleased Pharaoh and all his servants. ^{38}And Pharaoh said to his servants, "Can we find a man like this, in whom is the Spirit of God?"* (Genesis 41:37–38).

Comment:

How else could Joseph have done the work he did without God's Spirit at work in him? In fact, the entire story of Joseph is a testament of God's Spirit at work in him. Notice how Joseph grew spiritually as he became older and more experienced. Is there any doubt that Joseph now resides with Jesus (God) in heaven? Therefore, he must also have possessed the eternal Spirit of salvation.

E. Deuteronomy 34:9: *And Joshua the son of Nun was full of the spirit of wisdom, for Moses had laid his hands on him. So the people of Israel obeyed him and did as the LORD had commanded Moses.*

Comment:

This word *spirit* should be capitalized, because if we look in Proverbs 8, the Spirit of wisdom is its entire focus. There can only be one Spirit of wisdom, which is why there's a footnote on this verse that indicates the word could be capitalized.

F. Numbers 11:25 (related to Numbers 11:16–17, quoted on page 192): *Then the LORD came down in the cloud and spoke to [Moses], and took some of the Spirit that was on him and put it on the seventy elders. And as soon as the Spirit rested on them, they prophesied. But they did not continue doing it.*

Comment:

Note that the word *prophesied* here means to speak with divine inspiration (Hebrew: נָבָא *(naba'),* H5012). This manifestation of the Spirit can be temporary, as seen here and elsewhere. There is another gift of prophecy that comes when a person is saved and designated a prophet by God.[223]

See also:

---

[223] I'm wondering whether this gift or all other spiritual gifts might ever be lost. I'm thinking that not faithfully using the gifts God's Spirit gives us can lead to God taking them from us. Why? See the story of the Talents starting in Matthew 25:15 (and elsewhere) and ending with this admonition from Matthew 25:29 regarding the wicked servant: *"For to everyone who has will more be given, and he will have an abundance. But from the one who has not, even what he has will be taken away."*

        i   Numbers 11:26–27. The Spirit of prophecy came upon two men who were not present at the tent of meeting with the other elders.

        ii 1 Samuel 10:10–13. The Spirit of God comes upon Saul and he prophesies with others. This was clearly a temporary manifestation of the Spirit's influence, because the phrasing of verse 13 in this passage indicates that this gift left Saul.

        iii 1 Samuel 19:20–21, 23–24. The second passage is truly amazing. Saul is on his way to kill David, but the Spirit of God comes upon him (absolutely without doubt a temporary gift!) and he prophesies.

        iv Zechariah 7:12.

G. Speaking of God giving His Spirit to whomever he chooses, consider the following passage.

Numbers 24:2–3: *²And Balaam lifted up his eyes and saw Israel camping tribe by tribe. And the Spirit of God came upon him, ³and he took up his discourse and said, "The oracle of Balaam the son of Beor, the oracle of the man whose eye is opened..."*

    Comment:

    As made abundantly clear in Scripture, Balaam was a sorcerer and therefore a servant of Satan. We should not be surprised, however, that God's Spirit can work in anyone to accomplish His purpose, whether or not the person is devoted to Him. Note also that the phrasing indicates the Spirit's presence in Balaam was meant to be temporary.

H. 1 Samuel 10:6–7, Samuel speaking to Saul: ⁶ *"Then the Spirit of the L*ORD *will rush upon you, and you will* *prophesy with them and be turned into another man. ⁷Now when these signs meet you, do what your hand finds to do, for God is with you."*

Comment:

This prophecy is fulfilled in 1 Samuel 10:10. A careless reading of this verse might lead one to take the view that the Spirit given to persons prior to Pentecost was always a temporary gift, meaning that He could be taken away. This would justify believing that the Spirit of salvation, that eternal indwelling gift from God, was not given prior to Pentecost. We know that this last statement is false on its face, because many people were saved prior to Pentecost. And we know from John 6:44 no one can be saved unless God, through His Spirit, draws men to Him. (Jesus later clarifies in John 12:32 that it is He, His person, which is indistinguishable from the Person of God, who does this drawing.) We also know from Peter's sermon in Acts 2 that when you are saved you are given the gift of the Spirit. (Acts 2:38; see paragraph V7.A on page 167.) And of course we know that when the Spirit of salvation is given He is never taken away (Romans 11:29).[224]

Then how do we understand the words, *changed person*? Does it mean that Saul will become a faithful follower of the LORD? That's how we who have the Spirit of salvation view the words *changed person*. However, this is clearly not what this Scripture means, because as the story of Saul unfolds, he never becomes a faithful follower of the LORD. He is an evil man who does what he wants and tries to justify it later.

---

[224] We know that those who are saved are called by God from Romans 8:30. We also know that when saved, we are given the gift of the Holy Spirit. Since the calling of God is irrevocable, the gift of the Holy Spirit can never be taken away.

Eventually, the LORD substitutes this Spirit with an evil spirit who then hounds Saul literally to death. So what did the Spirit change in Saul? Maybe it was that he was given the courage he needed to govern as a king and go to battle. After all, when we meet Saul for the first time, he seems timid when Samuel first confronts him about his anointing as king (1 Samuel 9:21). Later we find Saul hiding behind the baggage, and the LORD Himself has to root him out (1 Samuel 10:22). I do not know precisely what the answer is, but clearly the Spirit given to Saul was not for his salvation. Otherwise, Saul would have been righteous before God and borne the fruit of righteousness, and God would not have rejected him.[225]

I. 1 Samuel 16:13a, speaking of the anointing of David as king over Israel: *Then Samuel took the horn of oil and anointed him in the midst of his brothers. And the Spirit of the LORD rushed upon David from that day forward.*

<u>Comment:</u>

From the phrasing this appears to be the same Spirit of power that had come upon Saul, Samson and other O.T. saints. This Spirit of power gave David the courage and wisdom to kill Goliath, a man who had terrified all the armies of Israel; to successfully withstand Saul's constant assaults without taking Saul's life; and then to rule the nation and fight God's battles. I don't believe this was the Spirit of salvation. Clearly, David had already been saved, otherwise he would not have been a man

---

[225] Jesus says you can tell whether one is saved by the fruit they bear. See Matthew 7:15–20. As to bearing godly fruit see Romans 7:4, Galatians 5:22, and Ephesians 5:8–9. Saul bore no godly fruit, ever.

after God's heart (1 Samuel 13:14). This is why God chose him to be king over Israel.

J. Judges 3:9–10a: *⁹But when the people of Israel cried out to the LORD, the LORD raised up a deliverer for the people of Israel, who saved them, Othniel the son of Kenaz, Caleb's younger brother. ¹⁰ The Spirit of the LORD was upon him, and he judged Israel. He went out to war...*

Comment:

This does not indicate that salvation took place here, though Othniel was probably saved. I do not believe that God would make an unsaved man a hero of Israel, and I think Hebrews 11 confirms this. Be that as it may, this particular spirit gave Othniel the wisdom he needed to be Israel's leader.

  i   See also Judges 6:34 and 11:29.

K. Ezekiel 11:22–25: *²²Then the cherubim lifted up their wings, with the wheels beside them, and the glory of the God of Israel was over them. ²³And the glory of the LORD went up from the midst of the city and stood on the mountain that is on the east side of the city. ²⁴And the **Spirit lifted me up** and brought me **in the vision by the Spirit of God** into Chaldea, to the exiles. Then the vision that I had seen went up from me. ²⁵And I told the exiles all the things that the LORD had shown me.*[226]

---

[226] According to Ezekiel 1:1, he was with the exiles southeast of Babylon near the Kebar River, a little over five hundred miles from Jerusalem. Then the Spirit lifted him up and took him away to Jerusalem (Ezekiel 3:14). The prophet is experiencing supernatural transport between Babylon and Jerusalem here. In the verse just quoted, the Spirit is returning him to his disciples in Babylon.

L. Joel 2:28–30: In this passage the LORD is speaking. *²⁸"And it shall come to pass afterward, that I will pour out my Spirit on all flesh; your sons and your daughters shall prophesy, your old men shall dream dreams, and your young men shall see visions. ²⁹Even on the male and female servants in those days I will pour out my Spirit. ³⁰And I will show wonders in the heavens and on the earth, blood and fire and columns of smoke."*

Comment:

The Spirit begins in Joel 2 by talking about the day of the LORD, the terrible day of judgment that will bring horror and fear, gloom and destruction and so on. In verse 4, we see the horses mentioned in Revelation 9:7 and following. We see the LORD's army, mentioned in Revelation 19:14. The *afterward* in Joel 2:28 above refers to the time after *that day*, which will see the restoration of Israel and the salvation of people from all the nations. The passage leading up to Joel 2:28 describes the wonderful things the LORD will do for all people whom He has saved. I believe that this describes the duration of Christ's thousand year reign, which clearly occurs before the White Throne Judgment, all of which are described in Revelation 20.

M. John 1:32–34: *³²And John* [the Baptist] *bore witness: "I saw the Spirit descend from heaven like a dove, and it remained on him. ³³I myself did not know him, but he who sent me to baptize with water said to me, 'He on whom you see the Spirit descend and remain, this is he who baptizes with the Holy Spirit.' ³⁴And I have seen and have borne witness that this is the Son of God."*

Comment:

Normally, the Spirit of God speaks to our minds and opens them so that we may gain insight, knowledge and wisdom. Here is an unusual manifestation of the Spirit.

I interpret this passage to mean that the Spirit of God, who lived in John, told him about the Spirit coming down. Again we see that the Holy Spirit can manifest His presence in many places and in many forms at once. See Ezekiel 1:28; 3:12, 23 and many other places where the prophet identifies *the glory of the* LORD, and *a figure like that of a man* and *the Spirit* interchangeably. See also the flaming tongues of fire at Pentecost in Acts 2:3.

N. Acts 2:17–18, Here, Peter quotes Joel 2:28–29: [17]*"'And in the last days it shall be, God declares, that I will pour out my Spirit on all flesh, and your sons and your daughters shall prophesy, and your young men shall see visions, and your old men shall dream dreams;* [18]*even on my male servants and female servants in those days I will pour out my Spirit, and they shall prophesy.'"*

Comment:

This reminds me of Ezekiel 36:26–27. It puts a bit of a kink in the widely held but erroneous belief there will be no prophets in the church age. Of course God will send prophets. The trouble is, unless the church changes its doctrine on prophets and prophecy, no one will hear them, because the devil has convinced everyone of power in the church (it seems) that such men and women would be evil.[227] Too bad for the church, especially when the Tribulation of the last days comes

---

[227] Probably based on a misapplication of Matthew 24:12. Jesus speaks of false prophets coming during this time. There is another reason people will not listen to God's messengers, which is given in Hosea 9:7: [7]*The days of punishment have come; the days of recompense have come; Israel* [the church, Abraham's spiritual seed as described in Romans 4:16–17] *shall know it. The prophet is a fool; the man of the spirit is mad, because of your great iniquity and great hatred.*

upon God's saints as described in Daniel and Revelation. (See **Tribulation of the Saints of God** on page 107.) Prophets will come to help God's people by preaching confession and repentance. If God's people do not listen, much of the church will be destroyed because of disobedience and faith that has grown cold.

i   See also Acts 6:3–7:60, describing Stephen, the first recorded martyr of the church.

ii See also Ephesians 1:17 where Paul keeps asking *...that the God of our LORD Jesus Christ, the Father of glory, may give you a spirit of wisdom and of revelation in the knowledge of him...*

Comment:

This manifestation of the Holy Spirit is not the deposit that gives eternal life. The Ephesians, to whom Paul was writing, already had that Spirit. Clearly, once this deposit is made, we don't have to keep asking for it. Here Paul is praying that God, through His Spirit, will give us certain types of gifts. Note also that here the *Spirit* in *Spirit of wisdom* is capitalized, unlike in Deuteronomy 34:9, previously quoted on page 146.

O. Ephesians 3:4–5: *^{4}When you read this, you can perceive* **my insight into the mystery of Christ**, *^{5}which was not made known to the sons of men in other generations* **as it has now been revealed** *to his holy apostles and prophets* **by the Spirit**.

P. 2 Chronicles 15:1–2: *^{1}The Spirit of God came upon Azariah the son of Oded, ^{2}and he went out to meet Asa and said to him, "Hear me, Asa, and all Judah and Benjamin: The LORD is with you while you are with him. If you seek him, he will be found by you, but if you forsake him, he will forsake you."*

Comment:

This phrasing, *the Spirit of God came upon Azariah*, is not unusual in the Scriptures. We saw previously that this same Spirit of prophecy descended on the new church at Pentecost. The phrasing clearly implies that this habitation is temporary, but it is also clear that this manifestation of the Spirit is not to bring Azariah to salvation. Who could doubt that Azariah had received that saving Spirit long before this incident? No, rather, it is to give Azariah the power to communicate something important to King Asa.

See also:

i   2 Chronicles 20:14–17. Here the Spirit of God temporarily comes upon Jahaziel to empower him to make a prophetic utterance.

ii 2 Chronicles 24:20. Here the Spirit of God temporarily comes upon Zechariah (not the prophet of the book, Zechariah) to empower him to make a prophetic utterance.

iii Isaiah 48:16. Here the Spirit empowers Isaiah to deliver the word of God to Israel.

iv Isaiah 61:1. Isaiah describes how He is filled with the Spirit of the Gospel. This is the verse Jesus quoted in Luke 4:18.

v   Micah 3:8. Here Micah is filled with the Spirit of power to declare God's message to Israel.

Q. Luke 1:41–45: *[41]And when Elizabeth heard the greeting of Mary, the baby leaped in her womb. And Elizabeth was filled with the Holy Spirit, [42]and she exclaimed with a loud cry, "Blessed are you among women, and blessed is the fruit of your womb! [43]And why is this granted to me that the mother of my* LORD *should come to me?* ^{44}*For behold, when the sound of your greeting came to my ears, the baby in my womb leaped for joy.* ^{45}*And blessed is she who believed that there would be a fulfillment of what was spoken to her from the* LORD.*"*

Comment:

This filling is indeed temporary. The Spirit came upon Elizabeth, and she prophesied concerning who Jesus would be. This is the same type of manifestation of the Spirit's power that happened to King Saul, although Elizabeth was certainly saved and a devoted servant of the LORD, unlike Saul.

See also:

i   Luke 1:67–79, where the Spirit fills John the Baptist's father Zechariah, and he prophesies concerning his son John's ministry.

ii   Luke 2:25–35. This passage shows the work of the Spirit in many ways. He filled Simeon with knowledge that he would not die before he saw his Savior. The Spirit then moved Simeon to go to the Temple. Simeon did not know that this was to introduce him to his Savior. Finally Simeon uttered wonderful prophecies about Jesus.

iii   Acts 28:25–27. This passage quotes Isaiah 6:9–10. This shows how the Holy Spirit inspired Isaiah's prophetic utterances.

R.   Ezekiel 2:1–2, the LORD commissioning Ezekiel; note the work of the Spirit here: ^{1}*And he said to me, "Son of man, stand on your feet, and I will speak with you." ^{2}And as he spoke to me, the Spirit entered into me and set me on my feet, and I heard him speaking to me.*

Comment:

Without the strength that God gives us through His Spirit we cannot do anything that pleases Him. (See Zechariah 4:6, for example.) Here, the Spirit allows Ezekiel to stand in the presence of Jesus, who is God in bodily form (Colossians 2:9). The Spirit that came into Ezekiel here was certainly not the Spirit of salvation (See Ezekiel 36:24–29a). Ezekiel had long ago received the gift of salvation, otherwise God would not have made him the great prophet he was. This Spirit was given to serve God's specific purpose, to send Ezekiel to the people of Israel and speak to them.

One other thing. Don't pass over the command, *"Son of man, stand up on your feet and I will speak to you."* It gives me chills to write this. Imagine the scene. The very LORD of creation speaking to Ezekiel. Imagine if that were you. Though I've tried, I know that on this side of eternity I can't ever fully appreciate the wonder and awe that must have been going through the prophet's mind at that moment.

S. 2 Peter 1:21: *For no prophecy was ever produced by the will of man, but men spoke from God as they were carried along by the Holy Spirit.*

T. Revelation 4:2–4: *²At once **I [John] was in the Spirit**, and behold, a throne stood in heaven, with one seated on the throne. ³And he who sat there had the appearance of jasper and carnelian, and around the throne was a rainbow that had the appearance of an emerald. ⁴Around the throne were twenty-four thrones, and seated on the thrones were twenty-four elders, clothed in white garments, with golden crowns on their heads.*

Comment:

This passage and the entire book of Revelation show dramatically how the Spirit is the key to making prophetic utterings and seeing and understanding spiritual things.

    i   See also Revelation 17:3.

U. Revelation 19:9–10: *⁹And the angel said to me, "Write this: Blessed are those who are invited to the marriage supper of the Lamb." And he said to me, "These are the true words of God." ¹⁰Then I fell down at his feet to worship him, but he said to me, "You must not do that! I am a fellow servant with you and your brothers who hold to the testimony of Jesus. Worship God." For the testimony of Jesus is the spirit of prophecy.*

V Contends with man and feels grief when we do not obey. He convicts a person of sin and after completing this process that could take years, He then gives a person power to accept Christ as his Savior and comes to dwell within him, bestowing on him eternal life.

1. Contends with Man.

    A. Genesis 6:3: *Then the LORD said, "My Spirit shall not abide in man forever, for he is flesh: his days shall be 120 years."*

Comment:

What can *contend with man* mean? I would guess that it means to chasten the unbeliever as well as the believer, and to make our consciences work. He convicts us of sin, for example, but there is a limit to this process. At some point mercy will stop and wrath will take over. For example, at some point God will send a powerful delusion upon all those who, as a pattern of life, have rejected God's grace in to lead them to destruction (2 Thessalonians 2:11).

B. Psalm 106:32–33: *^{32}They angered him at the waters of Meribah, and it went ill with Moses on their account, ^{33}for they made his spirit bitter, and he spoke rashly with his lips.*

Comment:

Recall that all the books of Exodus, Leviticus, Numbers and Deuteronomy, and through the rest of the O.T., are a record of how God contended with the stiff-necked Israelites. This verse gives some insight into how God dealt with them; it was through His Spirit. It is clear that God was constantly reaching out to their spirits through His own to get them to obey, worship and have faith in Him only, but they were unwilling (Isaiah 30:15c).[228] God finally had enough and destroyed them, as he had threatened repeatedly. (See Lamentations 2:17 and then all Lamentations 4, which testify that the destruction of Jerusalem was brought about according to God's plan as revealed to Israel by the prophets.)

C. Acts 7:51–53, Stephen speaking: *^{51}"You stiff-necked people, uncircumcised in heart and ears, you always resist the Holy Spirit. As your fathers did, so do you. ^{52}Which of the prophets did your fathers not persecute? And they killed those who announced beforehand the coming of the Righteous One, whom you have now betrayed and murdered, ^{53}you who received the law as delivered by angels and did not keep it."*

Comment:

Lest we doubt, this passage shows that the Spirit of God was with Israel during their history, calling them to repentance, but they would not obey. If He was there calling them to repentance, does it not make sense that

---

[228] The NIV has a stronger translation of this verse, that *they would have none of it*.

He would have given eternal life to those who heeded the call, which thousands undoubtedly did over the time from Adam through the time of Pentecost? No, you say? Well, then, consider the use of the word *uncircumcised* in the above passage. And then consider this passage:

Deuteronomy 10:15–17: *[15]Yet the LORD set his heart in love on your fathers and chose their offspring after them, you above all peoples, as you are this day. [16]Circumcise therefore the foreskin of your heart, and be no longer stubborn. [17]For the LORD your God is God of gods and Lord of lords, the great, the mighty, and the awesome God, who is not partial and takes no bribe.*

And this one also:

Deuteronomy 30:4–6: *[4]If your outcasts are in the uttermost parts of heaven, from there the LORD your God will gather you, and from there he will take you. [5]And the LORD your God will bring you into the land that your fathers possessed, that you may possess it. And he will make you more prosperous and numerous than your fathers. [6]And the LORD your God will circumcise your heart and the heart of your offspring, so that you will love the LORD your God with all your heart and with all your soul, that you may live.*

Comment:

By what agency of God specifically are our hearts circumcised? According to Romans 2:29, circumcision of the heart is done by the Spirit. The above passage also sounds like the promise of salvation to me! This must be one instance of the gospel message written about in Hebrews 3:17–4:2. We will speak more of the circumcision of the heart on page 174.

2. ***Feels grief when we do not obey.***

   A. Ephesians 4:30–32: *{superscript}30{/}And do not grieve the Holy Spirit of God, by whom you were sealed for the day of redemption. {superscript}31{/}Let all bitterness and wrath and anger and clamor and slander be put away from you, along with all malice. {superscript}32{/}Be kind to one another, tenderhearted, forgiving one another, as God in Christ forgave you.*

   Comment:

   The words *God in Christ* mean God, working through His revealed self, forgave us our sins, just as God, in Christ, created the heavens and the earth.

3. ***Convicts people of their sin.***

   John 16:8–11: *{superscript}8{/}And when he comes, he will convict the world concerning sin and righteousness and judgment: {superscript}9{/}concerning sin, because they do not believe in me; {superscript}10{/}concerning righteousness, because I go to the Father, and you will see me no longer; {superscript}11{/}concerning judgment, because the ruler of this world is judged.*[229]

4. ***Tells us specifically that Christ lives in us.***

   1 John 3:23–24: *{superscript}23{/}And this is his commandment, that we believe in the name of his Son Jesus Christ and love one another, just as he has commanded us.{superscript}24{/} Whoever keeps his commandments abides in God, and God in him. And by this we know that he abides in us, by the Spirit whom he has given us.*

---

[229] This is a worldwide manifestation of the Spirit. The Holy Spirit has been convicting individuals of sin since the beginning of time. See, for example, Psalm 51. We know this because thousands if not millions of people were saved before Pentecost. To be saved they had to be drawn to the LORD, and to be drawn to the LORD, they must first be convicted of sin.

Solid Food for the Mature Believer

5. ***Draws the elect to repentance and salvation, even before Pentecost.***

John 6:44, The LORD Jesus speaking: "*No one can come to me unless the Father who sent me draws him. And I will raise him up on the last day.*"

Comment:
It is clearly the Spirit who does the drawing, since He is the only agency with which God interacts with creation.

A. See also 2 Thessalonians 2:13: *But we ought always to give thanks to God for you, brothers beloved by the LORD, because God chose you as the first fruits to be saved, through sanctification by the Spirit and belief in the truth.*

Comment:

When thinking about what Spirit means by the word *chose*,[230] consider Proverbs 16:4 (NASB): *The LORD has made everything for its own purpose, even the wicked for the day of evil.*[231] It seems pretty black and

---

[230] Greek *eklegomai*, which means *to select*.

[231] I am quoting the NASB here, because the ESV translates the Hebrew word פָּעַל (*pa'al*, H6466), as *works out*. But according to Strong's dictionary, this word can also mean *to make*. This makes more sense to me, since the LORD forms all babies in the womb (Psalm 139:13), and knows who is going to be wicked before they are born. He doesn't have to work anything out as if He didn't know to begin with.

A word about *the wicked*, a phrase used well over two hundred times in the O.T. alone. While all of us would qualify as being *wicked* before we are saved, I believe that when the LORD speaks of the wicked, most of the time He is speaking of those whom He knows will never accept God's salvation. He is referring, I believe, to those who serve the Evil One (whether knowingly or not); who work with all their strength and soul to thwart God's righteous purposes; who consciously hate God and His people; who hate truth and what is right; and who are lawless in themselves and work to lead others down a lawless path. As Jesus said of the wicked, in this case the Pharisees of His time, *"Woe to you, scribes and Pharisees, hypocrites! For you travel across sea and land to make a single proselyte, and when he becomes a proselyte, you make him twice as much a child of hell as yourselves"* (Matthew
This note is continued on the next page.

white that God chose some to be saved and not others. See Romans 8:29 for the process. Knowing beforehand those who will be saved by an act of His sovereign will leads to the predestination to be conformed to the likeness of Christ, leads to a call, and so on. In addition to the above Scripture, in John 15:16a Jesus says, *"You did not choose me, but I chose you and appointed you..."* In the world today there are only two types of people, those who are to escape destruction and those made specifically for destruction, all for the LORD's righteous purposes. Also see Romans 9:14–18, 21–25. There is absolutely no question about this eternal truth. Just be glad, those of you who believe, that by an act of God's sovereign will you are spared the destruction that awaits all who belong to the Evil One.[232] This one truth will prove to be a stumbling block to many and, as it is known, many will fall away, but they were never saved in the first place. See 1 John 2:19. Either we accept that God makes such sovereign choices and glorify Him thereby, or we don't.

6. *Gives eternal life.*

   A. John 6:63, The LORD speaking: *"It is the Spirit who gives life; the flesh is no help at all. The words that I have spoken to you are spirit and life."*

23:15). We see many of these creatures in America, in the entertainment industry, the media, the halls of Congress, and, after November 2008, even the White House itself. They will certainly find themselves in the pit of hell one day.

[232] See Matthew 13:24–30 for the parable of the wheat and the tares (or weeds). The sons of God are the stalks of wheat; the sons of the evil one are the weeds, destined for destruction. If you are not a believer, which are you? To erase any doubt, bow before the Throne of Grace, confess that you are a sinner, repent, and ask Him to allow you to come into the Kingdom by accepting Jesus Christ as your LORD and Savior. Your very ability to do this will prove that you are wheat and not tare. And the LORD Himself promises to anyone who comes to Him with sincere heart that He will never drive him away (John 6:37).

Comment:

As mentioned in footnote 94 on page 47, the NIV translation is *the flesh counts for nothing*. In any case, the meaning here is pretty cut and dried. Without the Spirit of God at work in us, or in the pre-Pentecostal saints or in anyone else, we cannot follow God, much less be saved.

B. Romans 8:10–11: *[10]But if Christ is in you, although the body is dead because of sin, the Spirit is life because of righteousness. [11]If the Spirit of him who raised Jesus from the dead dwells in you, he who raised Christ Jesus from the dead will also give life to your mortal bodies through his Spirit who dwells in you.*

Comment:

Jesus said that He, Himself, would take up His life after He had laid it down (John 10:17–18). Sounds like the One who raised Jesus from the dead was Jesus, the eternal God, Himself.

C. Galatians 4:28-30: *[28]Now you, brothers, like Isaac, are children of promise. [29]But just as at that time he who was born according to the flesh persecuted him who was born according to the Spirit, so also it is now. [30]But what does the Scripture say? "Cast out the slave woman and her son, for the son of the slave woman shall not inherit with the son of the free woman."*

Comment:

So it is by the power of the Holy Spirit that new children of God are born.

D. Matthew 3:11–12: *[11]"I [John the Baptist] baptize you with water for repentance, but he who is coming after me is mightier than I, whose sandals I am not worthy to carry. He will baptize you with the Holy Spirit and fire.*

> *[12] His winnowing fork is in his hand, and he will clear his threshing floor and gather his wheat into the barn, but the chaff he will burn with unquenchable fire."*

E. Luke 11:11–13, The LORD speaking: *[11] What father among you, if his son asks for a fish, will instead of a fish give him a serpent; [12] or if he asks for an egg, will give him a scorpion? [13] If you then, who are evil, know how to give good gifts to your children, how much more will the heavenly Father give the Holy Spirit to those who ask him!"*

Comment:

This principle of God giving the Spirit to those who ask is eternal; it did not come into being at Pentecost. Since the time of Adam it has been true that God would happily give the Holy Spirit to those who asked Him. Moses says to the LORD's people, *[2] "You have seen all that the LORD did before your eyes...[3] the great trials that your eyes saw, the signs, and those great wonders. [4] But to this day the LORD has not given you a heart to understand or eyes to see or ears to hear"* (Deuteronomy 29:2a, 3–4). Their hard hearts made them unable to ask the LORD for them, which He would gladly have given through His Spirit.

F. John 3:5–8: Jesus telling Nicodemus how salvation happens: *[5] Jesus answered, "Truly, truly, I say to you, unless one is born of water and the Spirit, he cannot enter the kingdom of God. [6] That which is born of the flesh is flesh, and that which is born of the Spirit is spirit. [7] Do not marvel that I said to you, 'You must be born again.' [8] The wind blows where it wishes, and you hear its sound, but you do not know where it comes from or where it goes. So it is with everyone who is born of the Spirit."*

Comment:

Is there any born-again biblical scholar who would not agree that this birthing by the Spirit includes the Spirit coming to live in a person forever, never to be taken away? It follows that those who were saved prior to Pentecost also had to receive this eternal manifestation of the Spirit.

G. John 6:63–65, Jesus is speaking: *⁶³"It is the Spirit who gives life; the flesh is no help at all. The words that I have spoken to you are spirit and life. ⁶⁴But there are some of you who do not believe." (For Jesus knew from the beginning who those were who did not believe, and who it was who would betray him.) ⁶⁵And he said, "This is why I told you that no one can come to me unless it is granted him by the Father."*

Comment:

We are not astonished by the first verse quoted above, but many are astonished and quite offended by the last one. In fact, some of Jesus' disciples were so offended by this they turned away from Him. When I was struggling against the goads this verse really got me angry, but by the LORD's grace, I did not turn away. This key passage shows that the process of salvation begins before one can accept Jesus as his Savior. Jesus, through His Spirit, might work for years on a person before he finally surrenders to His call. This was true prior to Pentecost too. This is an eternal principle, the flesh counts for nothing. So Abraham, Moses, David, all the great prophets and other godly men and women who lived prior to Pentecost—all the godly Jews who were saved—had to go through a period where Jesus' Spirit worked in their hearts before they surrendered to God's saving grace. Once they did, they were saved forever.

7. *Comes to dwell in the believer (forever!).*

A. Acts 2:38–39: *[38]And Peter said to them, "Repent and be baptized every one of you in the name of Jesus Christ for the forgiveness of your sins, and you will receive the gift of the Holy Spirit. [39]For the promise is for you and for your children and for all who are far off, everyone whom the LORD our God calls to himself."*

Comment:

This gift of the Spirit is the deposit that Paul talks about in 2 Corinthians 1:22; 5:5, and Ephesians 1:13–14. This is clearly not about the Spirit of the church that came from God through Jesus to establish and empower the church at Pentecost. This is about the Spirit of salvation that comes to everyone who has ever, in the history of the world, believed, repented and accepted this wonderful gift from God. This didn't start with the cross. Salvation started with the creation of man and his fall from grace in the garden. The cross was the final seal on God's plan of salvation for each of us who are His, whom He had known from eternity past.

B. 2 Corinthians 1:20–22: *[20]For all the promises of God find their Yes in him. That is why it is through him that we utter our Amen to God for his glory. [21]And it is God who establishes us with you in Christ, and has anointed us, [22]and who has also put his seal on us and given us his Spirit in our hearts as a guarantee.*

Comment:

That the Spirit seals our salvation is an eternal principle. If people were saved prior to Pentecost, they too must have been given this deposit of ownership. For example, in this passage in 1 Kings Elijah is complaining to God; observe carefully how God answers him:

> ¹⁴*He said, "I have been very jealous for the* LORD, *the God of hosts. For the people of Israel have forsaken your covenant, thrown down your altars, and killed your prophets with the sword, and I, even I only, am left, and they seek my life, to take it away."* ¹⁵*And the* LORD *said to him, "Go, return on your way to the wilderness of Damascus. And when you arrive, you shall anoint Hazael to be king over Syria.* ¹⁶*And Jehu the son of Nimshi you shall anoint to be king over Israel, and Elisha the son of Shaphat of Abel-meholah you shall anoint to be prophet in your place.* ¹⁷*And the one who escapes from the sword of Hazael shall Jehu put to death, and the one who escapes from the sword of Jehu shall Elisha put to death.* ¹⁸*Yet I will leave seven thousand in Israel, all the knees that have not bowed to Baal, and every mouth that has not kissed him"* (1 Kings 19:14–18).

God would leave 7,000 alive, because they had not bowed to Baal. Why? John 6:63–65 tells us that He must have deposited His Spirit in them just as He had in Elijah. Certainly Elijah is saved. And certainly these people were saved, from death in this life as well as in the next.

See also:

i   2 Corinthians 3:3. It seems to me that a letter written on *tablets of human hearts* is a metaphorical way of saying the same thing.

ii   2 Corinthians 5:5. Paul says the deposit of the Spirit will *guarantee* what is to come, which is our resurrection from the dead and being clothed *with our heavenly dwelling.* Since salvation occurred in the O.T., how could, for example, Moses, David,

Zechariah and Elizabeth (Luke 1:5), and all the prophets not been given this same guarantee?

iii Galatians 4:6–7: *⁶And because you are sons, God has sent the Spirit of his Son into our hearts, crying, "Abba! Father!" ⁷So you are no longer a slave, but a son, and if a son, then an heir through God.*

Comment:

Since there is only one Spirit that comes into us,[233] and since it is common knowledge that when we are saved, it is the Person of Jesus Christ that comes to live in our hearts, there can be no distinction between the Person of Jesus and the person of His Spirit, who is also the Person and Spirit of God.[234] Through the Holy Spirit, we have constant and eternal communion with the Father, the God beyond our comprehension or understanding, through the person of His revealed self, Jesus Christ, incarnate as the Son of Man.

See also:

iv Ephesians 1:13. We are essentially marked with the seal of salvation by the Spirit. Compare this with Ezekiel 9, where the people who mourn the sins of Israel are also marked, and thereby shielded from

---

[233] Concerning the one Spirit, see Ephesians 4:4–6 and 1 Corinthians 12:9, 13. The implications of these passages are discussed more fully in the comment under paragraph IX1 204.

[234] Romans 8:9a and 10a read in part, *⁹You, however, are not in the flesh but in the Spirit, if in fact **the Spirit of God dwells in you**…¹⁰But **if Christ is in you**, although the body is dead because of sin, the Spirit is life because of righteousness.* This passage clearly equates the Person of the indwelling Spirit with the Person of Jesus Christ.

God's judgment of Jerusalem and its inhabitants. Do these marks not accomplish the same purpose?

v Ephesians 2:19–22: *¹⁹So then you are no longer strangers and aliens, but you are fellow citizens with the saints and members of the household of God, ²⁰built on the foundation of the apostles and prophets, Christ Jesus himself being the cornerstone, ²¹in whom the whole structure, being joined together, grows into a holy temple in the LORD. ²²**In him you also are being built together into a dwelling place for God by the Spirit**.*

Comment:

It is God Himself who lives in us, that we know. And He does it in the person of His Spirit, which means there can be no distinction between the Person of God and that of the Spirit, nor between the Person of Christ and that of the Spirit.[235]

VI Circumcises (transforms) hearts, shaping God's elect into Christ-likeness, giving them the desire—and enabling them—to follow God and to serve Him (Numbers 14:24; Deuteronomy 8:17–18; Zechariah 4:6; Romans 8:2–8; Philippians 2:13 and 4:13). He can also cause non-believers, even wicked men, to carry out His will.

1. It's all about the Holy Spirit's power.

Here's the keystone of our faith in God:

---

[235] The Godhead theologians would no doubt say this proves the entire Godhead dwells in us, and what dwells in us is the unique Person of God. The term Godhead is not mentioned here or anywhere else in the original Greek or Hebrew of the Bible. The term does appear in the KJV in Colossians 2:9, where the Greek word θεότης (*theotis*, G2320), which is an abstract term for divinity or God, is mistranslated as *Godhead*.

Zechariah 4:6: *Then [the* LORD] *said to me, "This is the word of the* LORD *to Zerubbabel: Not by might, nor by power, but by my Spirit, says the* LORD *of hosts."*[236]

A. Luke 1:13–17, Gabriel speaking of John the Baptist:

> *[13]But the angel said to him, "Do not be afraid, Zechariah, for your prayer has been heard, and your wife Elizabeth will bear you a son, and you shall call his name John. [14]And you will have joy and gladness, and many will rejoice at his birth, [15]for he will be great before the* LORD*. And he must not drink wine or strong drink, and **he will be filled with the Holy Spirit, even from his mother's womb**. [16]And he will turn many of the children of Israel to the* LORD *their God, [17]and he will go before him in the spirit and power of Elijah, to turn the hearts of the fathers to the children, and the disobedient to the wisdom of the just, to make ready for the* LORD *a people prepared."*

Comment:

This filling of the Spirit allowed John, son of Zechariah, to be the great man prophesied, and ultimately praised as the greatest man born of woman by Jesus Himself (Luke 7:28).

B. The following passage demonstrates that the power of obedience, even in the most difficult times, comes from Him:

> Luke 4:1–2: *[1]And Jesus, full of the Holy Spirit, returned from the Jordan and was led by the Spirit in the wilderness [2]for forty days, being tempted by the devil.*

---

[236] The Hebrew phrase יְהוָה צָבָא (Yĕhovah (H3068), *tsaba'* (H6635)) translated here literally as LORD *of hosts* is rendered as the LORD *Almighty* in the NIV. I like the second better because it provides a clearer image of the majestic power of the Person of God.

And he ate nothing during those days. And when they were ended, he was hungry.

Comment:

See how Jesus, the Son of Man, was not exempt from the necessity of being filled by the Spirit to do God's will, especially when God required extraordinary commitment of Him. But Jesus, the human man, was unique in this; he was filled with the Spirit without limit (John 3:34).

See also:

i   Luke 4:18. Jesus testifies that He was anointed with the Spirit so that He might do good and heal, etc.

ii Luke 10:21, where the indwelling Spirit fills Jesus with joy.

2. **With regard to being filled with the Spirit,** there seems to be a distinction made in Scripture between having the Holy Spirit dwell in us and being filled with that same Spirit. It seems to be a matter of degree. Here are several passages that make this distinction:

   A. Acts 2:2–3: *²And suddenly there came from heaven a sound like a mighty rushing wind, and it filled the entire house where they were sitting. ³And divided tongues as of fire appeared to them and rested on each one of them.*

   Comment:

   In this case, being filled with the Spirit gave the people supernatural power to speak in tongues. They were already believers; they already had the Spirit of Christ dwelling in them. This passage indicates a degree of effect beyond the saving work of the Spirit. One can also be *filled* this way and not be a believer. Saul, king of Israel, is a good example discussed previously. He was filled to the point that he stripped himself naked and lay on the ground, prophesying (1 Samuel 19:23).

B. Acts 4:8–10: *[8]Then Peter, filled with the Holy Spirit, said to them, "Rulers of the people and elders, [9]if we are being examined today concerning a good deed done to a crippled man, by what means this man has been healed, [10]let it be known to all of you and to all the people of Israel that by the name of Jesus Christ of Nazareth, whom you crucified, whom God raised from the dead—by him this man is standing before you well."*

Comment:

Here, Peter was filled with the Spirit for the purpose of preaching to the Jews and telling them, without equivocation, the awful thing they had done. The phrasing of this passage makes it clear that absent the Spirit, Peter would not have been able to make this speech.

i   See also Acts 4:31, which mirrors this previous passage.

C. Luke 12:11–12, The LORD speaking: *[11]"And when they bring you before the synagogues and the rulers and the authorities, do not be anxious about how you should defend yourself or what you should say, [12]for the Holy Spirit will teach you in that very hour what you ought to say."*

Comment:

Here is the Wonderful Counselor personified!

D. Acts 5:30–32: Peter speaking to the Jews: *[30]"The God of our fathers raised Jesus, whom you killed by hanging him on a tree. [31]God exalted him at his right hand as Leader and Savior, to give repentance to Israel and forgiveness of sins. [32]And we are witnesses to these things, and so is the Holy Spirit, whom God has given to those who obey him."*

Comment:

It's easy to read this verse and get the order of causation backward. This is the clear truth of all Scripture, that we obey God because He has given us His Spirit. Before we receive His Spirit we are incapable of obeying God, or even caring about obeying Him (Romans 8:7).[237] All who obey Him have been given the Spirit. Therefore, it must be that Noah, Abraham, Isaac, Jacob, Joseph, all the prophets, and indeed all the faithful saints who lived prior to Pentecost had the Spirit dwelling in them, otherwise they could not possibly have obeyed the LORD.

3. ***He strengthens groups of believers as well.***

   A. Acts 9:31: *So the church throughout all Judea and Galilee and Samaria had peace and was being built up. And walking in the fear of the LORD and in the comfort of the Holy Spirit, it multiplied.*

   Comment:

   As the Spirit of Jesus Christ (e.g. the Person of the divine LORD, Jesus Christ) moved throughout the land, the church grew in numbers and strength.

4. ***He circumcises (transforms) the heart.***

   Romans 2:28–29: *²⁸For no one is a Jew who is merely one outwardly, nor is circumcision outward and physical. ²⁹But a Jew is one inwardly, and circumcision is a matter of the*

---

[237] This is why Romans 7:15–24 cannot be the reflections of a non-believer, as I have heard some very godly people claim. No non-believer could ever delight in God's law in his *inner being* as in verse 22.

heart, by the Spirit, not by the letter. His praise is not from man but from God.

Comment:

Using the Jews as an example, Paul emphasizes that this principle is eternal; circumcision of the heart can only come by the work of the Spirit of Christ. God calls the people of the O.T. to circumcise their hearts. See, for example, Deuteronomy 10:16 and Deuteronomy 30:6. According to Paul, this act of God could not happen without the Holy Spirit, which means that God was willing to give the Holy Spirit to any of the pre-Pentecostal saints who asked Him (Luke 11:13).

5. **He shapes us into Christ-likeness.**
   A. By pouring His love into our hearts.

   Romans 5:1–5: *^{1}Therefore, since we have been justified by faith, we have peace with God through our LORD Jesus Christ. ^{2}Through Him we have also obtained access into this grace in which we stand, and we rejoice in hope of the glory of God. ^{3}More than that, we rejoice in our sufferings, knowing that suffering produces endurance, ^{4}and endurance produces character, and character produces hope, ^{5}and hope does not put us to shame,* **because God's love has been poured into our hearts through the Holy Spirit** *who has been given to us.*

   B. By releasing us from the law of sin and death.

   Romans 7:5–6: *^{5}For while we were living in the flesh, our sinful passions, aroused by the law, were at work in our members to bear fruit for death. ^{6}But now we are released from the law, having died to that which held us captive, so that we serve in the new way of the Spirit and not in the old way of the written code.*

   i See also Romans 8:2–4.

C. By giving us life and peace.

Romans 8:6: *For to set the mind on the flesh is death, but to set the mind on the Spirit is life and peace.*

   i   See also Romans 14:17.

D. He gives us hope.

Romans 15:13: *May the God of hope fill you with all joy and peace in believing, so that by the power of the Holy Spirit you may abound in hope.*

E. He produces in us the fruits of a righteous character.

Galatians 5:16–18, 22–26: *[16]But I say, walk by the Spirit, and you will not gratify the desires of the flesh. [17]For the desires of the flesh are against the Spirit, and the desires of the Spirit are against the flesh, for these are opposed to each other, to keep you from doing the things you want to do. [18]But if you are led by the Spirit, you are not under the law.*

[22]But the fruit of the Spirit is love, joy, peace, patience, kindness, goodness, faithfulness, [23]gentleness, self-control; against such things there is no law. [24]And those who belong to Christ Jesus have crucified the flesh with its passions and desires. [25]If we live by the Spirit, let us also walk by the Spirit. [26] Let us not become conceited, provoking one another, envying one another.

6. **He sets our minds on what God desires.**

Romans 8:5: *For those who live according to the flesh set their minds on the things of the flesh, but those who live according to the Spirit set their minds on the things of the Spirit.*

Comment:

How can what the Person of Spirit desires of us be distinguishable at all from what the Person of God or the

Person of Christ desires of us? This verse does not say, "What the Spirit heard that God desired and relayed to us," as one might expect if their persons were distinguishable in some way. The Spirit doesn't have to ask what God desires, because He is indistinguishable from God and therefore already knows.

A. By enabling us to put away our hostility toward God and submit to His will.

> Romans 8:7–9: *^{7}For the mind that is set on the flesh is hostile to God, for it does not submit to God's law;* **indeed, it cannot**. *^{8}Those who are in the flesh cannot please God. ^{9}You, however, are not in the flesh but in the Spirit, if in fact the Spirit of God dwells in you. Anyone who does not have the Spirit of Christ does not belong to him.*

Comment:

This is how we know that all the people who followed God prior to Pentecost had to be saved. Without the Spirit of God (Christ) working in them, they could not possibly have obeyed God or served Him faithfully. This is also how we know that the Spirit of salvation was given before the cross of Christ occurred in the creation timeline.

- i Companions of Romans 8:9 is Romans 9:13–14: *^{13}For if you live according to the flesh you will die, but if by the Spirit you put to death the deeds of the body, you will live. ^{14}For all who are led by the Spirit of God are sons of God.*

- ii See also Galatians 6:7–8: *^{7}Do not be deceived: God is not mocked, for whatever one sows, that will he also reap. ^{8}For the one who sows to his own flesh will from the flesh reap corruption, but the one who* *sows to the Spirit will from the Spirit reap eternal life.*

Comment:

In Romans 8:14 those who have the Spirit of God are led by Him to live according to the Spirit, implying that the Holy Spirit will lead us to *put to death the deeds of the body.* Since Romans 7:15–24 verifies this will be a source of struggle for all children of God, if someone claims to know the LORD Jesus Christ and is not on the path to put sin to death in his body, he should ask himself whether or not he is really saved. I would say that he is not.

B. By erasing a certain type of fear from our lives and establishing our relationship with our Father in heaven.

See, for example, Romans 8:15–17: *[15]For you did not receive the spirit of slavery to fall back into fear, but you have received the Spirit of adoption as sons, by whom we cry, "Abba! Father!" [16]The Spirit himself bears witness with our spirit that we are children of God, [17]and if children, then heirs—heirs of God and fellow heirs with Christ, provided we suffer with him in order that we may also be glorified with him.*

Comment:

It's very important to understand that the *fear* spoken of here does not refer to the fear of God that is the beginning of wisdom, which was described earlier. The *fear* mentioned above is the fear of doing God's will; to be afraid to step out in faith to accomplish our personal, holy, God-given mission in life. If you are presented with an opportunity to share your faith, but you do not because you are afraid, this fear comes from your sinful nature (and the Evil One). This fear does not come from God.

C. By helping us in our weakness and interceding for us in prayer.

See, for example, Romans 8:26–27: *^{26}Likewise the Spirit helps us in our weakness. For we do not know what to pray for as we ought, but the Spirit himself intercedes for us with groanings too deep for words. ^{27}And he who searches hearts knows what is the mind of the Spirit, because the Spirit intercedes for the saints according to the will of God.*

Comment:

See also Jude 1:20–21. We are to be in the Spirit when we pray. This means we are to be conscious of the truth of the above passage, realize that we cannot communicate with God adequately on our own, and be aware that we have a Wonderful Counselor to help us when we pray. For a good example of this, see Revelation 1:10. Wow, talk about being in the Spirit!

D. By sanctifying us (setting us apart) to God.

See, for example, Romans 15:15–16: *^{15}But on some points I have written to you very boldly by way of reminder, because of the grace given me by God ^{16}to be a minister of Christ Jesus to the Gentiles in the priestly service of the gospel of God, so that the offering of the Gentiles may be acceptable,* **sanctified by the Holy Spirit***.*

E. By giving us the desire and strength to obey God faithfully.

See, for example, Numbers 14:24, the LORD speaking: *"But my servant Caleb, because he has a different spirit and has followed me fully, I will bring into the land into which he went, and his descendants shall possess it."*

Comment:

What spirit did Caleb have? He must have had God's Holy Spirit in him, otherwise he would not have been able to follow the LORD. It is impossible for carnal man to follow God, because the flesh counts for nothing (John 6:63). Therefore every pre-Pentecostal saint who followed God and served Him faithfully must have had Jesus' Spirit living in him. Of course, under current doctrine, since the Spirit was not given prior to Pentecost, the Spirit of this verse must be some kind of general spirit, not the Holy Spirit. This erroneous doctrine leads to one crazy interpretation, doesn't it?

i   See also Numbers 27:18–19, where: *[18]...the LORD said to Moses, "Take Joshua the son of Nun, a man in whom is the Spirit, and lay your hand on him. [19] Make him stand before Eleazar the priest and all the congregation, and you shall commission him in their sight."*

ii See also 1 Kings 18:9–14, which refers to the Spirit of the LORD as carrying Elijah, stating in no uncertain words that Elijah was led by the Spirit of God to accomplish his mission. Obadiah's protest means that he expected the Spirit could pick Elijah up and carry him along. See 2 Kings 2:16. In this same vein, will He not carry us all if we are willing to be obedient? If you doubt that the answer is yes, check out Isaiah 40:11.

iii Ezekiel 3:22–27: *[22] And the hand of the LORD was upon me there. And he said to me, "Arise, go out into the valley, and there I will speak with you." [23] So I arose and went out into the valley, and behold, the glory of the LORD stood there, like the glory that I had seen by the Chebar canal, and I fell on my face. [24] But the Spirit entered into me and set* *me on my feet, and he spoke with me and said to me, "Go, shut yourself within your house. ^{25}And you, O son of man, behold, cords will be placed upon you, and you shall be bound with them, so that you cannot go out among the people. ^{26}And I will make your tongue cling to the roof of your mouth, so that you shall be mute and unable to reprove them, for they are a rebellious house. ^{27}But when I speak with you, I will open your mouth, and you shall say to them, 'Thus says the LORD God.' He who will hear, let him hear; and he who will refuse to hear, let him refuse, for they are a rebellious house."*

Comment:

The text does not distinguish between the LORD God (e.g. Sovereign LORD) speaking to Ezekiel and the Spirit speaking. According to the BHS Interlinear Bible, the original Hebrew text clearly implies that the *He* in verse twenty-four is the Spirit of God. Ezekiel refers to the glory of the LORD standing in the plain. Who is the very radiance of that Glory? The LORD Jesus Christ (Hebrews 1:3), who reveals God's glory to us by His Person and through his *glorious body*.[238]

F. By moving us to follow the LORD's laws and decrees:

   i Ezekiel 36:24–27, where Ezekiel is quoting the words the LORD gives him: *^{24} "I will take you from the nations and gather you from all the countries and bring you into your own land. ^{25}I will sprinkle clean water on you, and you shall be clean from all your uncleannesses, and from all your idols I will cleanse you. ^{26}And I will give you a new heart, and a new spirit I will put within you. And I will remove*

---

[238] See Philippians 3:21 and Colossians 1:22.

the heart of stone from your flesh and give you a heart of flesh. ²⁷***And I will put my Spirit within you, and cause you to walk in my statutes and be careful to obey my rules.***"

Comment:

There are two things going on here. The *new spirit* the LORD is speaking of is clearly the Spirit of salvation. There is also the Spirit that moves us to obedience, the same Spirit that is the eternal deposit given us when we are saved (2 Corinthians 1:22). This passage also clearly describes the *changed life* that Paul spoke of in 2 Corinthians 5:17—the new creation.

ii   2 Corinthians 6:4–7: *⁴But as servants of God we commend ourselves in every way: by great endurance, in afflictions, hardships, calamities, ⁵beatings, imprisonments, riots, labors, sleepless nights, hunger; ⁶by purity, knowledge, patience, kindness,* **the Holy Spirit***, genuine love; ⁷by truthful speech, and the power of God; with the weapons of righteousness for the right hand and for the left.*

Comment:

How else could Paul have endured the tremendous suffering of his ministry without the deposit of the Holy Spirit in his heart and the guiding hand of the Spirit (see Romans 8:9)?

iii   Galatians 5:4–6: *⁴You are severed from Christ, you who would be justified by the law; you have fallen away from grace. ⁵****For through the Spirit, by faith, we ourselves eagerly wait for the hope of righteousness****. ⁶For in Christ Jesus neither circumcision nor uncircumcision counts for anything, but only faith working through love.*

Comment:

It is by God's power working in us through His Spirit that we attain the character and the ability to perform works of righteousness that He has prepared in advance for us (Ephesians 2:10).

iv Galatians 5:16–18: *[16]But I say, walk by the Spirit, and you will not gratify the desires of the flesh. [17]For the desires of the flesh are against the Spirit, and the desires of the Spirit are against the flesh, for these are opposed to each other, to keep you from doing the things you want to do. [18]But if you are led by the Spirit, you are not under the law.*

Comment:

This *not do[ing] what you want* because of the Spirit's conflict with our flesh verifies that Romans 7:15, which says the same thing, is about believers. Here, Paul is clearly speaking of the struggle believers face in living the Christian life of righteousness.

G. By hemming us in behind and before to keep us on the path of righteousness and never leaving our side.

i Psalm 139:5–10: *[5]You hem me in, behind and before, and lay your hand upon me. [6]Such knowledge is too wonderful for me; it is high; I cannot attain it. [7]Where shall I go from your Spirit? Or where shall I flee from your presence? [8]f I ascend to heaven, you are there! If I make my bed in Sheol, you are there! [9]If I take the wings of the morning and dwell in the uttermost parts of the sea, [10]even there your hand shall lead me, and your right hand shall hold me.*

Comment:

The LORD our God guards His faithful ones. We are always in His presence whether we like it or not. He is relentless in this, all praise to His wonderful Name! That's why we can rest secure in His love, because...*the LORD is good; his steadfast love endures forever, and his faithfulness to all generations* (Psalm 100:5).

ii Haggai 2:4–5, the LORD speaking: *⁴"Yet now be strong, O Zerubbabel, declares the LORD. Be strong, O Joshua, son of Jehozadak, the high priest. Be strong, all you people of the land, declares the LORD. Work, for I am with you, declares the LORD of hosts, ⁵according to the covenant that I made with you when you came out of Egypt. My Spirit remains in your midst. Fear not."*

Comment:

It is clear that the LORD never leaves the side of those whose hearts are turned to Him. Jesus speaking in the N.T. says many times, *"I will never leave you nor forsake you."* But Scripture also teaches that while God may walk with a man by His Spirit to get him to do His bidding, if that man's heart is turned away from the LORD, if he has never yielded to the urgings of the Spirit to confess, repent and accept salvation, the LORD will eventually consign him to everlasting damnation. This is one thing the writer meant when he said in Hebrews 6:4–6:

> *⁴For it is impossible, in the case of those who have once been enlightened, who have tasted the heavenly gift, and have shared in the Holy Spirit, ⁵and have tasted the goodness of the word of God and the powers of the age to come, ⁶and then have fallen away, to restore them*

again to repentance, since they are crucifying once again the Son of God to their own harm and holding him up to contempt.

And again, in Hebrews 10:29–30: *[29]How much worse punishment, do you think, will be deserved by the one who has spurned the Son of God, and has profaned the blood of the covenant by which he was sanctified, and has outraged the Spirit of grace? [30]For we know him who said, "Vengeance is mine; I will repay." And again, "The LORD will judge his people."*

Comment:

Saul, in the book of 1 Samuel, is the best example of this. He, of course, was never saved, because his heart was never with God. He never received the Spirit of salvation, so God rejected him.[239]

I. By leading us on level ground, preserving us, making us fertile ground, enabling us to bear the fruit of righteousness, and filling us with grace.

   i Psalm 143:10–12: *[10]Teach me to do your will, for you are my God! Let your good Spirit lead me on level ground! [11]For your name's sake, O LORD, preserve my life! In your righteousness bring my soul out of trouble! [12]And in your steadfast love you will cut off my enemies, and you will destroy all the adversaries of my soul, for I am your servant.*

   ii Isaiah 32:14–20: *[14]For the palace is forsaken, the populous city deserted; the hill and the watchtower will become dens forever, a joy of wild donkeys, a*

---

[239] See 1 Samuel 15:23, 26, and 16:1.

pasture of flocks; ^{15}*until the Spirit is poured upon us from on high, and the wilderness becomes a fruitful field, and the fruitful field is deemed a forest.* ^{16}*Then justice will dwell in the wilderness, and righteousness abide in the fruitful field.* ^{17}*And the effect of righteousness will be peace, and the result of righteousness, quietness and trust forever.* ^{18}*My people will abide in a peaceful habitation, in secure dwellings, and in quiet resting places.* ^{19}*And it will hail when the forest falls down, and the city will be utterly laid low.* ^{20}*Happy are you who sow beside all waters, who let the feet of the ox and the donkey range free.*

Comment:

Here we have the Spirit creating richness out of poverty, fecundity out of a wasteland, and carrying justice, righteousness, peace, quietness and confidence with Him. Man cannot experience these things without the Spirit of Christ working around and in him.

   iii Zechariah 12:10, the LORD speaking: *"And I will pour out on the house of David and the inhabitants of Jerusalem a spirit of grace and pleas for mercy, so that, when they look on me, on him whom they have pierced, they shall mourn for him, as one mourns for an only child, and weep bitterly over him, as one weeps over a firstborn."*

J. By providing the tools we need to stand firm in our faith, even as all the forces of hell attack us.

   i Ephesians 6:10–18a: ^{10}*Finally, be strong in the LORD and in the strength of his might.* ^{11}*Put on the whole armor of God, that you may be able to stand against the schemes of the devil.* ^{12}*For we do not*

> *wrestle against flesh and blood, but against the rulers, against the authorities, against the cosmic powers over this present darkness, against the spiritual forces of evil in the heavenly places. [13]Therefore take up the whole armor of God, that you may be able to withstand in the evil day, and having done all, to stand firm. [14]Stand therefore, having fastened on the belt of truth, and having put on the breastplate of righteousness, [15]and, as shoes for your feet, having put on the readiness given by the gospel of peace. [16]In all circumstances take up the shield of faith, with which you can extinguish all the flaming darts of the evil one; [17]and take the helmet of salvation, and the sword of the Spirit, which is the word of God, [18]praying at all times in the Spirit...*

Comment:

Other Scriptures make it abundantly clear that we cannot do any of this on our own, but only with God working in us. Put on the things of God through the power of His Spirit working in you, so that you may stand victorious in the end. As God, revealed through the Person of Jesus Christ, said to King Ahaz, *"If you are not firm in faith, you will not be firm at all"* (Isaiah 7:9b).

See also:

a. Philippians 3:3. The Spirit enables us to worship God in a way acceptable to Him.

b. Colossians 1:8. The Spirit helps us to love one another.

c. 1 Thessalonians 1:6. The Spirit gives us joy.

7. He leads men, both good and evil, to do His bidding.

A. 2 Kings 19:7, the LORD, speaking of the king of Assyria: *"Behold, I will put a spirit in him, so that he shall hear a rumor and return to his own land, and I will make him fall by the sword in his own land."*

Comment:

And He did! See 2 Kings 19:36-37.

B. 1 Chronicles 5:26: *So the God of Israel stirred up the spirit of Pul king of Assyria, the spirit of Tiglath-pileser king of Assyria, and he took them into exile, namely, the Reubenites, the Gadites, and the half-tribe of Manasseh, and brought them to Halah, Habor, Hara, and the river Gozan, to this day.*

Comment:

Of course that *stirring* was done through the power of the Holy Spirit, the only agency through whom God interacts with His creation. See my comment on the next passage.

C. See Isaiah's prophecy concerning Cyrus (God's shepherd!) in Isaiah 44:28. See also Jeremiah 25:9 speaking of Nebuchadnezzar as the LORD's servant.

Comment on items B and C:

How did God cause the king of Assyia to go back to his own country? How did God stir the spirit of Pul? How did God move Cyrus to do His bidding? He did all these things through His Spirit. What did He want to accomplish? In the case of the king of Assyria, He was exercising righteous judgment to put him to death. With Pul, he wanted to banish the northern kingdom of Israel into captivity in order to remove them from His presence (2 Kings 17:20). And in the case of Cyrus, He raised him up specifically so that he would send God's people back to the land from which God had banished them in the first place.

D. Haggai 1:14: *And the LORD stirred up the spirit of Zerubbabel the son of Shealtiel, governor of Judah, and the spirit of Joshua the son of Jehozadak, the high priest, and the spirit of all the remnant of the people. And they came and worked on the house of the LORD of hosts, their God.*

E. Matthew 4:1–4: *[1]Then Jesus was led up by the Spirit into the wilderness to be tempted by the devil. [2]And after fasting forty days and forty nights, he was hungry. [3]And the tempter came and said to him, "If you are the Son of God, command these stones to become loaves of bread." [4]But he answered, "It is written, 'Man shall not live by bread alone, but by every word that comes from the mouth of God.'"*

Comment:

Jesus was hungry! This might be one of the greatest understatements in Scripture. I cannot imagine how much He must have wanted to create that bread and eat. Even the ultimate Good Man, the very Son of God, was led by the Spirit of God to do God's will. It was by the supernatural strength that God gave Jesus through the work of His Spirit that Jesus was able to resist the devil's temptations. Jesus testifies to this source of His power in Matthew 12:28.

F. Matthew 10:18–20, the LORD speaking: *[18]"And you will be dragged before governors and kings for my sake, to bear witness before them and the Gentiles. [19]When they deliver you over, do not be anxious how you are to speak or what you are to say, for what you are to say will be given to you in that hour. [20]For it is not you who speak, but the Spirit of your Father speaking through you."*

Comment:

God's Spirit will certainly do for us what He did for Jesus in the desert if we are willing to follow Him and trust Him completely, as Jesus did.

G. Matthew 12:18, which quotes Isaiah 42:1: *"Behold, my servant whom I have chosen, my beloved with whom my soul is well pleased. I will put my Spirit upon him, and he will proclaim justice to the Gentiles."*

H. Acts 8:26–30: ^{26}*Now an angel of the* LORD *said to Philip, "Rise and go toward the south to the road that goes down from Jerusalem to Gaza." This is a desert place.* ^{27}*And he rose and went. And there was an Ethiopian, a eunuch, a court official of Candace, queen of the Ethiopians, who was in charge of all her treasure. He had come to Jerusalem to worship* ^{28}*and was returning, seated in his chariot, and he was reading the prophet Isaiah.* ^{29}*And the Spirit said to Philip, "Go over and join this chariot."* ^{30} *So Philip ran to him and heard him reading Isaiah the prophet and asked, "Do you understand what you are reading?"*

Comment:

The term *angel of the* LORD is used throughout Scripture. Most of the time it designates the appearance of God (YHWH or Jesus Christ) among men. I believe it is used in that sense here, where Luke uses this term interchangeably with the *Spirit*. One person, two names, same entity, directing His servant in the way he should go. See, for example, Psalm 25:12; Psalm 32:8; Psalm 139:24 and Proverbs 4:11 among the many verses that teach this truth.

See also:

i   Acts 13:2, 4.

      ii   Acts 16:6–10. Here the Holy Spirit prevents Paul from going to one place and directs him to another, in accordance, obviously, with the will of God.

      iii Acts 20:22–23.

VII Enables the believer to know and relate to God personally.

1. ***By walking with His people to give them success and rest.***

    A. Isaiah 63:11–14: *[11]Then he remembered the days of old, of Moses and his people. Where is he who brought them up out of the sea with the shepherds of his flock?* **Where is he who put in the midst of them his Holy Spirit**, *[12]who caused his glorious arm to go at the right hand of Moses, who divided the waters before them to make for himself an everlasting name, [13]who led them through the depths? Like a horse in the desert, they did not stumble. [14]Like livestock that go down into the valley,* **the Spirit of the LORD gave them rest**. *So you led your people, to make for yourself a glorious name.*

2. ***By allowing us to choose to be filled with Him.***

    Ephesians 5:18 and 20: *[18]And do not get drunk with wine, for that is debauchery, but be filled with the Spirit... [20]giving thanks always and for everything to God the Father in the name of our LORD Jesus Christ...*

    Comment:

    This verse implies that we have a choice to make—to be filled with the Spirit or not. If it is our choice to make, and we live our lives not filled with the Spirit, we will have much to answer for when we stand before Christ in the Judgment. My one consolation is that I know I cannot make this choice on my own, but only with the power of the LORD working in me in the person of His Spirit. If I am not making the choices I should as a child of God, I can go to the Father through the Spirit of Jesus, confess this, repent and ask God to fill me with the power of the Spirit so that I can make the right choices.

VIII Bestows talents, skills and abilities, as well as spiritual gifts, as He sees fit. He also provides what we would call miraculous power to any sapient being God chooses.

1. ***Regarding the skill of design and crafts, and all artistic skills.***

Exodus 31:1–5: *[1]The LORD said to Moses, [2]"See, I have called by name Bezalel the son of Uri, son of Hur, of the tribe of Judah, [3]and I have filled him with the Spirit of God, with ability and intelligence, with knowledge and all craftsmanship, [4]to devise artistic designs, to work in gold, silver, and bronze, [5]in cutting stones for setting, and in carving wood, to work in every craft."*

Comment:

If God chose this man to make the most holy artifacts of worship, He would have saved him as well. I sincerely believe that we who are God's children will meet Bezalel in the Kingdom. See also Exodus 35:30–35.

2. ***Regarding the gift of administration and sound (godly) judgment, given when Moses complained that the burden God placed on him was too great.***

Numbers 11:16–17: *[16]Then the LORD said to Moses, "Gather for me seventy men of the elders of Israel, whom you know to be the elders of the people and officers over them, and bring them to the tent of meeting, and let them take their stand there with you. ¹⁷And I will come down and talk with you there. And I will take some of the Spirit that is on you and put it on them, and they shall bear the burden of the people with you, so that you may not bear it yourself alone."*

3. Regarding how God gave David the plans for the temple to be built, which he dutifully passed onto his son Solomon.

1 Chronicles 28:11–12 (NIV)²⁴⁰: *¹¹Then David gave his son Solomon the plans for the portico of the temple, its buildings, its storerooms, its upper parts, its inner rooms and the place of atonement. ¹²He gave him **the plans of all that the Spirit had put in his mind** for the courts of the temple of the* LORD *and all the surrounding rooms, for the treasuries of the temple of God and for the treasuries for the dedicated things.*

4. Gives gifts to each of us in the body of Christ.

1 Corinthians 12:7–11: *⁷To each is given the manifestation of the Spirit for the common good. ⁸For to one is given*

---

²⁴⁰ I have chosen to quote the NIV here. The ESV translates the emphasized phrase in verse 12 as *the plan of all that he had in mind*, but this phrase in the Hebrew text is: וְתַבְנִית כֹּל אֲשֶׁר הָיָה (*tabniyth kol hayah ruwach;* H8403 H3605 H1961 H7307*).* Taking the definitions of these words from the Reverse Interlinear Bible as given by the Blue Letter Bible(https://www.blueletterbible.org/esv/1ch/28/11/t_conc_366012) one can translate these words as: *tabniyth* meaning *pattern, form* or *figure*; *kol* meaning *everything, all, whatsoever*; *hayah* meaning *was, come to pass, came*; *ruwach* meaning *Spirit* or *spirit* as well as *mind*. Thus we have the phrase, loosely translated as, *and the **pattern** of **all** that **came from the Spirit**.* The KJV translates *ruwach* as *Spirit* or *spirit* 232 times and as *mind* only five times. The same numbers apply more or less to how the ESV has translated this word. I can't imagine the thought process of the ESV translators, ignoring the influence of God on David when he drew the plans for the Temple, especially in light of what David is recorded as saying in verse 19 of this chapter: *"All this," David said, "I have in writing as a result of the* LORD*'s hand on me, and he enabled me to understand all the details of the plan"* (1 Chronicles 28:19 NIV).

through the Spirit the utterance of wisdom, and to another the utterance of knowledge according to the same Spirit, ⁹to another faith by the same Spirit, to another gifts of healing by the one Spirit, ¹⁰to another the working of miracles, to another prophecy, to another the ability to distinguish between spirits, to another various kinds of tongues, to another the interpretation of tongues. ¹¹All these are empowered by one and the same Spirit, who apportions to each one individually as he wills.

Comment:

Probably one of the most famous passages in Scripture, the above passage applies to everyone in the body of Christ. We all know that. But look at the last sentence in this passage. Paul says it is the Spirit who determines who will receive what gifts. It doesn't say that it is after consultation with God that He gives us these gifts. No, it is the Spirit who determines this. But if that is true, then how can the Spirit's person be distinct from God's person, since it is God who determines all things according to His will? The will of the Spirit and the will of God must have the same mind, which is the mind of the divine Person of Jesus Christ, the exact revelation of the Person of God to us, who also inhabits the transformed human man, the Son of Man.

5. *Gives power to obey and do good works.*

Ephesians 3:14a, 16–19: ¹⁴*...I bow my knees before the Father...¹⁶that according to the riches of his glory he may grant you to be strengthened with power through his Spirit in your inner being, ¹⁷so that Christ may dwell in your hearts through faith—that you, being rooted and grounded in love, ¹⁸may have strength to comprehend with all the saints what is the breadth and length and height and depth, ¹⁹and to know the love of Christ that surpasses knowledge, that you may be filled with all the fullness of God.*

6. *Gives gifts of supernatural power to perform miraculous works among men.*

A. Judges 14:5–6: *⁵Then Samson went down with his father and mother to Timnah, and they came to the vineyards of Timnah. And behold, a young lion came toward him roaring. ⁶Then the Spirit of the LORD rushed upon him, and although he had nothing in his hand, he tore the lion in pieces as one tears a young goat. But he did not tell his father or his mother what he had done.*

Comment:

A literal translation of the Hebrew here would be something like, "God breathed power into Samson." Clearly this Spirit was not permanent, nor was it the Spirit of salvation, which is never withdrawn. This Spirit of power also came upon Samson in Judges 14:19 and 15:14, but it was temporary. When Samson disobeyed the LORD by marrying Delilah, a pagan woman from the Valley of Sorek, and gave in to her demands, the LORD's Spirit of power left him (Judges 16:19–20), and he became as weak as any other man.

B. 1 Samuel 11:6–7: *⁶And the Spirit of God rushed upon Saul when he heard these words, and his anger was greatly kindled. ⁷He took a yoke of oxen and cut them in pieces and sent them throughout all the territory of Israel by the hand of messengers, saying, "Whoever does not come out after Saul and Samuel, so shall it be done to his oxen!" Then the dread of the LORD fell upon the people, and they came out as one man.*

Comment:

Clearly this gift is temporary also, because nowhere else in this story does it mention Saul having any supernatural power. The phrase *the terror of the* LORD recalls the earlier discussion of how have we forgotten to be terrified by God's majestic, incomprehensible power and His demonstrated willingness to use it to destroy anything or anyone that justly deserves it.

C. Ezekiel 3:12–15: *²Then the Spirit lifted me up, and I heard behind me the voice of a great earthquake: "Blessed be the glory of the LORD from its place!" ¹³It was the sound of the wings of the living creatures as they touched one another, and the sound of the wheels beside them, and the sound of a great earthquake. ¹⁴The Spirit lifted me up and took me away, and I went in bitterness in the heat of my spirit, the hand of the LORD being strong upon me. ¹⁵And I came to the exiles at Tel-abib, who were dwelling by the Chebar canal, and I sat where they were dwelling. And I sat there overwhelmed among them seven days.*

Comment:

This has the same feel as the supernatural transportation of Philip after he had baptized the Ethiopian Eunuch (Acts 8:39–40). Ezekiel's in one place, and then, suddenly, he's in another.

i   See also Ezekiel 8:3, 11:1, 11:24 and 37:1.

D. Matthew 12:25–28: *²⁵Knowing their thoughts, he said to them, "Every kingdom divided against itself is laid waste, and no city or house divided against itself will stand. ²⁶And if Satan casts out Satan, he is divided against himself. How then will his kingdom stand? ²⁷And if I cast out demons by Beelzebul, by whom do your sons cast them out? Therefore they will be your judges. ²⁸**But if it is by the Spirit of God that I cast out demons**, then the kingdom of God has come upon you."*

Comment:

The Son of Man's supernatural power came from God's Spirit working in and through Him. We'll see this happen at Pentecost as well, where the Spirit comes gives the disciples supernatural power and gives birth to the church.

E. Acts 1:4–8: *⁴And while staying with them he ordered them not to depart from Jerusalem, but to wait for the promise of the Father, which, he said, "You heard from me; ⁵for John baptized with water, but you will be baptized with the Holy Spirit not many days from now." ⁶So when they had come together, they asked him, "LORD, will you at this time restore the kingdom to Israel?" ⁷He said to them, "It is not for you to know times or seasons that the Father has fixed by his own authority. **⁸But you will receive power when the Holy Spirit has come upon you**, and you will be my witnesses in Jerusalem and in all Judea and Samaria, and to the end of the earth."*

Comment:

Here Jesus talks about the work of the Spirit in the church age. He defines the baptizing they are to receive as a gift of supernatural power. There is no mention of salvation here, but only of power to be Jesus' witnesses throughout the world. All through Acts, Scripture tells of the Apostles laying hands on people and saying to them, "Receive the Holy Spirit." I don't know anyone who received the Spirit of salvation by the laying on of hands. In Romans 10:9, Paul says that to be saved you must acknowledge Jesus as LORD and believe that God raised Him from the dead. He doesn't mention anything about the laying on of hands to receive the Spirit. Rather, as Peter says in Acts 2, once you have done these two things you will receive the gift of the Holy Spirit. Peter never mentions the laying on of hands either. Scripture makes clear that the only way anyone can satisfy these two requirements is to have God, through His Spirit, draw him to Himself, move him to repent and then move him to receive the gift of salvation. It is clear, therefore, that it is not the Spirit of salvation that Jesus is talking about in this passage.

F. Acts 2:32–34, Peter speaking of Jesus, saying, *[32]"This Jesus God raised up, and of that we all are witnesses. [33]Being therefore exalted at the right hand of God, and having received from the Father the promise of the Holy Spirit, he has poured out this that you yourselves are seeing and hearing. [34]For David did not ascend into the heavens, but he himself says, 'The LORD said to my LORD, Sit at my right hand...'"*

Comment:

At a loss for how to interpret this incredibly opaque passage, I went to three commentators, *Adam Clarke*, *Barne's Notes*, and *Jamison, Faucet and Brown*. All these sources agree that Peter is not implying that there were two entirely spiritual entities in heaven. Rather, they indicate there was a human entity in heaven (the incarnation of YHWH) sitting in a seat of power and authority; that's what the *right hand of God* means. This point is touched on briefly on page 34, that the human Jesus is acting temporarily as God's prime minister, who will *step down* when all of His enemies have been defeated.

They also agreed that Jesus Himself was not receiving the Holy Spirit. This *promised Holy Spirit* was the Spirit of Power sent to the church as Jesus promised. To summarize: From God the Transcendent Majesty and through Jesus Christ comes the Holy Spirit of power, the Spirit of the church, to give the apostles, and all of us believers, the power to do the work required of us.

G. Acts 8:15–19: *15Who came down and prayed for them that they might receive the Holy Spirit, 16for he had not yet fallen on any of them, but they had only been baptized in the name of the LORD Jesus. 17Then they laid their hands on them and they received the Holy Spirit. 18Now when Simon saw that the Spirit was given through the laying on of the apostles' hands, he offered them money, 19saying, "Give me this power also, so that anyone on whom I lay my hands may receive the Holy Spirit."*

Comment:

This was the Spirit of power, as proved by Simon the sorcerer's desire to also receive this Spirit, because he had seen the miracles that were performed.

i See also Acts 10:44–46, where the Spirit of power is poured out on the gentiles, giving them supernatural gifts.

H. Romans 15:18–19a: *18For I will not venture to speak of anything except what Christ has accomplished through me to bring the Gentiles to obedience—by word and deed, 19by the power of signs and wonders, **by the power of the Spirit of God**...*

Comment:

Same for Paul as for Jesus and any other human being who performs miraculous works.

IX Shapes God's church according to His will (1 Corinthians 3:9-10; 2 Corinthians 5:1; and Ephesians 2:21).

1. **By unifying the body of Christ.**

   Ephesians 4:3–6: *3...eager to maintain the unity of the Spirit in the bond of peace. 4There is one body and one Spirit—just as you were called to the one hope that belongs to your call— 5one LORD, one faith, one baptism, 6one God and Father of all, who is over all and through all and in all.*

2. **By directing the church's leaders.**

    A. Acts 1:1–2: *¹In the first book, O Theophilus, I have dealt with all that Jesus began to do and teach, ²until the day when he was taken up, after he had given commands through the Holy Spirit to the apostles whom he had chosen.*

    Comment:

    I can only interpret this verse to mean that the Holy Spirit filling Jesus without limit moved Jesus to give these instructions to His apostles. All Jesus' work was the work of the Holy Spirit, expressing Himself in Jesus' physical flesh. Without the Holy Spirit dwelling in Him, Jesus would have been able to do nothing (John 5:30a).

3. **By giving God's chosen leaders faithful followers who will do His will.**

    1 Chronicles 12:18, speaking of David preparing to assume the kingship over Judah: *Then the Spirit clothed Amasai, chief of the thirty, and he said, "We are yours, O David, and with you, O son of Jesse! Peace, peace to you, and peace to your helpers! For your God helps you." Then David received them and made them officers of his troops.*

    Comment:

    Does God not do this in the modern church? To every faithful pastor, He raises up servants who will make His ministry function properly. As for nations, God has done this in the past for the United States of America. He raised up the right men and women at the right time to accomplish His purpose. Think of our founding fathers, a truly amazing collection of men. Think of Abraham Lincoln, whom the

LORD our God, Jesus Christ, used to direct America through the civil war. There are dozens of examples of this in American history.[241]

4. **By giving us all instruction how to follow the LORD.**

Nehemiah 9:19–20, where Nehemiah is praying, recalling how the LORD brought instruction for righteousness to his people: *[19]You in your great mercies did not forsake them in the wilderness. The pillar of cloud to lead them in the way did not depart from them by day, nor the pillar of fire by night to light for them the way by which they should go. [20]You gave your good Spirit to instruct them and did not withhold your manna from their mouth and gave them water for their thirst.*

Comment:

Through His Spirit, our LORD provides all our physical needs. He also provides protection for His saints, if they are careful to abide in Him. (Psalm 34 and 91 are good examples of God's promises in this regard.)

   i   See also Nehemiah 9:30.

X Raises the dead whom God has chosen (again the life-giving Spirit; the Spirit of salvation), to all who were, are, or who are ever going to be saved in this age (Isaiah 26:19; Acts 2:28–39).

A. Ezekiel 37:11–14: *[11]Then [the LORD] said to me, "Son of man, these bones are the whole house of Israel. Behold, they say, 'Our bones are dried up, and our hope is lost; we are indeed cut off.' [12]Therefore prophesy, and say to them, Thus says the LORD GOD: Behold, I will open your graves and raise you from your graves, O my people. And I will*

---

[241] See, for example, *Under God* by Toby Mac and Michael Tait, for many examples of how the LORD our God influenced America's history.

Solid Food for the Mature Believer

bring you into the land of Israel. ¹³And you shall know that I am the LORD, when I open your graves, and raise you from your graves, O my people. ¹⁴And I will put my Spirit within you, and you shall live, and I will place you in your own land. Then you shall know that I am the LORD; I have spoken, and I will do it, declares the LORD."

Comment:

This is crystal clear evidence that the Gospel of resurrection to eternal life is not only a N.T. doctrine.

A wonderful companion to this testimony from God in the O.T. is found in Job 19:25–27: *²⁵"For I know that my Redeemer lives, and at the last he will stand upon the earth. ²⁶And after my skin has been thus destroyed, yet in my flesh I shall see God, ²⁷whom I shall see for myself, and my eyes shall behold, and not another. My heart faints within me!"*

Another example is Hebrews 4:2, which refers to the gospel being preached in the time of Moses: *For good news came to us just as to them, but the message they heard did not benefit them* [did not benefit those who, as a pattern of life, disobeyed God], *because they were not united by faith with those who listened.*

This concludes my very brief study on the Holy Spirit. I hope this has been helpful.

APPENDIX 2

A FEW OF GOD'S COMMANDS APPLICABLE TO ALL BELIEVERS

Reference	Command
Love God, your neighbor, other believers, even your enemies!	
Matthew 22:37–38	And he said to him, "You shall love the LORD your God with all your heart and with all your soul and with all your mind. ^{38}This is the great and first commandment."
Matthew 22:39	"And a second is like it: You shall love your neighbor as yourself."
Matthew 5:44	"But I say to you, Love your enemies and pray for those who persecute you..."
John 13:34–35	^{34}"A new commandment I give to you, that you love one another: just as I have loved you, you also are to love one another. ^{35}By this all people will know that you are my disciples, if you have love for one another."
John 15:9–10	^{9}"As the Father has loved me, so have I loved you. Abide in my love. ^{10}If you keep my commandments, you will abide in my love, just as I have kept my Father's commandments and abide in his love."
Romans 12:9a and 10a	^{9}Let love be genuine. ^{10}Love one another with brotherly affection.

Reference	Command
Leviticus 19:17–18	[17]"**You shall not hate your brother in your heart**, but you shall reason frankly with your neighbor, lest you incur sin because of him. [18]You shall not take vengeance or bear a grudge against the sons of your own people, **but you shall love your neighbor as yourself**: I am the LORD."
	Hate [only] what is evil.[242]
Exodus 18:21	*Moreover, look for able men from all the people, men who fear God, **who are trustworthy and hate a bribe**, and place such men over the people as chiefs of thousands, of hundreds, of fifties, and of tens.*
Psalm 31:6	*I hate those who pay regard to worthless idols, but I trust in the LORD.*
Psalm 36:2–	*[2]For he flatters himself in his own eyes that his iniquity cannot be found out and hated. [3]The words of his mouth are trouble and deceit; he has ceased to act wisely and do good.* [243]
Psalm 45:7	*You have loved righteousness and **hated***

---

[242] Hatred is an emotion of which we have to be very careful. Probably 90% of the time that we feel hatred, it is an ungodly and unrighteous emotion based on justifying ourselves at the expense of others. Nevertheless, it is not a sin to hate what is evil; in fact, we are commanded to do so. Nor do I think it is a sin to hate those who hate God, or those who, with premeditated malice, work actively to harm His people or to thwart His will. We shall see verses to this effect in this section. The LORD Himself hates certain types of people. See the section entitled **Hatred/Wrath** on page 58.

[243] We are commanded to hate our own sin here, in a roundabout way.

Reference	Command
	wickedness. *Therefore God, your God, has anointed you with the oil of gladness beyond your companions.*
Psalm 97:10	***O you who love the LORD, hate evil!*** *He preserves the lives of his saints; he delivers them from the hand of the wicked.*[244]
Psalm 101:3–4	*³I will not set before my eyes anything that is worthless. I hate the work of those who fall away; it shall not cling to me. ⁴A perverse heart shall be far from me; I will know nothing of evil.*
Psalm 119:163	*I hate and abhor falsehood, but I love your law.*
Romans 12:9b	*Abhor what is evil; hold fast to what is good.*[245]

---

[244] Many will say, "I am a Christian," while they support abortion, homosexual rights, and other detestable things in this society. This verse says, in effect, you can't hate what the LORD loves, love what the LORD hates, and claim to have a viable fruit-bearing relationship with Him. Doesn't work that way. All those in the so-called *evangelical community* who support certain politicians *because they are* pro-abortion or pro-homosexual rights, or both, are like the thieves that try to sneak into the sheep pen (John 10:1). They are like those in Psalm 1:1–2 who walk in the counsel of the wicked and follow the paths of mockers. They are essentially spitting in the LORD's face every time they mention His Name. The warning in Matthew 7:21–23 applies to these poor souls. Let them repent or be destroyed by God's great anger!

[245] To sum up this section of the table, we are commanded to hate what is evil. Christians can experience the emotion of hatred without sinning against God. Psalm 139:19–22: *¹⁹Oh that you would slay the wicked, O God! O men of blood, depart from me! ²⁰They speak against you with malicious intent; your enemies take your name in vain! ²¹Do I not hate those who hate you, O LORD? And do I not loathe those who rise up against you? ²²I hate them with complete hatred; I* This note is continued on the next page.

Solid Food for the Mature Believer

Reference	Command
Talk the talk: Sharing what we have with unbelievers/ making disciples	
Matthew 28:18–20	*[18]And Jesus came and said to them, "All authority in heaven and on earth has been given to me. [19]Go, therefore, and make disciples of all nations, baptizing them in the name of the Father and of the Son and of the Holy Spirit, [20]teaching them to observe all that I have commanded you. And behold, I am with you always, to the end of the age."*
1 Thessalonians 2:2–4	*[2]But though we had already suffered and been shamefully treated at Philippi, as you know, we had boldness in our God to declare to you the gospel of God in the midst of much conflict. [3]For our appeal does not spring from error or impurity or any attempt to deceive, [4]but just as we have been approved by God to be entrusted with the gospel, so we speak, not to please man, but to please God who tests our hearts.*
Romans 1:14–17	*[14]I am under obligation both to Greeks and to barbarians, both to the wise and to the foolish. [15]So I am eager to preach the gospel to you also who are in Rome. [16]For I am not ashamed of the gospel, for it is the power of God for salvation to everyone who believes, to the Jew*

---

count them my enemies. The very next words out of David's mouth are to ask God to test his heart, to see *if there is any offensive way in me.*

Reference	Command
	first and also to the Greek. ¹⁷For in it the righteousness of God is revealed from faith for faith, as it is written, "The righteous shall live by faith."[246]
2 Corinthians 9:12–13	*¹²For the ministry of this service is not only supplying the needs of the saints but is also overflowing in many thanksgivings to God. ¹³By their approval of this service, they will glorify God because **of your submission flowing from your confession of the gospel of Christ**, and the generosity of your contribution for them and for all others.*
Walk the walk: Letting God's righteousness shine through us	
Leviticus 19:14	*"You shall not curse the deaf or put a stumbling block before the blind, but you shall fear your God: I am the LORD."*
Romans 12:1–2	*¹I appeal to you therefore, brothers, by the mercies of God, **to present your bodies as a living sacrifice**, holy and acceptable to God, which is your spiritual worship. ²**Do not be conformed to this world**, but be transformed by the renewal of your mind, that by testing you may discern*

---

[246] Paul is quoting Habakkuk 2:4.

Solid Food for the Mature Believer

Reference	Command
	what is the will of God, what is good and acceptable and perfect.[247]
Romans 12:3–4	*³For by the grace given to me I say to everyone among you **not to think of himself more highly than he ought to think**, but to think with sober judgment, each according to the measure of faith that God has assigned. ⁴For as in one body we have many members, and the members do not all have the same function…*
Romans 12:10b–13	10 *Honor one another above yourselves.*
	11 *Never be lacking in zeal, but keep your spiritual fervor, serving the LORD.*
	12 *Be joyful in hope, patient in affliction, faithful in prayer.*
	13 *Share with the LORD's people who are in need. Practice hospitality.*
Romans 12:17–18	17a *Repay no one evil for evil,*[248]
	17b *but give thought to do what is honorable in the sight of all.*
	18 *If possible, so far as it depends on you, live peaceably with all.*

---

[247] This last admonition is where the American church has failed and allowed itself to be corrupted by the world.

[248] This might be the hardest command to obey. Everyone's first inclination in his Romans 7 struggle with sin is to want revenge on those who do harm, whether to him or to others, but God says, *The anger of man does not produce the righteousness of God* (James 1:20). Nevertheless, it is hard not to harbor *This note is continued on the next page.*

Reference	Command
Romans 12:19–21	19 *Beloved, never avenge yourselves, but leave it to the wrath of God, for it is written, "Vengeance is mine, I will repay," says the LORD.*[249]
	20 *To the contrary*
	"if your enemy is hungry, feed him; if he is thirsty, give him something to drink; for by so doing you will heap burning coals on his head."[250]
	21 *Do not be overcome by evil, but overcome evil with good.*
1 Corinthians 16:13–14:	
	13a *Be watchful*
	13b *stand firm in the faith*
	13c *act like men*
	13d *be strong*
	14 *Let all that you do be done in love.*
2 Corinthians 8:7	*But as you excel in everything—in faith, in speech, in knowledge, in all earnestness, and in our love for you—see that you excel in this act of grace also.*

---

unrighteous anger and hatred in one's heart. As is true of all God's commands, only the Spirit can give us the power to obey.

[249] Paul is quoting Deuteronomy 32:35
[250] Paul is quoting Proverbs 25:21–22.

Reference	Command
Ephesians 4:17	*Now this I say and testify in the LORD, that you must no longer walk as the Gentiles do, in the futility of their minds.*
Ephesians 5:22	*Wives, submit to your own husbands, as to the LORD.*
Ephesians 5:25	*Husbands, love your wives, as Christ loved the church and gave himself up for her.*
Colossians 3:12–14	
	12 *Put on then, as God's chosen ones, holy and beloved, compassionate hearts, kindness, humility, meekness, and patience*
	13a *bearing with one another and, if one has a complaint against another, forgiving each other*
	13b *as the LORD has forgiven you, so you also must forgive*
	14 *And above all these put on love, which binds everything together in perfect harmony.*
Pray! All the time!	
Matthew 26:41	*"Watch and pray that you may not enter into temptation. The spirit indeed is willing, but the flesh is weak."*
Ephesians 6:18	*[Pray] at all times in the Spirit, with all prayer and supplication. To that end keep alert with all perseverance, making supplication for all the saints.*

Reference	Command
Luke 6:2	"...*bless those who curse you, pray for those who abuse you.*"
Store up the word in your heart and meditate on it	
Joshua 1:8–9	[8]"*This Book of the Law shall not depart from your mouth, but you shall meditate on it day and night, so that you may be careful to do according to all that is written in it. For then you will make your way prosperous, and then you will have good success.*[251] [9]*Have I not commanded you? Be strong and courageous. Do not be frightened, and do not be dismayed, for the* LORD *your God is with you wherever you go.*"
Commands that will keep us healthy, wealthy, wise and of good repute	
Proverbs 3:1–12	1-2 *My son, do not forget my teaching, but let your heart keep my commandments for length of days and years of life and peace they will add to you.*
	3-4 *Let not steadfast love and faithfulness*

---

[251] I have not seen or heard or met anyone in today's church who believes this promise literally. Everyone explains this promise away, to say, in essence, "Well, the LORD *doesn't really mean* 'prosperous' as we might otherwise understand the word." But He does. Time and again in the O.T. when the LORD is with someone, everything he does prospers. See, for example, the story of Joseph starting in Genesis 37. The LORD wants us to succeed at whatever we do whether it be at our jobs or in our ministries. That means He wants us to prosper, as an unbeliever might understand the word. What loving father would not want his children to prosper? Then, how much more so our loving Father in heaven? See Matthew 7:11.

Solid Food for the Mature Believer

Reference	Command
	forsake you; bind them around your neck; write them on the tablet of your heart. So you will find favor and good success in the sight of God and man.
5-6	*Trust in the LORD with all your heart, and do not lean on your own understanding. In all your ways acknowledge him, and he will make straight your paths.*[252]
7-8	*Be not wise in your own eyes; fear the LORD, and turn away from evil. It will be healing to your flesh and refreshment to your bones.*
9-10	*Honor the LORD with your wealth and with the first fruits of all your produce; ¹then your barns will be filled with plenty, and your vats will be bursting with wine.*
11-12	*My son, do not despise the LORD's discipline or be weary of his reproof, ¹²for the LORD reproves him whom he loves, as a father the son in whom he delights.*

---

[252] Everyone quotes Proverbs 3:5–6, but no one quotes the other ten verses in this passage. Why? Because they don't believe them. They don't believe that God wants to extend our lives, to keep us healthy, to make us financially successful as well as spiritually strong. This is truly sad. They will say, look at all the sick poor Christians. While there can be many reasons that believers will experience poor health or poverty (when, for example, God is testing them), I will still reply: yes, because the church does not know and understand the LORD, and it does not believe His word or trust Him as it ought. The body of Christ in the America is sick, because it harbors spiritual and moral corruption and is becoming more corrupt with every passing year.

Reference	Command
Where to set your heart and mind	
1 Peter 1:13–16	*[13]Therefore, preparing your minds for action, and being sober-minded, set your hope fully on the grace that will be brought to you at the revelation of Jesus Christ. [14]As obedient children, do not be conformed to the passions of your former ignorance, [15]but as he who called you is holy, you also be holy in all your conduct, [16]since it is written, "You shall be holy, for I am holy."*
1 Peter 3:15–16a	*[15]But in your hearts honor Christ the LORD as holy, always being prepared to make a defense to anyone who asks you for a reason for the hope that is in you; yet do it with gentleness and respect, [16]having a good conscience, so that, when you are slandered, those who revile your good behavior in Christ may be put to shame.*
Forgive [253]	
Mark 11:25	*"And when you stand praying, if you*

---

[253] This is another hard command to obey. For example, I can't imagine how hard it would be for a child who grew up with abusive parents to forgive them. Or for a parent whose child was murdered, to forgive the murderer. But God seems to make no distinction about the depth of the transgression we must forgive, because we are all abusers and blasphemers and murderers in our heart (*Anyone who hates his brother is a murderer*, (1 John 3:15)), and God has forgiven us. Indeed, God would have forgiven Hitler had he truly repented of his colossal sins. In fact, He demonstrated this in King Manasseh's life. Read his story in 2 Chronicles 33 and how the LORD saved him in verse 13. Nevertheless, how hard it is for us to forgive! It can only be done by the Holy Spirit giving us strength!

Reference	Command
	hold anything against anyone, forgive them, so that your Father in heaven may forgive you your sins."
Luke 6:37	*"Do not judge, and you will not be judged."*
	"Do not condemn, and you will not be condemned."
	Forgive, and you will be forgiven.
Luke 17:3–4	*³"So watch yourselves. If your brother or sister sins against you, rebuke them; and if they repent, forgive them. ⁴Even if they sin against you seven times in a day and seven times come back to you saying 'I repent,' you must forgive them."*
Colossians 3:13	*Bear with each other and forgive one another if any of you has a grievance against someone. Forgive as the LORD forgave you.*

BIBLIOGRAPHY OF NON-SCRIPTURAL SOURCES

Behe, Michael, *Molecular Machines: Experimental Support for the Design Inference by* Michael Behe [1997] at http://www.arn.org/docs/BEHE/mb_mm92496.htm.

Brown, Michael L., *Can You Be Gay and Christian?* Front Line Publishing, Lake Mary, Fla., 2014.

De Young, James B., *Burning Down the Shack.* WND Books, New York, NY, 2002.

Fee, Gordon D., and Stuart, Douglas, *How to Read the Bible for All Its Worth.* Zondervan, Grand Rapids, Michigan, 1981 & 1993.

Ferris, Timothy, *Coming of Age in the Milky Way.* Anchor Books–Doubleday, NY, NY, 1988.

Horton, et al., *The Agony of Deceit.* Moody Press, Chicago, Ill, 1992.

Keller, Timothy, *The Reason for God.* Riverhead Books, NY, NY, 2008.

Mac, Toby and Tait, Michael, *Under God.* Bethany House, Bloomington, Minnesota, 2004.

MacArthur, John, *The Truth War,* Thomas Nelson, Nashville, TN, 2007.

Maier, Paul L., *Eusebius–the Church History: A New Translation with Commentary.* Kregal Publications, Grand Rapids, MI, 1999.

Microsoft Bookshelf in FN20, 1996-1997 edition.

Miller, Kevin and Stein, Ben, *Expelled, No Intelligence Allowed.* Documentary film directed by Nathan Frankowski. Released to the public for general viewing in April 2008.

Wald, Dr. George, "The origin of life," *Scientific American,* August 1954.

White, Dr James, *The Forgotten Trinity*. Bethany House, Minneapolis, MN., 1998.

White, Dr. James, *King James Only Controversy*. Bethany House, New York, NY, 2009.

INDEX OF SCRIPTURE REFERENCES

There are two types of Scripture references. Those verses I quote, paraphrase or excerpt from the ESV (and occasionally the NASB and NIV), and those I merely refer to, relying on the reader to look them up. To distinguish between these, when Scripture verses are quoted or paraphrased in part or in full it is noted in the Index.

Book, Chapter, and Verse	Page	Book, Chapter, and Verse	Page
Genesis 1:1 FN15	10	Exodus 3:14 FN30	15
Genesis 1:26a	11	Exodus 3:5 FN40	19
Genesis 1:26–27	97	Exodus 15:14 FN152	85
Genesis 3:8–10	19	Exodus 18:21 Quoted	204
Genesis 3:9 FN58	29	Exodus 20:18	15
Genesis 6:3 FN85	43	Exodus 20:20 Quoted	84-85
Genesis 6:3 Quoted	158	Exodus 31:1–5 Quoted	192
Genesis 8:21	55	Exodus 31:1–6 FN90	44
Genesis 12:1 FN100	49	Exodus 31:3	97
Genesis 18	19	Exodus 33:10–11	19
Genesis 18:1	19	Exodus 33:19 Quoted	68
Genesis 19:19 FN105	56	Exodus 35:30–35	192
Genesis 22:1–14 FN100	49	Leviticus 7:13, 15 FN166	96
Genesis 32:22–30	19	Leviticus 10:1–2	85
Genesis 37 FN251	211	Leviticus 18:22 Quoted	62
Genesis 41	146	Leviticus 18:22 FN180	110
Genesis 41:37–38 Quoted	146	Leviticus 19:14 Quoted	207
Genesis 41:41–44 Quoted	35	Leviticus 19:17–18 Quoted	204

219

Solid Food for the Mature Believer
Scripture Reference Index

Book, Chapter, and Verse	Page	Book, Chapter, and Verse	Page
Leviticus 20:13 FN180	110	Deuteronomy 10:12–13 Quoted	80
Numbers 6 FN191	122	Deuteronomy 10:12	82, 83
Numbers 6:1–4	124	Deuteronomy 10:12–13	96
Numbers 11:16–17	147	Deuteronomy 10:15–17 Quoted	160
Numbers 11:16–17 Quoted	192	Deuteronomy 10:16	175
Numbers 11:25 Quoted	147	Deuteronomy 14:24–26 Quoted	123
Numbers 11:26–27	148	Deuteronomy 22:5 Quoted	62
Numbers 12:6	97	Deuteronomy 25:15–16 Quoted	62
Numbers 14:20–23 FN130	73	Deuteronomy 28	38
Numbers 14:24	44, 170	Deuteronomy 28:58–63 Quoted	117
Numbers 14:24 Quoted	179	Deuteronomy 28:63 FN138	79
Numbers 15:30 Quoted	125	Deuteronomy 29:4	43, 143
Numbers 23:19 FN93	45	Deuteronomy 29:2a, 3–4 Quoted	165
Numbers 24:2–3 Quoted	148	Deuteronomy 30:4–6 Quoted	160
Numbers 27:18–19 Quoted	180	Deuteronomy 30:6	175
Numbers 28:7	123	Deuteronomy 31:20 FN138	79
Deuteronomy 4:6 FN145	82	Deuteronomy 32:35 FN249	209
Deuteronomy 4:24	14, 40, 85	Deuteronomy 32:43b	59
Deuteronomy 6:4	21	Deuteronomy 34:9 Quoted	146
Deuteronomy 7:9–10	58	Deuteronomy 34:9	154
Deuteronomy 8:17–18	44, 170	Joshua 1:8–9 Quoted	211-211

Solid Food for the Mature Believer
Scripture Reference Index

Book, Chapter, and Verse	Page	Book, Chapter, and Verse	Page
Joshua 5:13–16	19	1 Samuel 13:14	80, 151
Joshua 5:15 Quoted FN40	19	1 Samuel 15:1–3 Quoted	119
Joshua 10:12–13 FN203	128	1 Samuel 15:10–12 Quoted	119-119
Joshua 11:18–20 Quoted	64	1 Samuel 15:15–23 Quoted	120-120
Judges 3:9–10a Quoted	151	1 Samuel 15:23, 26, and 16:1 FN239	185
Judges 6:34 and 11:29	151	1 Samuel 16:13a Quoted	150
Judges 13:18 (also in FN17)	11	1 Samuel 19:20–21, 23–24	148
Judges 14:5–6 Quoted	195	1 Samuel 19:23	173
Judges 14:19 and 15:14	195	2 Samuel 23:2–5	53
Judges 16:19–20	195	2 Samuel 24:14	88
1 Samuel 1:3b Quoted	63	1 Kings 3:5	19
1 Samuel 2:12–17 Quoted	63	1 Kings 8:27	12, 18, 140
1 Samuel 2:22–25 Quoted	63-64	1 Kings 9:2	19
1 Samuel 9:21	150	1 Kings 18:9–14	180
1 Samuel 10:6 FN91	44	1 Kings 19:18 FN97	48
1 Samuel 10:6–7 Quoted	148	1 Kings 19:14–18 Quoted	168-168
1 Samuel 10:10–13	148	2 Kings 2:16	180
1 Samuel 10:10	149	2 Kings 17:20	188
1 Samuel 10:22	150	2 Kings 19:7 Quoted	188-188
1 Samuel 11:6–7 Quoted	195	2 Kings 19:36-37	188
1 Samuel 11:7	15	1 Chronicles 5:26 Quoted	188

Solid Food for the Mature Believer
Scripture Reference Index

Book, Chapter, and Verse	Page	Book, Chapter, and Verse	Page
1 Chronicles 12:18 Quoted	200	Nehemiah 12:8, 24, 27, and 46 FN166	96
1 Chronicles 16:30 FN152	85	Job 9:1–13	14
1 Chronicles 16:36 Excerpt	15	Job 11:13–20	80
1 Chronicles 28:11–12 Quoted (NIV)	193-193	Job 12:10 Quoted (FN217)	141, (141)
1 Chronicles 28:19 Quoted (NIV) FN240	193-193	Job 19:25–27 FN220	142
1 Chronicles 29:10	55	Job 19:25–27 Quoted	202
2 Chronicles 2:6	140	Job 23:15 FN152	85
2 Chronicles 6:18	140	Job 28:28 FN147	83
2 Chronicles 7:14 FN120	67	Job 29:4	97
2 Chronicles 15:1–2 Quoted	154	Job 32:8	97,190
2 Chronicles 20:14–17	155	Job 32:8 Quoted	143
2 Chronicles 24:20	155	Job 33:4	43
2 Chronicles 33 FN253	213	Job 33:4 Quoted	142
Ezra 3:11 FN166	96	Job 34:13–15	14
Ezra 9:3–4 Quoted	87	Job 34:14–15 Quoted	142
Nehemiah 9:5	11	Job 36:26	11
Nehemiah 9:19–20 Quoted	201	Job 39:13–17	14
Nehemiah 9:29–31 Quoted	69-70	Psalm 1:1–2 Quoted	93
Nehemiah 9:30	201	Psalm 1:1–2 FN244	205
Nehemiah 11:17 FN166	96	Psalm 5:5–6 Quoted	61

Solid Food for the Mature Believer
Scripture Reference Index

Book, Chapter, and Verse	Page	Book, Chapter, and Verse	Page
Psalm 9:1–2 Quoted	92	Psalm 78:40	97
Psalm 9:10 Quoted	93	Psalm 89:26 FN52	27
Psalm 11:5 FN108	58	Psalm 89:7	16
Psalm 14:1	11	Psalm 95:2 FN166	96
Psalm 14:1 Quoted	127	Psalm 96:1–2 FN163	93
Psalm 19:1–4	11	Psalm 96:9 FN152	85
Psalm 23:6	97	Psalm 97:10 Quoted	205
Psalm 25:12	190	Psalm 100:4 FN166	96
Psalm 31:6 Quoted	204	Psalm 100:5 Quoted	184
Psalm 36:2– Quoted	204	Psalm 101:3–4 Quoted	205
Psalm 37:4 Quoted	93	Psalm 102	26
Psalm 38	15	Psalm 102:1; 12, 18–19, 24–27 Quoted	25
Psalm 40:5	98	Psalm 103 FN169	98
Psalm 45:1–7 Quoted	25	Psalm 104:15 FN194	123
Psalm 45:7 Quoted	204	Psalm 106:32–33 Quoted	159
Psalm 45:6–7 Quoted	61	Psalm 110:1 FN71, FN222	35,145
Psalm 50:4 FN114	61	Psalm 111:10aQuoted	83
Psalm 51 FN229	161	Psalm 114:7 FN152	85
Psalm 51:11–12 Quoted	53	Psalm 119:46–48 Quoted	93
Psalm 52:8–9 Quoted	94	Psalm 119:96 (& FN21)	12,(12)
Psalm 65:4	97	Psalm 119:163 Quoted	205
Psalm 69:30 FN166	96	Psalm 139:5–10 Quoted	183

Solid Food for the Mature Believer
Scripture Reference Index

Book, Chapter, and Verse	Page	Book, Chapter, and Verse	Page
Psalm 139:7–10	140	Proverbs 16:4	14
Psalm 139:13 FN231	162	Proverbs 16:4 (NASB)	162
Psalm 139:19–22 Quoted FN245	205	Proverbs 25:21–22 FN250	209
Psalm 139:24	190	Ecclesiastes 3:11b	11
Psalm 143:10–12 Quoted	185	Ecclesiastes 3:11c	11
Psalm 147:4	14	Ecclesiastes 8:17b	11
Proverbs 1:8–9 Quoted	75	Isaiah 3:10–11 FN161	89
Proverbs 2:1–8	15	Isaiah 6:9–10 (FN175)	(105),156
Proverbs 2:6	97	Isaiah 7:9b Quoted	187
Proverbs 3:5–6 FN252	212	Isaiah 8:13	16
Proverbs 3:11–12	15, 98	Isaiah 8:14 FN142	82
Proverbs 3:1–12 Quoted	211-212	Isaiah 9:6	54
Proverbs 3:31–32a Quoted	62	Isaiah 24:1	40
Proverbs 3:34–35 Quoted	75	Isaiah 24:1–3 (FN156)	77,(87)
Proverbs 4:11	190	Isaiah 26:10	72-72
Proverbs 6:16–19 Quoted	60	Isaiah 26:10 Quoted	76
Proverbs 8:15–16	111	Isaiah 26:19	45,201
Proverbs 9:10 FN147	83	Isaiah 28:16 FN142	82
Proverbs 12:10 Quoted	73	Isaiah 30:15c	159
Proverbs 15:8a Quoted	62	Isaiah 32:14–20 Quoted	185
Proverbs 15:26a Quoted	62	Isaiah 33:6 FN147	83
Proverbs 15:33 FN147	83	Isaiah 40:11	15,180

Solid Food for the Mature Believer
Scripture Reference Index

Book, Chapter, and Verse	Page	Book, Chapter, and Verse	Page
Isaiah 40:28c FN56	28	Jeremiah 16:5–7 Quoted	65
Isaiah 42:1	190	Jeremiah 17:9a Quoted (also KJV) FN109	59
Isaiah 44:6 Quoted	20	Jeremiah 19:4–6 Quoted	66
Isaiah 44:28	188	Jeremiah 23:24	13
Isaiah 45:5–7 Quoted	78	Jeremiah 23:23–24 Quoted	140
Isaiah 45:7	14	Jeremiah 25:9	188
Isaiah 45:19c Quoted	78	Jeremiah 29:11	74
Isaiah 46:9c–10 Quoted	79	Jeremiah 35 in FN188	121
Isaiah 48:12 FN43	20	Lamentations 2:17	159
Isaiah 48:16	155	Lamentations 4	159
Isaiah 55:3 FN103	54	Ezekiel 1	22
Isaiah 61:1	155	Ezekiel 1 FN177	107
Isaiah 63:9	19	Ezekiel 1:26–28	20
Isaiah 63:11–14 Quoted	191	Ezekiel 1:28; 3:12, 23	153
Isaiah 64:8	55	Ezekiel 2:1	20
Isaiah 64:6a Quoted FN143	82	Ezekiel 2:1–2 Quoted	156
Isaiah 66:5 FN152	85	Ezekiel 3:11 FN51	26
Jeremiah 2:12 FN32	16	Ezekiel 3:12–15 Quoted	196-196
Jeremiah 5:20–22a Quoted	85	Ezekiel 3:14 FN226	151
Jeremiah 5:22	16	Ezekiel 3:22–27 Quoted	180
Jeremiah 9:23–24 FN138	79	Ezekiel 5:8–10 Quoted	65
Jeremiah 9:23–24	97	Ezekiel 6:9	97

Solid Food for the Mature Believer
Scripture Reference Index

Book, Chapter, and Verse	Page	Book, Chapter, and Verse	Page
Ezekiel 6:9b Excerpt FN167	97	Daniel 10(FN185)	111,(116)
Ezekiel 8:3, 11:1, 11:24 and 37:1	196	Daniel 10:5	19
Ezekiel 9 (FN151)	15, 118 169, (85)	Daniel 10:5–6 FN182	111
Ezekiel 11:22–25 Quoted	151-151	Daniel 10:7–10 FN153	86
Ezekiel 28:12-13	79	Daniel 11 (FN185)	111,(116)
Ezekiel 33:11 FN138	79	Daniel 11:29–39 Quoted	111-112
Ezekiel 36:22–23 FN117	65	Daniel 11:36a Quoted	113
Ezekiel 36:24–27 Quoted	181	Daniel 12 FN185	116
Ezekiel 36:24–29a	157	Daniel 12:1–3 Quoted	112
Ezekiel 36:24–29a Quoted	135	Hosea 4:1–6a Quoted	117-118
Ezekiel 36:26–27	153	Hosea 9:7 Quoted FN227	153
Ezekiel 37:11–14 Quoted	201-202	Joel 2	152
Daniel 7 (FN185)	107,115,(116)	Joel 2:28–30	43, 143
Daniel 7:16b–22 Quoted	107-108	Joel 2:28–30 Quoted	152
Daniel 7:23–25	115	Joel 2:28–29	153
Daniel 7:23–27 Quoted	108-109	Amos 5:20–22 Quoted	61
Daniel 7:9	107	Jonah 3:9 120	67
Daniel 8 (FN185)	109,(116)	Jonah 4:11 Paraphrased FN111	60
Daniel 8:22–25 Quoted	110	Micah 3:8	155
Daniel 8:8–12 Quoted	109	Micah 5:2	52

Solid Food for the Mature Believer
Scripture Reference Index

Book, Chapter, and Verse	Page	Book, Chapter, and Verse	Page
Micah 6:8 Quoted	89	Matthew 10:28 (FN154)	86, (86)
Habakkuk 2:4 FN145, FN246	82, 207	Matthew 10:29–30 Quoted	77
Haggai 1:14 Quoted	189	Matthew 11:19	123
Haggai 2:4–5 Quoted	184-184	Matthew 11:27	17, 21, 97
Zechariah 4:6	44, 157, 170	Matthew 12:18 Quoted	190
Zechariah 4:6 Quoted	171	Matthew 12:25–28 Quoted	196
Zechariah 12:1	15	Matthew 12:28 (FN91)	28, 189, (44)
Zechariah 12:10 Quoted	76, 186	Matthew 12:31–32 Quoted	124
Malachi 2:10 FN52	27	Matthew 13:13–14 FN175	105
Malachi 2:16a (NASB and ESV)	5	Matthew 13:24–30 FN232	163
Malachi 2:16	61	Matthew 13:47–50	40
Matthew 2:3–6	52	Matthew 17:2–3 FN67	33
Matthew 3:11–12 Quoted	164	Matthew 19:29	81
Matthew 4:1–4 Quoted	189	Matthew 22:13	40
Matthew 4:2 FN56	28	Matthew 22:37–38 Quoted	203
Matthew 5:44 Quoted	203	Matthew 22:37–39 Excerpts quoted	82
Matthew 5:48 Quoted	136	Matthew 22:39	203
Matthew 7:21–23 (FN244)	40, 80, 130, (205)	Matthew 22:43–44 Quoted	145
Matthew 8:24 FN56	28	Matthew 23:15 Quoted FN231	162
Matthew 10:18–20 Quoted	189	Matthew 24:12 FN227	153

Solid Food for the Mature Believer
Scripture Reference Index

Book, Chapter, and Verse	Page	Book, Chapter, and Verse	Page
Matthew 24:50–51	40	Luke 8:45 Excerpt	29
Matthew 25:21a Quoted	96	Luke 9:15 Paraphrased	39
Matthew 25:23 Excerpt	80	Luke 9:30	48
from Matthew 25:29 Quoted FN223	147	Luke 10:20 Excerpt	48
Matthew 26:41 Quoted	210	Luke 10:21	172
Matthew 28:18–20 Quoted	206	Luke 10:22	21
Mark 6:5 Excerpt	29	Luke 11:11–13 Quoted	165
Mark 6:4–6	146	Luke 11:13	175
Mark 11:25 Quoted	213	Luke 12:4–5	16
Mark 13	104	Luke 12:4-5 FN154	86
Mark 13:18–20 Quoted	101	Luke 12:5b Quoted	86
Mark 14:34 excerpt from KFV FN61	29	Luke 12:11–12 Quoted	173
Luke 1:13–17 Quoted	171	Luke 13:28	48
Luke 1:41–45 Quoted	155	Luke 14:26–27 Quoted	91
Luke 1:67–79	156	Luke 17:3–4	214
Luke 2:25–35	156	Luke 17:7–10	94
Luke 4:1–2 Quoted	171	Luke 17:7–10 Quoted	96
Luke 4:18	155, 172	Luke 19:12, 14, 27 Quoted	39
Luke 6:2 Quoted	211	Luke 24:39	16, 24, 32
Luke 6:37 Quoted	214	Luke 24:39, 43 FN68	34
Luke 7:28	171	*John 1:1* referenced by Dr. White	9
Luke 7:34	123	John 1:1 FN15	10

Solid Food for the Mature Believer
Scripture Reference Index

Book, Chapter, and Verse	Page	Book, Chapter, and Verse	Page
John 1:12–13 FN95	47	John 6:44a Quoted	46
John 1:14 (1:14a quoted)	24, (31)	John 6:44	149
John 1:18 Quoted	20	John 6:44 Quoted	162
John 1:32–34 Quoted	152	John 6:44 FN86,92	44,45
John 2 FN195	123	John 6:44a Quoted	46
John 2:10 FN195	123	John 6:63 Quoted	163
John 3:34	172	John 6:63–65 Quoted	47, 166, 168
John 3:5–8 Quoted	165	John 6:63	180
John 4:1 FN55	28	John 7:25–27 Quoted	52
John 4:1–3 Quoted	143	John 7:37–39 Quoted	46
John 4:24	15, 16, 27	John 7:38b	48
John 4:7 FN56	28	John 8:58	4, 17
John 5:19 FN56	16	John 8:58 Quoted FN30	15
John 5:26	14	John 8:58 Excerpt, Full	23, 55
John 5:27	40	John 10:1 FN244	205
John 5:30a	200	John 10:10	98
John 5:37 Excerpt	19	John 10:17–18	164
John 5:37	20, 139	John 10:28b Quoted FN90	45
John 6:37 FN232	163	John 10:28–29	45
John 6:38 FN61	29	John 10:30 Paraphrase	21
John 6:41–42	24	John 12:27 FN61	29
John 6:44 FN86	44	John 12:32	149
John 6:44 FN92	45	John 13:34–35 Quoted	92, 203

Solid Food for the Mature Believer
Scripture Reference Index

Book, Chapter, and Verse	Page	Book, Chapter, and Verse	Page
John 14:9 Paraphrase	21	Acts 1:4–8 Quoted	197
John 14:10 Quoted	27	Acts 1:8; 6:8; 10:38 referred to by Fee and Stuart	50
John 14:10	30	Acts 2	45,53,149,197
John 14:15,21 Quoted	82	Acts 2:3	153
John 14:17 Excerpt FN98	48	Acts 2:2–3 Quoted	172
John 14:23–24 Quoted	91	Acts 2:17–18 Quoted	153
John 14:26	48	Acts 2:28–39	45,201
John 14:28 Quoted	16, 36	Acts 2:38–39 Quoted	45, 167
John 15:6 FN138	79	Acts 2:31–35 Quoted	35-35
John 15:9–10 Quoted	203	AcActs 2:32–34 Quoted	198
John 15:15 FN55	28	Acts 2:38	149
John 15:16a Quoted	163	Acts 2:38 FN86	44
John 15:26	49	Acts 4:8–10 Quoted	173
John 16:8 FN86	44	Acts 4:31	173
John 16:8–11 Quoted	161	Acts 5	86
John 16:13	49	Acts 5:1–11 FN128	73
John 19:28 FN56	28	Acts 5:1–10	83
John 20:22 FN183	114	Acts 5:11 Quoted	86
John 20:27 FN68	34	Acts 5:29–30 FN69	34
John 21:25 FN15	11	Acts 5:30–32 Quoted	173
Acts 1:1–2 Quoted	200	Acts 5:31 Quoted	34

Solid Food for the Mature Believer
Scripture Reference Index

Book, Chapter, and Verse	Page	Book, Chapter, and Verse	Page
Acts 6:3–7:60	154	Romans 2:29	160
Acts 7:51–53 Quoted	159	Romans 3:20,4:13,5:20 FN145	82
Acts 8:14–17	49	Romans 4:16–17 FN227	153
Acts 8:14–17 Quoted by Fee and Stuart	50	Romans 5:1–5 Quoted	175
Acts 8:15–19 Quoted	199	Romans 5:6–10	97
Acts 8:26–30 Quoted	190	Romans 5:10	55
Acts 8:39–40	196	Romans 6	105
Acts 9:31 Quoted	174	Romans 6:1–10 Quoted	105-106
Acts 10:44–46	199	Romans 7 (FN155)	90,(87) 136
Acts 11:4–10 FN192	122	Romans 7:5–6 Quoted	175
Acts 11:9 Quoted	122	Romans 7:15–24 FN237	174
Acts 13:2, 4	190	Romans 7:15–24	178
Acts 16:6–10	191	Romans 7:15	183
Acts 17:24-28 Quoted	141	Romans 7:24–25a	90
Acts 19:1b–7 Quoted	51-51	Romans 8:1–11	90
Acts 20:22–23	191	Romans 8:2–4	175
Acts 28:25–27	156	Romans 8:2–8	44,170
Romans 1:9 NIV	94	Romans 8:5 Quoted	176
Romans 1:9 Quoted FN165	94	Romans 8:6 Quoted	176
Romans 1:14–17	206	Romans 8:6–7	55
Romans 1:26–27 FN115	62	Romans 8:7 FN94	47
Romans 2:28–29 Quoted	174	Romans 8:7	174

Solid Food for the Mature Believer
Scripture Reference Index

Book, Chapter, and Verse	Page	Book, Chapter, and Verse	Page
Romans 8:7–9 Quoted	177	Romans 11:29	45, 149
Romans 8:9	177, 182	Romans 12:1b Quoted	95
Romans 8:9 FNs 81, 213	42, 139	Romans 12:2	106
Romans 8:9a and 10a Quoted FN234	169	Romans 12:1–2, 3–4 Quoted	207
Romans 8:10–11 Quoted	164	Romans 12:9a and 10a Quoted	203
Romans 8:14	178	Romans 12:9b Quoted	205
Romans 8:15–17 Quoted	178-178	Romans 12:10b–13	208
Romans 8:16	144	Romans 12:19–21	209
Romans 8:26–27 Quoted	179	Romans 14:17	176
Romans 8:28	44, 70, 97	Romans 15:13 Quoted	176
Romans 8:29	163	Romans 15:15–16 Quoted	179
Romans 9:5	17	Romans 15:18–19a Quoted	199
Romans 9:13–14 Quoted	177	1 Corinthians 2:6–15 Quoted	144
Romans 9:14–18 Quoted	68	1 Corinthians 2:14	43, 143
Romans 9:14–18, 21–25	163	1 Corinthians 3:9–10	44, 199
Romans 9:30–33 Quoted	81-82	1 Corinthians 3:12–15 FN128	73
Romans 10:9 FN171	99	1 Corinthians 3:15	38
Romans 10:9	197	1 Corinthians 3:14–15	83
Romans 11:22 Excerpt FN102	53	1 Corinthians 4:9–13 Quoted	95
Romans 11:19–22 Quoted	88	1 Corinthians 6:9 FN115	62

Solid Food for the Mature Believer
Scripture Reference Index

Book, Chapter, and Verse	Page	Book, Chapter, and Verse	Page
1 Corinthians 6:9–11 FN180	110	2 Corinthians 5:1	44, 199
1 Corinthians 11:27–30	124	2 Corinthians 5:5	167, 168
1 Corinthians 11:30	83	2 Corinthians 6:4–7	182-182
1 Corinthians 12:1–11 FN90	44	2 Corinthians 8:7 Quoted	209
1 Corinthians 12:7–11 Quoted	193	2 Corinthians 9:8, 14	98
1 Corinthians 12:9, 13	46	2 Corinthians 9:12–13 Quoted	207
1 Corinthians 12:9, 13 FN233	169	Galatians 4:6–7 Quoted	169
1 Corinthians 15:20b Quoted FN66	33	Galatians 4:28-30 Quoted	164
1 Corinthians 15:20–28 Quoted	36	Galatians 5:4–6 Quoted	182
1 Corinthians 15:24–28	4	Galatians 5:16–18, 22–26 Quoted	176
1 Corinthians 15:27–28	32	Galatians 5:16–18 Quoted	183
1 Corinthians 15:53	32	Galatians 6:7–8 Quoted	177
1 Corinthians 15:51–54	33	Ephesians 1:1–7	98
1 Corinthians 16:13–14 Quoted	209	Ephesians 1:7–8	74
2 Corinthians 1:22 FN86	45	Ephesians 1:13–14	167
2 Corinthians 1:22	45, 167, 182	Ephesians 1:13	169
2 Corinthians 1:20–22 Quoted	167	Ephesians 1:17	43, 143
2 Corinthians 3:3	168	Ephesians 1:17 Quoted	154
2 Corinthians 3:12–18 Quoted	41-42	Ephesians 1:23 (FN25)	(13), 30
2 Corinthians 4:7	28	Ephesians 2:8	46

Solid Food for the Mature Believer
Scripture Reference Index

Book, Chapter, and Verse	Page	Book, Chapter, and Verse	Page
Ephesians 2:1–9 Quoted	76-77	Ephesians 6:18 Quoted	210
Ephesians 2:10 and 4:1	82	Philippians 1:29 FN77	39
Ephesians 2:10	183	Philippians 2:6 Excerpt	18
Ephesians 2:19–22 Quoted	170	Philippians 2:6–8	24
Ephesians 2:21	44, 199	Philippians 2:9–11 Quoted	34-34
Ephesians 3:4–5	43, 143	Philippians 2:13 (FN163)	44, 90,(93),170
Ephesians 3:4–5 Quoted	154	Philippians 3:3	187
Ephesians 3:10–13 Quoted	51	Philippians 3:7–11 Quoted	91-92
Ephesians 3:14a, 16–19 Quoted	194	Philippians 3:8–14 Quoted	136
Ephesians 4:3–6 Quoted	199	Philippians 4:4 Quoted	93
Ephesians 4:4	46	Philippians 4:13	44, 170
Ephesians 4:10 FN25	13	Colossians 1:8	187
Ephesians 4:10	30	Colossians 1:10	82
Ephesians 4:17 Quoted	210	Colossians 1:15	33
Ephesians 4:30 FN86	44	Colossians 1:15–17 Quoted	17, 78
Ephesians 4:30–32 Quoted	161	Colossians 1:16a Quoted	42-42
Ephesians 5:18 and 20	191	Colossians 1:18–20 Quoted	32-32
Ephesians 5:22 Quoted	210	Colossians 1:27 Excerpt FN89	44
Ephesians 5:25 Quoted	210	Colossians 2:9 Excerpt	18
Ephesians 6:10–18a Quoted	186	Colossians 2:9	157

Solid Food for the Mature Believer
Scripture Reference Index

Book, Chapter, and Verse	Page	Book, Chapter, and Verse	Page
Colossians 2:9 FN235	170	1 Timothy 4:1–5 Quoted	122
Colossians 3:12–16 Quoted	89-90	1 Timothy 4:1–3 Quoted	145
Colossians 3:12–14 Quoted	210	1 Timothy 6:4 FN176	106
Colossians 3:13 Quoted	214	2 Timothy 3:16–17	145
Colossians 3:16 Quoted	96	Hebrews 1:1	31
1 Thessalonians 1:6	187	Hebrews 1:2	31
1 Thessalonians 2:2–4 Quoted	206-206	1 Timothy 4:1–5 Quoted	122
1 Thessalonians 4 FN176	106	Hebrews 1:3	9, 11, 181
1 Thessalonians 4:13–17 Quoted	103	Hebrews 1:3 FN82	42
1 Thessalonians 5:16–18 Quoted	98	Hebrews 1:3 Quoted	17, 140
2 Thessalonians 2	113	Hebrews 1:6 Quoted	32
2 Thessalonians 2:1–4 Quoted	113	Hebrews 1:8–9 Quoted	26
2 Thessalonians 2:5–12 Quoted	113-114	Hebrews 1:8–12	24
2 Thessalonians 2:7–12 (Quoted)	60,(67)	Hebrews 1:10–12 Quoted	26-26
2 Thessalonians 2:11	158	Hebrews 3:17–4:2	160
2 Thessalonians 2:13 Quoted	162	Hebrews 4:2 Quoted	202
1 Timothy 1:3–4 FN176	106	Hebrews 4:13 FN157	87
1 Timothy 1:14	98	Hebrews 5:8 Excerpt	29
1 Timothy 3:14–15 FN49	24	Hebrews 5:8 FN55	28
1 Timothy 3:16 FN49	24	Hebrews 5:11–14 Quoted	1

Solid Food for the Mature Believer
Scripture Reference Index

Book, Chapter, and Verse	Page	Book, Chapter, and Verse	Page
Hebrews 6:1–3 Quoted	1	2 Peter 1:21 Quoted	157
Hebrews 6:4–6 Quoted	184	2 Peter 2:1 FN46	22
Hebrews 7:3 Quoted	31	2 Peter 3:12	79
Hebrews 8:1	11	1 John 1:9 FN130	73
Hebrews 10:29–30 Quoted	185	1 John 2:19	163
Hebrews 10:30 FN114	61	1 John 2:22–23 FN99	49
Hebrews 10:31 Quoted	40	1 John 3:1	74
Hebrews 11:6	81	1 John 3:15 Quoted FN253	213
Hebrews 12:5–11	98	1 John 3:23–24 Quoted	161-161
Hebrews 12:21	15	1 John 4:1 Excerpt	3
Hebrews 12:29	14, 40, 85	1 John 4:2–3 FN99	49
James 1:2–5 Quoted	99-99	1 John 4:10 Paraphrased	94
James 1:6b Quoted	98	1 John 4:13	144
James 1:20 Quoted FN248	208	1 John 4:16 Quoted	57
James 2:14–17	82	1 John 4:20–21 Quoted	92
James 2:19 FN32	16	1 John 5:6	144
James 5:14–15	146	1 John 5:11	98
1 Peter 1:10–12 Quoted	139	Jude 1:4	17
1 Peter 1:11 FN81	42	Jude 1:20–21	179
1 Peter 1:13–16 Quoted	213-213	Revelation 1 FN41, 177 and 182	19, 107, 111
1 Peter 3:15–16a Quoted	213	Revelation 1:4; 3:1; 4:5 and 5:6	42

Solid Food for the Mature Believer
Scripture Reference Index

Book, Chapter, and Verse	Page	Book, Chapter, and Verse	Page
Revelation 1:10	179	Revelation 13	114, 115
Revelation 1:17	20	Revelation 13:4	116
Revelation 1:17 FN153	86	Revelation 13:1–10 Quoted	114-115
Revelation 2:7, 11, 17 and 29	139	Revelation 13:11–17 Quoted	115-116
Revelation 2:8	20	Revelation 17:3	158
Revelation 3	2	Revelation 19:9–10 Quoted	158
Revelation 3:6, 13 and 22	139	Revelation 19:14	152
Revelation 3:14–19 FN159	88	Revelation 20	104, 106, 152
Revelation 3:14–22 (FN161)	38 (89)	Revelation 20 FN176	106
Revelation 3:20	60	Revelation 20:4b–6 Quoted	104-105
Revelation 4 through 19	106	Revelation 20:4–5	112
Revelation 4:2–4 Quoted	157	Revelation 20:11–15	40
Revelation 4:9	96	Revelation 22:1–5 Quoted	37
Revelation 5:6	32	Revelation 22:3–5	98
Revelation 7	106	Revelation 22:9 FN40	19
Revelation 7:9 Quoted	103	Revelation 22:13	20
Revelation 7:11–12	96	Revelation 22:15 FN107	58
Revelation 7:13–17 Quoted	102		
Revelation 7:14	101		
Revelation 9:7	152		

TOPICAL INDEX

A Great War	112
Abortion	2, 66, 67, 69, 93
	110, 119, 128, 206
Abraham	15, 19, 23, 47, 48
	49, 55, 65, 75, 154, 167, 175, 201
Adam	19, 29, 36, 44, 47
	75, 79, 161, 166, 199
Almighty God	31, 42, 54, 76, 139
	143, 144, 172
Almighty Spirit	31, 76
Animating Spirit	43, 142
BHS Version of Masoretic Text	5
Bible	2, 3, 4, 5, 7, 8,
	11, 14, 15, 16, 23, 51, 56, 57, 72
	75, 85, 90, 91, 94, 91, 94, 105, 125
	126, 127, 127, 129, 130, 135, 136
	145, 145, 171, 182, 194, 217
Bible Translation ESV	3
Bible Translation KJV	5
Bible Translation NASB	4
Bible Translation NIV	4
Blaspheme	125, 126
Blaspheme the Holy Spirit	125, 126
Blue Letter Bible	5
Body of Christ	1, 2
Breath of God	143

Child Sacrifice	66, 67, 119
Child Sacrifice in Canaan	71
Christ-likeness	44, 171, 176
Consequences of Sin	86
Convicting Spirit	145
Could We With Ink the Ocean Fill Poem	57
Covenant Law	79, 83
Covenant of Grace	51
Creation	10, 11, 12, 14, 16
	17, 18, 19, 20, 21, 22, 23, 27, 30
	31, 32, 33, 34, 35, 36, 41, 42, 43
	54, 55, 56, 57, 77, 79, 80, 88, 92
	98, 102, 127, 131, 133, 139, 140
	141, 158, 163, 168, 178, 183, 189
Daniel	19, 47, 87, 108, 109
	110, 111, 112, 113, 114, 116, 117
	155, 226
David	35, 48, 53, 54, 65
	76, 81, 89, 146, 149, 151, 167, 169
	187, 194, 199, 201, 207
Definition of a Person	8
Delusion from God	115
Disobedience	59, 71, 73, 77, 84
	88, 89, 119, 120, 137, 155
Divine Jesus	18
Divinity of Jesus	16

Solid Food for the Mature Believer
Topical Index

Divorce	6	God is One	21, 33, 37, 92, 143
DNA	14, 131, 132, 133	God Manifesting as a Man	22
Dr. James White	2, 7, 9, 10, 24	God our Father and LORD	7
ESV	5, 11	God the Father	9
ESV Quoted by permission	3	God the Holy Spirit	9
Eternal life	44, 48, 75, 99	God the Son	9
	143, 155, 159, 161, 164, 179, 203	God's Covenant with Israel	71
Eternal Security	48	God's Hatred	39, 59, 61
Eusebius Church Historian	22, 217	God's Person	18
Everlasting Covenant	54	God's Transcendence	19, 32, 36
Evil Nations Condemned	64	Godhead	2, 7, 8
Ezekiel	15, 20, 22, 26, 65	Godhead Theology	7, 8, 9, 10, 17
	66, 79, 86, 98, 108, 119, 136, 137		22, 23, 27, 29, 37, 38, 42, 55, 127
	152, 154, 157, 158, 170, 181, 182		130, 143
	197, 202, 225, 226	God-is-Love mantra	58
Ezra and the Fear of God	88	Godly Fear	85
	97, 222	Godly Wisdom	145
Father, Son and Holy Spirit	16	God's Majesty	12, 25, 56, 76
Fear	84		85, 87, 100
Firstborn of All Creation	33, 78	God's Decision to Grant Mercy	
Geocentric Theory	129, 130	Is His Sovereign Choice	68
Giving thanks	70, 93, 97, 99	God's Omnipresence	141
	100, 163	God's Presence	13, 14, 16, 18
God as a Consuming Fire	3, 14		42, 46, 53, 85, 87, 89, 98, 101, 103
	40, 86		140, 158, 184, 189
God as Creator	78, 79	God's Sovereign Will	69, 77
God in a Tiny Box	56		78, 80, 164
God in Human Flesh	32	God's Sovereignty	14, 47
God is Love	3, 38, 57, 100, 111	God's Transcendence	10, 28, 30

Solid Food for the Mature Believer
Topical Index

Goodness	8, 11, 56, 68, 69	Incarnation	4, 8, 10, 16, 17
	70, 71, 77, 82, 177, 185		18, 22, 23, 24, 27, 30, 31, 36, 37
Grace	25, 56, 60, 69, 75, 76		55, 199
	77, 81, 82, 99, 106, 107, 110, 135	Indwelling Spirit	44, 46, 49, 51
	139, 159, 164, 167, 168, 176, 180		52, 54, 143, 150, 170, 173
	183, 186, 187, 209, 210, 214, 244	Irrevocable Gift of Salvation	45, 150
Greek Word/Words	4, 5, 17, 29	Israel	6, 20, 34, 38, 54
	47, 49, 56, 104, 111, 115, 129		61, 63, 64, 65, 70, 79, 81, 82, 83
	139, 142, 163, 171, 207		88, 118, 120, 121, 148, 149, 151
Heaven	8, 11, 15, 17, 18		152, 153, 154, 156, 158, 160, 169
	19, 21, 22, 24, 25, 27, 28, 30, 31		170, 172, 173, 174, 189, 193, 196
	32, 33, 34, 42, 42, 48, 49, 78, 79		198, 202
	81, 89, 97, 104, 108, 109, 110, 116	Jehovah	8, 16, 23, 24, 26
	118, 140, 141, 142, 143, 147, 153		29, 30, 32, 34, 37, 38, 48, 55, 76
	158, 161, 173, 179, 184, 199, 207		92, 141
	212, 214	Jesus	17, 18, 20
Hebrew Word/Words	5, 11, 12	Divine and Human	30
	21, 26, 43, 56, 75, 79, 98, 115	Firstborn From the Dead	32
	126, 139, 142, 146, 148, 163, 171	Firstborn of all Creation	17
	172, 182, 194, 196	Jesus as Both Flesh and Bone and Spirit	18
Heliocentric Theory	129, 130		
Hidden Wisdom	145	Jesus as Creator	17, 23, 42, 54
Holiness	3, 7, 19, 25, 89	Jesus as Human Being	5, 9, 11, 12
	90, 105, 111, 123, 155, 171, 179		15, 16, 17, 18, 23, 24, 27, 28, 29
	193, 208, 211, 214		30, 31, 32, 33, 34, 35, 36, 43, 46
Holy Covenant	112, 185		54, 57, 68, 69, 71, 75, 76, 82, 87
Homosexual Rights	93, 119, 206		92, 102, 117, 127, 128, 131, 142
Human wisdom	145		144, 173, 195, 199, 200
		Jesus as Judge	40

Solid Food for the Mature Believer
Topical Index

Jesus as Prime Minister Ruling Over Creation   34, 35, 36
Jesus as Spirit   17, 194
Jesus Subordination to God   36
Jesus the I AM (YHWH)   23
Jesus, Son of Man
    Learning Things   28
Jesus' Coexistent Natures   16
Jesus' Human Limitations   28
Jesus' Resurrection   7, 28, 32, 33, 34, 35, 75, 93, 137, 165, 174, 198
Judgment and Condemnation of Unrepentant Sinners   67
Judgment of Israel   65, 66
Justice   67, 69, 71, 79, 90, 110, 187, 191
Justification   81, 82, 83
Kindness   3, 53, 56, 71, 72, 77, 89, 90, 177, 183, 211
King Saul   44, 120, 121, 122, 149, 150, 151, 157, 173, 186, 196
Laodicean Church   2
Later Times   123, 146
Law of Love   39, 111
Leftist Liberalism   59
Life Giving Spirit   142
Living water   4, 46, 48, 103

LORD Jesus Christ   17, 23, 33, 46, 69, 78, 102, 114, 140, 155, 176, 179, 182, 192
LORD of Hosts   20, 54, 61, 120, 172, 185, 190
LORD our God   8
Lucifer   79
Majesty of God's Being   12
Mercy   2, 51, 56, 58, 64, 65, 67, 68, 69, 70, 76, 77, 78, 79, 81, 82, 88, 110, 127, 135, 159, 187
Miracles   30, 48, 147, 195, 200
Modern Church   1
Moses   19, 21, 23, 33, 41, 47, 48, 64, 68, 70, 75, 85, 147, 148, 160, 166, 167, 169, 181, 192, 193, 203
Nazirite Vow   123
New Covenant   186
NIV   5
Obedience   28, 29, 34, 49, 83, 92, 172, 183, 200
Obey   43, 70, 82, 84, 87, 91, 93, 95, 110, 118, 121, 136, 159, 160, 162, 175, 180, 183, 195, 209, 210, 214
Old Covenant   41

Solid Food for the Mature Believer
Topical Index

Omnipotence	8
Omnipresent Spirit	141
Omniscience	8, 9, 28, 29
Oppression of the Saints	109
	110, 111
Opression of the Saints	112
Organized Religion	128
	129, 131
Our Universe	13
Pentecost	22, 38
44, 46, 47, 48, 49, 51, 52, 53, 54	
75, 82, 150, 154, 156, 161, 162, 163	
166, 167, 168, 175, 178, 181, 198	
Person of Christ	41, 42
	140, 171, 178
Person of God	9, 21, 23, 24
27, 33, 41, 42, 54, 150, 171, 172	
	177, 195
Person of Jesus Christ	9, 10
19, 38, 40, 42, 53, 54, 139	
	170, 188, 195
Person of the Spirit = Person of Christ	139
Personhood of God	15
Pleasing God	81
Pre-Pentecostal saints	47, 48
	75, 165, 176
Rebellion of Lawlessness	110, 114

Reference to N.T.	4, 5, 27, 38, 44
49, 56, 67, 83, 87, 91, 139, 142	
	185, 203
Reference to O.T.	5, 16
19, 20, 21, 24, 25, 27, 31, 33, 38	
49, 54, 75, 83, 87, 91, 97, 115, 119	
120, 124, 140, 151, 160, 163, 169	
	176, 203, 212
Repent/Repentance	1, 34, 45, 51
70, 100, 126, 155, 160, 163, 165	
	168, 174, 186
Resurrected	34, 37
Resurrection of the Damned	105
the second resurrection	113
Resurrection of the dead	1, 35
Resurrection of the Saints	45, 93
93, 104, 105, 106, 107, 137, 169	
	202, 203
The First Resurrection	36, 113
Revelation of God's Person	9, 10
16, 17, 18, 20, 22, 23, 27, 54, 78, 214	
Salvation	33, 44, 45, 46, 48
49, 51, 52, 53, 54, 63, 68, 69, 77	
82, 86, 105, 126, 135, 139, 147	
150, 151, 152, 153, 156, 158, 161	
163, 166, 167, 168, 169, 170, 178	
183, 185, 186, 188, 196, 198, 199	
	202, 207

Solid Food for the Mature Believer
Topical Index

Samuel the Prophet	15, 44, 53, 63
	64, 81, 89, 120, 121, 149, 150, 151
	152, 174, 186, 196, 221
Satan	67, 74, 78, 79
	111, 112, 115, 117, 149, 197
Scripture	2, 3, 5, 7, 9, 17
	19, 22, 23, 27, 28, 32, 34, 35, 36
	38, 39, 41, 44, 45, 46, 48, 49, 52
	53, 54, 56, 59, 62, 64, 68, 77, 79
	89, 97, 104, 105, 106, 107, 108
	110, 112, 113, 114, 119, 123, 124
	128, 139, 145, 146, 149, 150, 164
	165, 173, 175, 185, 190, 191, 195
	198, 219
Serve / Serving God	1, 7, 14, 37
	44, 53, 81, 95, 96, 97, 98, 103, 110
	158, 163, 171, 176
Sin	1, 16, 38, 39, 43, 56, 58, 59
Sin Nature	27
Sinful Man	59
Sinner/Sinners	47, 60, 64, 68
	69, 80, 94, 121
Sinner/Sinners	45, 60, 164
Sovereign LORD	17, 22, 78, 140
	182
Spirit of Godly Wisdom	145
	147, 148
Spirit of Holy Testimony	145
Spirit of Life	143
Spirit of Prophecy	149, 156
Spirit That Enables Understanding	144
Spiritual Fruit of Jesus' Resurrection	34
Spiritual gifts	44, 148
	155, 193, 195
Stern-Faced King	111, 114, 117
Supernatural Gifts	200
Supreme Being	128
Surrender	91, 93, 126
Sustaining Spirit	140
Tempoary Spirit	148
Terrifying God	15
Testing Spirit	3, 102, 144
The Catholic Church	129
The Church	1, 2, 16, 21, 32, 38
	39, 48, 51, 54, 55, 61, 82, 88, 102
	103, 104, 105, 107, 108, 110, 114
	117, 119, 122, 123, 125, 127, 128
	129, 130, 133, 136, 140, 154, 155
	168, 175, 198, 199, 201, 211, 213
The Devil	14, 79
	126, 154, 172, 187, 190
The Face of God	37, 63, 68
The Father	8, 9, 10, 15, 16
	19, 20, 21, 22, 23, 24, 27, 31, 32
	34, 35, 36, 42, 46, 47, 55, 92, 106
	140, 155, 162, 163, 167, 170, 192

Solid Food for the Mature Believer
Topical Index

The Father (contd)	193, 195
	198, 199, 204, 207
The Fear of God	2, 3, 16, 38, 40
	56, 73, 81, 84, 86, 87, 88, 89, 118
	175, 179, 205, 208, 212
The First Resurrection	105
The Flesh	46, 47, 144, 164
	165, 166, 167, 170, 176, 177, 178
	181, 184, 211
The Four Beasts	108
The Fourth Beast	109
The Gift of the Holy Spirit	45
The Great Tribulation	82, 102
	103, 105, 107, 108, 109, 110, 111
	113, 117, 154, 155
The Holy Spirit	5, 8, 9, 16, 18
	21, 27, 28, 31, 33, 35, 38, 41, 42
	44, 45, 46, 48, 49, 51, 52, 53, 54
	60, 115, 117, 125, 139, 140, 141
	142, 143, 150, 153, 154, 155, 156
	157, 158, 160, 162, 165, 166, 168
	170, 171, 172, 173, 174, 175, 176
	177, 179, 180, 181, 183, 185, 192
	198, 199, 200, 201, 203, 207, 214
The Indwelling Spirit	
of Salvation	52, 53
The Judgment	39, 81
	92, 131, 192
The Kingdom	45, 48
	62, 71, 81, 111, 130, 164, 193
The Lamb	32, 36
	37, 103, 104, 116, 159
The LORD	6, 11, 15, 16, 17
	19, 20, 23, 24, 25, 26, 31, 37, 41
	42, 44, 45, 49, 51, 55, 56, 60, 61
	62, 63, 64, 65, 66, 67, 68, 69, 70
	71, 72, 73, 74, 75, 76, 78, 79, 81
	83, 84, 85, 86, 87, 89, 90, 91, 93
	94, 96, 98, 101, 102, 103, 104
	110, 114, 117, 118, 120, 121, 122
	124, 125, 126, 127, 128, 135, 139
	140, 141, 145, 148, 149, 150, 151
	152, 153, 154, 157, 159, 161, 162
	163, 164, 166, 167, 168, 169, 171
	172, 175, 179, 180, 181, 182, 183
	185, 187, 189, 190, 191, 192, 193
	194, 196, 197, 200, 202, 204, 205
	206, 208, 209, 210, 211, 212, 213
	214, 215
The LORD as Creator	78
The LORD Jesus	3, 4
	16, 18, 20, 21
The LORD Our God	1
The Man of Lawlessness	67
	114, 115, 116, 117
The Parable of the Ten Minas	39

Solid Food for the Mature Believer
Topical Index

The Person of Jesus   9, 19, 20, 22
    30, 38, 40, 53, 54, 139, 170, 188
The Radiance of God's Glory   17
    18, 27
The Reign of the Son of Man   35
The Revelation of John   102
    117, 119
The Saints   48, 54, 107, 108
    109, 110, 116, 117, 118, 171, 180
    195, 208, 211
The Seven Spirits of God   42
The Son   8, 9, 16, 17, 23
    26, 27, 31, 32, 36, 55, 66, 92, 153
    186, 190, 207
Tthe Son of Man   5, 8, 16, 17
    18, 23, 24, 27, 28, 29, 31, 32, 33
    34, 36, 37, 40, 44, 55, 57, 76
    92, 125, 170, 173, 195, 198
The Spirit   3, 4, 8, 9, 19
    20, 26, 27, 28, 29, 30, 33, 35, 41
    42, 43, 44, 45, 47, 48, 49, 50, 51
    54, 60, 81, 91, 94, 106, 107, 110
    117, 123, 125, 126, 135, 138, 139
    140, 141, 143, 144, 145, 146, 147
    148, 149, 150, 151, 152, 153, 155
    156, 157, 158, 160, 161, 162, 163
    164, 165, 166, 167, 168, 169, 170
    171, 172, 173, 174, 175, 176, 177
    178, 179, 180, 181, 182, 183, 184

The Spirit (contd)   185, 186, 187, 188
    190, 191, 192, 193, 194, 195, 196
    197, 198, 199, 200, 201, 202, 211
The Spirit of Christ   140
Tthe Spirit of Joy, Peace,
    Contentment   53
Theory of Evolution   131, 132
Three Distinct Persons   9
Throne of God   24, 25, 26, 27
    36, 37, 55, 61, 103, 104, 108, 115
    158
Timeline of Creation   32
Transcendent   11
Transcendent being   10, 15
Transcendent Majesty   11, 15
    16, 20, 21, 22, 23, 29, 34, 41, 54
    78, 140, 199
Tremble Before God   16
Tribulation of the
    Saints/Church   108, 119
Trustworthy Saying   20
Truth Revealing Spirit   144
Unrepentant Sinners Condemned   63
Westboro Baptist Church   2, 58
When Do We Give Thanks?   99
What and Why God Hates   59
    61, 62
Why Be Thankful to God?   98

Solid Food for the Mature Believer
Topical Index

Wisdom	51, 79, 84, 89 91, 97, 100, 106, 122, 148, 151 152, 153, 155, 172, 179, 195	YHWH	4, 10, 16, 17, 18, 23, 24 25, 26, 27, 28, 31, 33, 36, 38, 41 54, 57, 69, 108 140, 191
		YHWH as O.T. Jews' Father	55

Other works by Kenneth John Marks include:

The Prophet's Son trilogy: Descent to Darkness; Sojourn in the Desert; Return to Grace

My God and Saviour, an anthology of short stories

Rebellion

A Wolf in Sheep's Clothing

www.ingramcontent.com/pod-product-compliance
Lightning Source LLC
Chambersburg PA
CBHW070052080526
44586CB00013B/1023